DOING GLOBAL FIELDWORK

DOING GLOBAL FIELDWORK

A SOCIAL SCIENTIST'S GUIDE TO MIXED-METHODS RESEARCH FAR FROM HOME

JESSE DRISCOLL

Columbia University Press
New York

Columbia University Press
Publishers Since 1893
New York   Chichester, West Sussex
cup.columbia.edu
Copyright © 2021 Columbia University Press
All rights reserved

Library of Congress Cataloging-in-Publication Data
Names: Driscoll, Jesse, 1978– author.
Title: Doing global fieldwork : a social scientist's guide to mixed-methods
research far from home / Jesse Driscoll.
Description: New York : Columbia University Press, [2021] | Includes bibliographical
references and index.
Identifiers: LCCN 2020036369 (print) | LCCN 2020036370 (ebook) |
ISBN 9780231195287 (hardcover) | ISBN 9780231195294 (trade paperback) |
ISBN 9780231551281 (ebook)
Subjects: LCSH: Social sciences—Fieldwork. | Social sciences—
Research—Methodology.
Classification: LCC H62 .D75 2021 (print) | LCC H62 (ebook) |
DDC 300.72/3—dc23
LC record available at https://lccn.loc.gov/2020036369
LC ebook record available at https://lccn.loc.gov/2020036370

Cover design: Noah Arlow

At last one little spider took time enough to stop and talk to Wilbur before making its balloon.

"We're leaving here on the warm updraft. This is our moment for setting forth. We are aeronauts and we are going out into the world to make webs for ourselves."

"But *where*?" asked Wilbur.

"Wherever the wind takes us. High, low. Near, far. East, west. North, south. We take to the breeze, we go as we please."

—E. B. White, *Charlotte's Web*

CONTENTS

FIGURES AND TABLES

FIGURES

TABLES

PREFACE

I spent much of my twenties living in some combination of Yemen, Turkey, Kyrgyzstan, Georgia, and Tajikistan. Then I spent most of my thirties publishing with the data that I collected. Along the way I learned more about my craft and outgrew some youthful opinions. I feel gratitude to political science, my home discipline. I consider myself lucky to be a professional author with a job that gives me the opportunity to listen to graduate students' half-baked research plans. In doing so, I can sometimes catch glimpses of a younger, brasher version of myself with startling clarity. Graduate students who come through my office often project brazen confidence that they have what it takes to do this job at a high level, even if they are not sure what is involved. I have assembled a book's worth of advice I keep repeating to these students. Graduate students tend to be left to their own devices when it comes to figuring out how to collect high-integrity data from subjects or transform their observations into persuasive tests. When I was in graduate school I had more reading than time to do it, but what I recall that I needed, but did not have, was a how-to of directions to get to the field and start collecting stories. Hence this book.

Much of what is required to succeed in the discipline cannot be reliably taught: a strong work ethic, creativity, a knack for innovating on others' work, the ability to work without supervision or direction, to take criticism, to delay gratification, and more. A book cannot teach any of that. Nor can a book instill confidence, which must be acquired solo. What a book can do is provide advice on issues of psychological and physical preparation, professionalization, research practice, and self-presentation. Some of the advice is sufficiently general to apply to master's students, natural scientists, or scholars of the humanities, but I write with more confident authority on the needs of social scientists, especially political scientists. I do not imagine it possible for a poor field researcher to become a great one with this kind of advice, but maybe a mediocre field researcher can become a competent one.

If this book succeeds, it will be by infusing readers with an ethos-based *improvisational pluralism*. The meaning of this phrase will be explicated as the book unfolds. Once one gets serious about making the best of unexpected discoveries, "fake it till you make it" often requires starting over from scratch and leaving half-formed pieces of multiple vestigial dissertation prospectuses on the cutting-room floor. This is psychologically painful. I have concluded that there is no viable alternative. It is not uncommon for students to get in over their heads, having embarked for the field with superficial understandings of the history, politics, or language associated with their chosen site. Few in their third year of graduate training have much knowledge of the literature, or how it is evolving, or how stiff the competition is. If you want to make field-work a part of your academic persona, however, the prescription is always the same: Weigh foreseeable consequences, plan as best you can, then jump. Supervised preparation and textbook knowledge can help, but these are never enough. You must also jump.

What does it mean to "jump"? How can one forge a sufficient plan? How does one go about writing oneself into the political science canon? Having seen many projects flounder or drag on for years—my own included—most of the chapters in this book are organized attempts to provide no-nonsense practical things to consider if one wants to collect high-integrity data. It ought not to be read as a methods manifesto. I do not feel confident enough to be evangelical about high theory debates. My advice is organized into seven signposted chapters assuming a busy reader who will skip around. I assume this book will be reread in fits and starts rather than absorbed in one sitting. Chapter 1 sorts three kinds of pre-fieldwork writing by audience (mentors, bureaucrats, donors). Chapter 2 provides a preplanning checklist to get out the door. Chapter 3 is filled with tips for planning self-presentation. Chapter 4 discusses basic interview, archival, and participant observation strategies. Chapter 5 sketches strategies for data collection as a manager of a small local team. Chapter 6 addresses specific planning concerns for designs in zones of contested sovereignty and authoritarian governance, trying to demystify and devalorize extreme fieldwork. Chapter 7 concludes with a discussion of coming home, putting the past where it belongs, and writing up findings. Between the chapters are small "FAQ" inserts, written informally, directly answering the six most common questions that I receive regarding fieldwork.

Since I am sometimes writing to a younger version of myself, the prose jumps a bit haphazardly between first, third, and second person. I sometimes slip between past and present tense. I am grateful to Columbia University Press for indulging me. The book draws heavily on my own lived experience and develops an extended analogy about fieldworkers as apprentices and journeymen in a guild, so some material in this book may be alienating to a non-American reader planning fieldwork in her own society and then a career in her home country. My intent is to write about what I know, not to offend. I do not wish to give the impression that I believe the "real" academy exists only in Europe and North America. That is not my belief.

There are many ways to make sausage. This book shares my favorite recipe notes from a moment in my life. It is not the only recipe, nor the only good one. But it *will* be helpful.

DOING GLOBAL FIELDWORK

1

WELCOME TO THE GUILD

Graduate school ceases being an IQ test immediately after comprehensive exams. A disorienting, unstructured, empty-feeling gray zone lies between the end of formal coursework and a sense that one's day-to-day labor is contributing to a research agenda worth pursuing. This chapter will encourage a few different kinds of writing, along with some preliminary strategic planning, to guide you as you begin to navigate a track through the gray.

Your path should begin with the realization that there are extremely strong professional incentives to collecting your own data. This book aims to minimize start-up costs for initially getting out the door. The expectation is that you will come back, regroup, forge a better plan, and head back out again. This may occur multiple times. I assume you are a reader overloaded with required readings who has muddled through your program thus far, picked up some buzzwords, and is considering decamping sooner rather than later. Upon your return you will know better whether it is a good use of your time to carefully reread some sections of *Mostly Harmless Econometrics* or to mine the footnotes of assembled essays in *Political Ethnography*.[1] This chapter provides structure for a process of orderly departure and provides a gloss on professional ethics. First, however, it is important to introduce the concept of improvisational pluralism, as it will provide conceptual scaffolding for the rest of the book.

IMPROVISATIONAL PLURALISM

My standard answer to the "Why do fieldwork?" question is simple: "To collect measurement indicators for a variable that you cannot measure from the safety and comfort of your home institution."[2] This is a narrow and instrumental rationale for a multiyear expedition. The goal of the fieldwork this book envisions is the publication of an academic book or article, not to impress your loved ones with a hero's journey, nor to send a costly signal to a competitive job market, nor to immerse yourself in a different culture for its own sake, nor to dramatize the renunciation of the world like a wandering monk. These goals can become hopelessly conjoined. Separate them.

The first step of the scientific method is observation. Conducting high-integrity observations of another society requires special kinds of preparation and a certain degree of methodological flexibility. Fieldwork also rewards an ability to improvise and adapt when things go wrong, especially in social contexts that are rapidly shifting (such as certain war zones). To many readers fresh from methods courses that emphasize predetermined and repeatable procedures, improvisation may have the feel of cheating. This is simply not true. If you spend a lot of time observing, generate unique expertise with a study community, and do *not* emerge with your research question altered and pre-fieldwork suppositions challenged, something is wrong. Your ideas should change while in the field. It follows that you will need to modify your research to reflect these unexpected new understandings.

What about pluralism? The way the term is being used here, improvisational pluralism requires a broader view of academia than can emerge from the narrow careerist point of view (with its ruthless focus on pleasing the citation-counters, publishing and not perishing, etc.). The highest form of labor, for most of us, is specialist reading. Academic disciplines are self-organized readers guilds. We discipline what we read so that we can accurately predict what other guild members would see as a worthy contribution to an ongoing conversation.

Reading patterns within our guilds are uneven, however, so in a healthy discipline there is bound to be a cacophony of debate about argument originality and a healthy diversity of aesthetic tastes. A mature attitude toward pluralism begins by taking the diversity of aesthetic opinions seriously and listening, with genuine respect, to the positions of people other than your favorite advisor. There are many different ways of understanding what "counts" as a contribution. Different measurement strategies are also always trending in a dynamic empirical discipline.

In the best of all worlds, prior to venturing into the field, one would acquire a working knowledge of many different methodologies, including a broad training in and respect for interdisciplinary work. In reality, there is only so much time, and some fads get more attention in training sequences than others. Since no one can understand all of the constraints of a site in advance, it is also not uncommon for advisors to give their students perfunctory "signoffs" to go to the field, to crash a few times, and to adapt, hoping they will find something interesting along the way and write up what they observe. Success under these circumstances requires not just DIY adaptation, but also an anchor to center the project and prevent excessive drift.

Professional ethics are a good anchor. You will need to develop a personal code. You are sure to get mixed signals from the market, your discipline, your mentors, and the profession, so your code must be your own. Different mantras work for different people. Consider the following excerpt from my own as a jumping-off point:

- Your goal must be to write something useful. Everything else is self-indulgence.
- You are a privileged observer. Not everyone has your freedom to just come and go.
- If anything goes wrong because of your thoughtlessness, admit responsibility.

Anchoring your own ethos in personal introspection is necessary. It will be clear in the chapters that follow that I believe that fieldwork has the potential to change the researcher permanently, for better and for worse. It is easy to find and repeat good rhetorical lines ("strive to leave no footprints . . . like visitors to nature preserves"[3]), but early-career scholars are under terrible pressure to get noticed, so the impulse to disseminate key findings on social media, attract attention, get bigger grants, and maximize visibility is real. Values can be in tension.

Some professional ethical standards are explicitly codified. The Belmont Report was written in 1979 by the National Commission for the Protection of Human Subjects of Biomedical and Behavioral Research. It is a living document that rewards multiple close rereadings, so acquaint yourself with its contents. The grind of discouraging referee reports, the presence of many compromised and unsympathetic models of professional success, and the cacophony of contradictory design advice (some provided disingenuously by people with no investment in your project or care for your subjects) can contribute to the impression that there is no ethical center to your discipline beyond careerism. The result can be a lonely nihilism. More broadly, the data on why some ethical training programs produce quantifiable results (e.g., human rights trainings for professional soldiers) show that what really works is iterative retraining repeated over years, as practitioners develop life experience to contextualize the curriculum personally. No one believes a one-time required module in basic training is of much practical use to professional soldiers, and the same goes for professional researchers.[4]

Not codified in the Belmont Report, but just as critical in their everydayness, are ethical concerns relating to personal relationships with people who may not be one's human subjects. Encounters begin in the field and relationships continue. This can present a variety of challenges. It is easier to describe trade-offs that can feel like dilemmas (e.g., the day-to-day adaptations and judgment calls necessary to conduct research under conditions of ubiquitous government surveillance) or to issue warnings based on high-profile projects that "splash" publicly, rippling beyond a subject pool. There was an unusual amount of publicity, for instance, around a 2014 field experiment in Montana, which created a stir based on the perception that distant social scientists were trying to meddle in a nonpartisan judicial election. Too often these dramatic anecdotes, or outliers in the social sciences such as the Milgram experiment or the Stanford Prison Experiments, become focal points for discussions of ethical matters.

The more far-reaching implications that affect a researcher's well-being, for better and worse, are often natural outgrowths of living a full life in an engaged way. Decisions made upstream for pragmatic reasons in the logistics and planning stage can have unforeseeable implications downstream. Because the mechanisms are complex, subtle, and inevitably context-specific, I devote a great deal of space in the following chapters to candid discussions of strategic dissimulation (e.g., whether and how much to lie) and documenting common psychological harms associated with fieldwork (e.g., trauma, exhaustion, secondary trauma, paranoia, and impostor syndrome). When you are writing social science and purporting to represent facts about how people live or what they believe, the stakes expand beyond the personal. When you are exhausted, you are prone to making lazy observations or inadvertently fudging data—especially if you are (ethically speaking) flying by the seat of your pants.

Redlines for stopping your research are particularly salient. There is a temptation by young researchers to view ethics solely through an instrumental lens (e.g., concerns for your professional reputation or negotiating institutional review board paperwork). The problem with taking a completely utilitarian approach is that perceived risk–reward ratios, in which you weigh the promise of a project landing in a high-impact venue against whatever costs accrue to you or your subjects, is that the weighing calculus is susceptible to motivated reasoning. Projects often drift and morph and come to feel personal. Adaptation is inevitable, so developing some core ethical principles and trying to stick to them provides a measure of stability and comfort.

Another anchor is to try to discipline oneself to remain focused on a single political outcome (dependent variable). Many researchers in the social sciences argue that systematic study of a normatively important outcome, such as order, democratization, war recurrence, civilian victimization in war zones, development, or identity change, is a good way to approach the dissertation prospectus. After all, the purpose of academic research is to produce articles, chapters, or books tied to a set of slow-moving topical debates so that the same materials can appear in course syllabi on similar topics at universities worldwide. A field of knowledge is analogous to a literary canon, in the sense that similar material is predictably taught in "voter behavior," "development economics," or "urban sociology" classes everywhere. There is an economy of scale to getting real depth in a narrow slice of the literature. Locate a part of the library that you want to responsibly curate on behalf of the academy, the way a palace gardener chooses a portion of the grounds to tend for life.

Within comparative politics, I believe in the value of compelling, locally valid narratives. An ability to interpret nuances in the politics of a field site is necessary in order to do credible storytelling as well as test-ing. Assembling original data is usually a prerequisite for both tasks. We do a lot in the field that has nothing to do with data collection, and a lot of this is important *to us* as we do it, but we are a guild of readers and writers, so it must all come together in a well-written causal narrative in the end. People ultimately learn by stories.

Table 1.1 is a gloss on how various kinds of questions can be answered using different methods. A few things should be clear at a glance. First, there are many ways to do empirical social science with integrity. We occupy a big tent. Few scholars can credibly claim to have mastered all of these methods, even at the end of a successful career. Entire classes, indeed multipart sequences, would only skim the surface of any single row, making a table like this one an idiosyncratic and haphazard survey. You will need to make hard choices and specialize at some point, because mastering an empirical skill set trades off with dabbling in formal the-ory, normative political philosophy, history, language acquisition (see FAQ #1), overcoming fear of public speaking, learning to teach, and other things you may want to know to please your advisors or prepare yourself for the life of the mind. Recognizing the breadth of possibility does not mean that every row is equally useful (to you), or that you would or could be equally good at every row. It is humbling and liberating to realize that you are not actually going to be good at everything. This is an entry point to an appreciation of pluralism. Improvisation comes later.

Second, embedded in each row are different ways of thinking about data. Depending on which part of the political science literature you want to write to, you will have to think differently about design, methods of data analysis, sampling, how to frame your puzzle, and a great deal more. Diana Kapiszewski, Lauren M. MacLean, and Benjamin Read are absolutely correct that the process of giving fieldwork advice involves "reaching across what may seem like stark dividing lines, speaking to scholars in different subfields, who employ different analytic methods, and who have contrasting epistemological philosophies . . . [because] scholars hailing from different traditions think about the processes and products of field research differently."[5] This is just a book on methods and strategies to assist data collection, not an attempt at a field synthesis. Consult different readings for more on research design, how to analyze and present your data, strategies of publication to turn earnest energy into academic outputs, and the like.

Third, some approaches are more time- and capital-intensive than others. Some social science emerges from million-dollar grants that employ dozens of subcontracted laborers over years. Other scholars purchase commercial datasets collected by survey professionals. Still others have fine careers subsisting on much more modest amounts—small grants for housing, food, transport, insurance, and perhaps a research assistant or two.

Fourth, because this is a book on fieldwork, it is easy to overlook the fact that a lot of what goes into a finished academic book or article can be written without leaving home. It is not cheating to write entire chapters of your dissertation from your desktop. While many young researchers are anxious to get to the field, there is no virtue in doing things in some distant place that could have been done at home. With every passing year, as the amount of information at one's fingertips grows, "desktop dissertations" become more impressive. Indeed, much of what will fill the dissertation does not require travel at all: It requires a library card, discipline, and a huge amount of unstructured time to curate scattered facts into a good causal narrative. There is probably more in your home library than you realize.[6] It is usually possible to write at least three chapters—at least half of the dissertation measured in page-counts—from your home work station. This will happen, in most cases, either before or after you venture to the field. Some people do the serious library work early; others delay it and come back later. Either way, comparative politics is not just about going somewhere new. It is possible to lean on family connections, languages one already speaks fluently, and other personal advantages to pass completely on self-transforming or immersive fieldwork. There are a lot of ways to do this job.

Fifth, methods in every row are being pushed ahead rapidly by the march of technology and the availability of new kinds of data with ever-more-granular units of analysis. Reliable survey data, for example, are more accessible from a distance today than when many classic design texts were written. Technological changes now permit self-publication in various forms. Many social scientists post working papers early on their personal websites and post replication datasets along with published

TABLE 1.1 Overview to Methods of Data Collection

Method of observation	For inferences the method leverages	Closest sister discipline	Solo, team, or desktop?	Grant size needed	What kinds of questions can these methods answer? What is a recent/teachable example of the method used with integrity?
Ethnography (chapters 3–4)	Patience and participant observation	Anthropology	Solo	$	Did NATO military intervention reduce or enhance the salience of ethnic status hierarchies in the Balkans?[a]
					How were Abkhaz perceptions of collective threat constructed in the early 1990s?[b]
					How does "border control" work, in practice, in the Ferghana Valley?[c]
In-depth interviews (chapter 4)	A hard-to-access sample + depth of rapport	Communication	Solo	$–$$	Why do some commercial elites collude with jihadis?[d]
					When do mass rapes force tighter group bonds?[e]
					How is "random" violence in a military occupation different from "retributive" violence?[f]
					Why are rural Wisconsin voters aggrieved?[g]
Using archives (chapters 2–4)	Responsible historiography + systematizing and analyzing data	History	Solo	$	Why was Ottoman state centralization challenged by bandits instead of peasant revolts?[h]
					Can newspaper reports of protests map the "tidal waves" of nationalism that ended the USSR?[i]
					Do Stalin-era police records suggest that population resettlement "works"?[j]

Method of observation	For inferences the method leverages	Closest sister discipline	Solo, team, or desktop?	Grant size needed	What kinds of questions can these methods answer? What is a recent/teachable example of the method used with integrity?
Surveys (chapter 5)	Aggregation of a large sample of responses + design tricks	Sociology	Team	$$$	Is Vladimir Putin's popularity exaggerated?[k]
					How is endorsing a hypothetical war—described in a survey vignette—different from endorsing real war up close?[l]
					Does anger at foreign electoral interference increase support for military retaliation?[m]
Experiments (chapter 5)	Laboratory-like control of confounding variables	Economics + psychology	Team	$$$$$	Which mechanisms best explain the demonstrated ability of co-ethnics to cooperate more effectively?[n]
					Do election monitors or police officers reduce malfeasance, or do they more often just displace it to nearby neighborhoods?[o]
Natural experiments	Clever identification strategies + panel datasets	Economics	Desktop	N/A	Do election monitors reduce election fraud?[p]
					Did the experience of WWI conscription permanently transform "German-Americans" into Americans?[q]
					Do income shocks affect armed conflict differently for agricultural shocks than natural resource shocks?[r]

(continued)

TABLE 1.1 Overview to Methods of Data Collection (continued)

Method of observation	For inferences the method leverages	Closest sister discipline	Solo, team, or desktop?	Grant size needed	What kinds of questions can these methods answer? What is a recent/teachable example of the method used with integrity?
"Found" large-n samples	Clever construct validity + new measurement tools	Data science	Desktop	N/A–$$	Are radical Muslim clerics kicked out of school because of their ideas, or are they more likely to give voice to radical ideas *after* they are kicked out?[δ] What can we learn, by observing controlled perturbations, about the effectiveness of Chinese government strategies to control the internet?[τ]

[a] Roger Petersen, *Western Intervention in the Balkans: The Strategic Use of Emotion in Conflict* (Cambridge: Cambridge University Press, 2011).

[b] Anastasia Shesterinina, "Collective Threat Framing and Mobilization in Civil War," *American Political Science Review* 110, no. 3 (2016): 411–27.

[c] Madeline Reeves, *Border Work: Spatial Lives of the State in Rural Central Asia* (London: Cornell University Press, 2014).

[d] Aisha Ahmad, *Jihad & Co: Black Market and Islamist Power* (New York: Oxford University Press, 2017).

[e] Dara Cohen, *Rape during Civil War* (Ithaca, NY: Cornell University Press, 2016).

[f] Emil A. Soulemianov and David S. Siroky, "Random or Retributive? Indiscriminate Violence in the Chechen Wars," *World Politics* 68, no. 4 (2016): 677–712.

[g] Katherine J. Cramer, *The Politics of Resentment: Rural Consciousness in Wisconsin and the Rise of Scott Walker* (Chicago: University of Chicago Press, 2016).

[h] Karen Barkey, *Bandits and Bureaucrats: The Ottoman Route to State Centralization* (Ithaca, NY: Cornell University Press, 1994).

[i] Mark Beissinger, *Nationalist Mobilization and the Collapse of the Soviet State* (Cambridge: Cambridge University Press, 2002).

[j] Yuri Zhukov, "Population Resettlement in War: Theory and Evidence from Soviet Archives," *Journal of Conflict Resolution* 59, no. 7 (2015): 1155–85.

[k] Timothy Frye, Scott Gehlbach, Kyle L. Marquardt, and Ora John Reuter, "Is Putin's Popularity Real?," *Post-Soviet Affairs* 33, no. 1 (2017): 1–15.

[l] Jesse Driscoll and Daniel Maliniak, "Did Georgian Voters Desire Escalation in 2008? Experiments and Observations," *Journal of Politics* 78, no. 1 (2016): 265–80.

[m] Michael Tomz and Jessica Weeks, "Public Opinion and Foreign Electoral Intervention. *American Political Science Review*, forthcoming, 2020, https://web.stanford.edu/~tomz/pubs/TomzWeeks-APSR-2020.pdf.

[n] James Habyarimana, Macartan Humphreys, Daniel N. Posner, and Jeremy Weinstein, *Coethnicity: Diversity and the Dilemmas of Collective Action* (New York: Russell Sage, 2011).

[o] Nahomi Ichino and Matthias Schündeln, "Deterring or Displacing Electoral Irregularities? Spillover Effects of Observers in a Randomized Field Experiment in Ghana," *Journal of Politics* 74, no. 1 (2012): 292–307; Christopher Blattman, Donald Green, Daniel Ortega, and Santiago Tobón, "Place Based Interventions at Scale: The Direct and Spillover Effects of Policing and City Services on Crime, NBER Working Paper, Development Economics, 2019. https://www.nber.org/papers/w23941.

[p] Susan Hyde, "The Observer Effect in International Politics: Evidence From a Natural Experiment," *World Politics* 60, no. 1 (2007): 37–63.

[q] Soumyajit Mazumder, "Becoming White: How Military Service Turned Immigrants into Americans," SocArXiv Papers, 2019, https://osf.io/preprints/socarxiv/agjsm/.

[r] Oeindrila Dube and Juan Vargas, "Commodity Price Shocks and Civil Conflict: Evidence from Colombia," *Review of Economic Studies* 80 (2013): 1384–421.

[s] Richard Neilsen, *Deadly Clerics: Blocked Ambition and the Path to Jihad* (New York: Cambridge University Press, 2017).

[t] Margaret Roberts, *Censored: Distraction and Diversion inside China's Great Firewall* (Princeton, NJ: Princeton University Press, 2019).

papers as a matter of pride. We may be moving quickly toward an era of ubiquitous public data. All of this is going to change what comparative politics means and where fieldwork fits. It is an exciting time to be a social scientist for this reason—but it is disorienting. If you acquire basic data management skills before venturing into the field, it will allow you to make good use of unexpected opportunities as they emerge (see chapter 2).

My hope is that table 1.1, viewed through a lens of improvisational pluralism, will illuminate alternative virtuous pathways that you might choose to take advantage of. Begin your appreciation of narrative with the observation that writing (especially about causes) can be constitutive. Every writer imagines an idealized reader. Graduate students develop a narrative in which they are an ethical and sympathetic character, acting within constraints to unravel a normatively important puzzle about the world. Begin to write this narrative as a story in the third person. When you are ready, share it. The process involves three distinct writing tasks: (1) documenting a research plan formally with your home institution; (2) constructing an adaptable funding narrative that you can use to begin to "pitch" the project to nonspecialists; and (3) sculpting a prospectus with advisors who will help you navigate the academic shoals.

FORMALIZING YOUR ROLE AS A UNIVERSITY REPRESENTATIVE

This book prioritizes the need for researchers to have a personal code of ethics. Improvisational pluralism in the field is not the same thing as "improvisational tinkering with the lives of your subjects because it is fun." There are separate instrumental reasons to think about how to present yourself, in writing, as a thoughtful and ethical person. You have only one reputation. The community you are trying to write your way into is small. People have long memories. If you acquire a reputation as a mad scientist, it may be because your behaviors have led people to the conclusion that you are a bad person. If a consensus forms that you cannot be trusted, your career is doomed. Graduate students, intuiting this, watch their professionally successful advisors carefully for hints about what kinds of behavior are rewarded and acceptable. A kind of forum shopping occurs as risk-acceptant students pair themselves off with risk-acceptant advisors—a process of social matching described in the next section on forming a committee.

Formal permission to represent your university to conduct research is a completely separate formal process that is your responsibility, not your advisor's. Research universities are businesses. For many students who went "straight through" from undergraduate into graduate school, filing paperwork with the university human subjects and institutional review boards (IRBs) is their first real foray into adulthood. Most people do not want to file IRB applications. They believe themselves to be ethical and so quietly resent the fact that IRBs have the power to stop their research before it begins.[7] Until a subset of social science researchers organizes and collectively demands that our subdisciplines be treated as offshoots of the humanities and not the natural sciences, however, the biomedical model of IRB review for social science research is here to stay, so before going to the field, you must file a formal research plan. If you consider fieldwork from the perspective of a risk-averse, brand-conscious bureaucracy, it is easy to understand why oversight is necessary. If anything goes wrong in the field, or if your study is published but then criticized as unethical, your university will be dragged into the news. It is good to think of yourself from the beginning as a high-status representative of an elite institution and an ambassador for your profession. While you will inevitably play other roles, and can proceed far without taking any of this seriously, if you get in trouble you will probably be forced to seek other work. Working with the IRB can minimize risk of trouble. If you can manage to treat your application to them as a serious two-way relationship instead of just a bureaucratic barrier, a variety of indirect benefits will accrue to you and your subjects.

The questions for the plan are designed by professional social scientists. They will force you to think through issues from the perspective of your subject pool. Taking the exercise seriously will produce better research. If you plan to use interviews or surveys, you will be forced to put thought into which "set piece" questions you plan to ask over and over again and the exact phrasing, in translation, of how you will solicit information in the course of your research. It is not an onerous task. If you are planning work using a vetted design, the forms you are expected to fill out often require about a day's worth of work.

Some research practices will predictably raise flags. If you propose doing anything with vulnerable populations, especially institutionalized persons, prisoners, or children, expect special scrutiny. The same is true if you intend to collect biological specimens of any kind. If your project involves deception, the research design will have to pass a higher threshold of scrutiny. If the study seems likely to generate friction with a government—by violating local standards of morality or political norms—the IRB may stop it unless you can articulate why there is no risk to subjects or implementers.[8]

Recruitment of acutely vulnerable subjects using financial inducements (often used in behavioral games) presents a Goldilocks problem: too little money and the researcher does not actually incentivize the behaviors the study is trying to capture, but too much money and the whole enterprise begins to reek of something coercive and ethically dubious. A standard set of arguments about minimal risk typically alleviates these concerns, and mentors or experienced researchers can help you find the right language choices (*"everyone wins but a control group wins less"*), but rhetorical presentations of arguments are not always as persuasive or effective as they need to be in a first draft by a novice. There is a generic set of issues related to authorial voice as it relates to relative disparities in power and associated disparities in privilege. It is not uncommon for ambitious or controversial projects to spend months caught in limbo.

Above all, the IRB provides a set of nonnegotiable rules that distinguish "real" research from preliminary scouting trips. You can get a tourist visa and go somewhere any time you want. Nothing stops you from meeting people and asking preliminary questions. What you do on a study abroad trip or an exotic vacation is not interchangeable with research. Your plan must be signed off on officially, so begin a few months in advance. Leave a few months for your proposal to be rejected, to make what revisions are necessary, to resubmit it, and to get it approved on a second or third try. This does slow you down. The delays can be irksome. It is easy to understand how an edgy adversarial relationship might develop between well-intentioned young people (who just want to get started) and aloof middle-aged bureaucrats (who only convene meetings once a month), but the most damaging and counterproductive caricatures are driven by immaturity.[9] Use the formal process to begin to construct a barrier between your professional and personal travel. It may be helpful to remind yourself that all of these "hoops" result in legal protection for the university and, by extension, yourself. Because that can sound abstract, here is an incomplete list of the kinds of things all universities can provide that can assist you in doing research:

- *Official forms/contacts.* In addition to help with visas, your university can serve as an official point of contact for when you register yourself with your home country's embassy.
- *Legal assistance.* Your university has every interest in helping to find you a lawyer in-country in advance to vet any aspect of a project that may seem dodgy. This is especially important if you are planning research in an overseas setting where there is an ongoing war—not only because of the potential need for legal assistance overseas, but also because you also do not want to inadvertently violate any US laws in the course of research.[10] If there is any possibility that your research will draw the attention of the host government, the United States government, or a third-party government, discussions with campus legal counsel can set your mind at ease and help you avoid costly missteps.
- *Introduction props.* If your work involves archives, or if you plan to interview high-ranking government or military officials, it is useful to acquire a formal letter of introduction to formally "borrow" institutional authority. You will want it to be on official letterhead with an ornate university seal and as many stamps as possible, written in the appropriate language by a native speaker. Make it look as important as you can. Arrange to have it signed by people with impressive-sounding titles (e.g., "Vice Chancellor for Research," "Head Librarian"). Keep an uncreased copy of each letter in a plastic binder for safekeeping. Reveal them only selectively. Act as if they should be treated as revered objects. Your affiliation with a research university sends a signal that you are someone worth talking to. Bring paper embossed with your department letterhead for special kinds of communication.
- *Mementos.* Business cards bearing an official university seal, a title, your name, and an official-looking permanent telephone number are also valuable. Hand-write a local cellular phone number on the back.

Members of a university's scholarly community receive voluntary assistance and many invisible social protections. You are a junior professional scholar. Always remember this.

GRANT APPLICATION PRELIMINARIES

Getting from a first draft to a polished grant proposal can take months, followed by a long wait, uncertain outcomes, and (even if you are lucky) more time before a check arrives, so it is best to get started early. Grant writing is a craft distinct from academic writing for publication. The process of framing a proposal for potential donors can be complementary with the task of framing research for advisors, referees, and journal editors—but it is a lot of work. Identifying potential sources, keeping track of deadlines, assembling materials, and organizing letters of support can feel like a full-time hustle. Aggregating grants is an important part of how entrepreneurial graduate students learn the ropes of self-promotion, however. Those who can weave a compelling narrative of how their university coursework and preparation support a research plan will have an early leg up.

There are relatively immediate psychological and material payoffs. Acquiring money for fieldwork is a source of external validation that you are on the right track and, as a practical matter, mitigates a common source of stress. The best scenario is to string together overlapping grants for a cushion of financial security in the field. Like a travel air mattress, however, this cushion will need to be refilled—manually. In contrast to assembling a committee or filing a research plan with your university, the search for funding is totally self-directed. Competition for scarce funds is not as fierce as the competition for scarce space in top journals, but there is not enough money for everyone. Insufficient funding for fieldwork forces trade-offs and compromises. If you do not succeed immediately, do not panic or lose hope. It is likely that applying widely and dealing with rejection by donors will eventually come to comprise a big part of your job if you remain in academia.[11] Modify expectations, rethink the framing, get assistance from your university writing center, follow instructions in the grant to the letter, apply aggressively for smaller pools of money, and keep trying. Grant applications will be revisited in the next chapter.

A RENEGOTIABLE COMMITMENT TO A READER COALITION

The primary appeal of joining a professional readers guild is predictability. You can anticipate that specialists with familiar reading habits and specialized knowledge—people equipped to appreciate the nuances of your design—will eventually read your words. If you are lucky, they will also distribute your work to their students. The trade-off is that, unlike journalists, social scientists have no commercial market for their writing. For some people, it helps productivity to imagine that a readership exists (or will exist) somewhere in the policy realm. However, this is mostly a self-serving illusion.[12] We labor for each other. Academic disciplines are the last of the great guilds. Housed within modern research universities, academia proved capable of enduring the social dislocations of the industrial revolution by enforcing codes and arcane membership rules impenetrable to outsiders, even well-read ones. An academic discipline is an independent, hierarchically organized, specialized, self-reproducing labor cartel that bestows labor protections (especially tenure) on high-ranked members. Its grandmasters control who receives early-career awards, who is asked to contribute to edited volumes apprentices will read, and more. There is an invisible prestige hierarchy, yet at our major conferences we all ride the same bus. We are a society of working- and middle-class teachers who really like to read.

At early stages of the profession, mentors and peers serve the role of the idealized readership face-to-face, providing feedback on papers, grant proposals, and initial plans. The graduate student should not shoulder responsibility for designing a viable research plan alone. Initial vetting of research design ideas begins with peers. Subsequent to this, discussions of feasibility and planning provide an opportunity to assess the student's fit with potential mentors. Shopping around a research design to gauge enthusiasm and mutual compatibility is a natural way to begin an advisor–advisee relationship. In more advanced stages, as a research plan is formalized, it metamorphoses into a prospectus. A reader coalition is eventually institutionalized as a department committee that signs off on a dissertation. Committee members assume a fiduciary responsibility to assist the apprentice in navigating the road to journeyman status. The relationships that form in this committee can be with you for a very long time. You never reach a stage of your career in the discipline when you don't need letters. In the short term, these people will assist with preparation of grant materials and recommendation letters to get you to the field. In the medium and long term, they are the avatars of the discipline, in the literal sense that their professional obligation will be to discipline you. It is not really an adversarial relationship, however, and usually not meant to be infantilizing. Everyone's career needs help getting started.

For you, as a graduate student, a plan for fieldwork begins by attempting to link a literature (which you can know only superficially but are trying to master) to a site (to which you intuit you want to go, but may also know only superficially). To connect the field site to the literature, begin to solicit feedback on how the committee members think about three questions: (1) What is the field site usually considered to exemplify? (2) Where does the site fit in a distribution of other cases that are sufficiently similar to form a natural comparison set? (3) What are the variables (and the possible values that variables can hold) that require fieldwork to assess? While the answer to (3) is preliminary, and may change once you are in the field and discover interesting new opportunities, I advocate for it as a springboard for conversations to sharpen measurement details and clear conceptual cobwebs. You can fake many things indefinitely in graduate school if you are glib. However, it is difficult to fake your way through conversations with guild professionals in which you act as if you care about an outcome if you are not acquainted with the trending strategies to measure the thing you say you care about. When you have inevitable moments of disorientation in the field, remember why you told your advisors you were there. Recall from earlier that a solid answer to the "Why do fieldwork?" question is "To collect measurements on a theoretically-important variable that I cannot observe or measure using library and internet resources alone."

A final write-up, whether a book or a paper, will be expected to conform with guild standards. The burden falls on graduate students to figure out what those are, including how a paper is supposed to look at the moment of submission. Many intrepid fieldworkers are surprised to discover that publication is often more difficult than the process of data collection itself (which can be rewarding and fun). Many students cheat themselves by delaying this process, faking their way through classes and thinking they are getting away with something. As table 1.1 suggests, there is no general answer on what should "count" as a good puzzle or an acceptably robust answer—one that is student-, project-, and coalition-specific—but the final product is always expected to appear to have emerged from research conducted in a systematic fashion. The beginning of a project, when many things are fluid, is a good time for honest reflection about what outcomes you want to spend years trying to observe, document, and describe to the guild, and what methods you believe are likeliest to be your comparative advantage in doing so.

Leaving the comfort and safety of the ivory tower is a gamble that requires confidence that your finished project will make a contribution to the literature. You will borrow this confidence, at first, from your committee. Before finalizing any logistical planning, identify a set of readers, all of whom are informed about what you are trying to do. Everyone involved in the committee should be able to count on each other to write consistent letters of support and provide advice that does not run at cross-purposes. That said, committees sometimes have complex social dynamics. Views of what "the literature" demands of future generations of researchers vary. Different people will expect different things from a great project and demand different things from a marginal one. Additional complexity can be introduced depending on who is in the room (and who wants to be), who is at the head of the table (and which people wish they were), and so on. The committee should be able to work together to cooperatively articulate a worthy puzzle, consider a range of answers that would fit into debates in the existing literature, think about what kind of evidence would be necessary to make a meaningful contribution, and consider the sample needed to select one answer from the set of possibilities. Different advisors will predictably push in different directions based on their own aesthetic judgements. Some friction is natural. Sometimes advisors do not get along with each other for personal or professional reasons. If you fear being put in a position of mediating a proxy war between powerful patrons, consider revising your committee's composition.

At the level of nuts-and-bolts design, there needs to be a meeting of the minds on practical questions. Is the question sufficiently well-asked such that the answer will be valuable? Does everyone in the room understand the question in the same way? Assuming the purpose of a journey to the field is empirical, what are you trying to estimate, and how are you planning to do it? What are the mechanisms consistent with the theory you are testing that will lead to heterogeneous effects (variation) on the quantity of interest? What would a test look like? Will you have sufficient power? What are the best measurement strategies on offer for the theoretical concepts you claim to care about? How will you troubleshoot foreseeable issues that might arise in the field (attrition, noncompliance, fraud, ethical violations)? These are basic science problems across all fields and methods, even if the language and mode of inquiry vary.[13]

For a fieldwork-heavy dissertation, institutionalizing informal relationships is a main purpose of the prospectus. The dissertation prospectus is analogous to a soft contract articulating what "counts for credit" in the minds of future letter-writers, even if things do not go completely according to plan. It is less a renegotiation-proof document and more a blueprint to repair one's ship at sea. Everyone wants to help get your career started. The conversations that take place within a committee (especially an interdisciplinary committee, as different fields translate their biases) are often unexpectedly revealing and productive. What is the evidence for the argument in its strong form supposed to look like? Does the answer change if we think not as narrow guild specialists, but rather as if we were going to use evidence the way other disciplines do? Does the answer change if the goal is to sell the project to a dean, or at an interdisciplinary meeting, or in the court of public opinion, or to make the most convincing courtroom case? In the course of discussions, even if everyone signs, it can become clear that the site needs reconsideration, that different methods need to be employed, that the committee membership needs to be altered, or that the project was never realistic or viable from the beginning. Sometimes more than one is true. Problems may arise because of a nonnegotiable matter of design ("*I do not think you have a viable strategy to isolate causal relationships of interest in the face of confounds*"); country-specific concerns ("*There is no way you are going to get government permission to do this, and, if you do, you will spend years in mid-career limbo because local scholars won't believe you did*"); an ethical discomfort with the project ("*I do not care if you have IRB approval—unlike my colleagues, I think something smells funny*"); mundane concerns ("*I don't think there's any reason for anyone to trust your observations. I happen to know that you don't speak Tagalog . . .*"); or a clash of strong personalities ("*I'm just not intellectually interested in this*"). You want to identify people who want to read what you write. If your proposed project is not a good fit, it is not the end of the world. Adapt to your committee members' expectations or remove them from the reader coalition.

Norms for "how complete" a plan needs to be to get committee sign-off obviously vary. During my graduate training sequence, the norm was for all students to attempt engagement with the tripartite method, consisting of three pillars: game theory, large-N quantitative analysis, and narrative.[14] I recall being initially daunted by the prescription. ("*Learn formal theory well enough to convince economists that your argument is original and internally coherent, demonstrate an ability to analyze high-dimensional data with competence, and, while you're at it, learn a language or two and master the politics of a distant place.*") Doing all of that before heading to the field was out of the question. I still got sign-off. The tripartite method is less a "how-to" for a dissertation and more a "how-to" for peripatetic inquiry over a lifetime. When it works, it provides a program to stay focused on an important outcome, to make sure your model explaining changes in the outcome is coherent (that you have not subtly changed the subject searching for rhetorically pleasing synthesis), and to design multiple tests. The ethos of improvisational pluralism requires faith that as your understanding of the field site becomes more authentic, it will be more obvious which findings are important ("real") and how these findings should fit into the literature. Your corner of the library will eventually find you.

Site-specific constraints may overwhelm even the best-laid-plans, but you still need to have a plan. Improvisation will happen in the field, but, as in jazz, it takes place around a chord progression. If the jazz analogy seems too facile, consider the analogy between a dissertation prospectus and a business plan. A business plan is necessary in order to get a loan from a bank to start a business. Start-ups that run exactly according to the initial plan usually fail.

The advice in this first chapter sits somewhat apart from the rest of the book. Preparation can reduce paralysis and disorientation in later stages. A viable research question, honed and embedded in a defensible review of the existing literature, a measurement strategy, and a set of institutionalized permissions, transforms overseas travel into research. It is easy, frankly, to give this kind of advice in a confident voice of authority, providing textbook answers to basic black-and-white questions. Much of what follows will be in shades of gray. Some advice varies by site and design. Some important questions just do not have easy answers. If one does this job with integrity, luck becomes increasingly important. In light of that, how is a young researcher to choose between an exciting new prospect and the well-laid plan already pitched to donors and advisors? If one seeks out cases with extremely vulnerable subject populations, the process of observation will likely change the researcher permanently—but what of the consequences? The only general answer to these kinds of personal questions is that three types of writing—for scholarly peers, IRBs, and donors—will continue to be a part of your professional footprint. It's not uncommon to redo everything more than once, essentially from scratch, in the course of completing a graduate school dissertation. Acquaint yourself with the rhythm of these writing tasks as soon as possible. We are a guild. Our craft involves writing.

FREQUENTLY ASKED QUESTION #1

How much language training am I supposed to have?

Knowledge of foreign languages is like running to maintain basic cardiovascular health: A little is better than none and when there is an emergency you always wish you had more. A fine answer is "just go and find out."

Some people have an ability to learn some languages much more easily than others, making this question difficult to answer in the abstract. If you are a native Russian speaker, you are sure to have an easier time "picking up" serviceable Ukrainian or Polish than Chinese or Arabic. Many people struggle to shed accents after decades. Whether this holds you back from doing work is often a matter of internal psychology. Some people get embarrassed and incapacitated if they make a grammar mistake. Others bluster forward unashamed and get 80 percent of what they want, laughing the whole time. It is important to remember that good observation often has nothing to do with erudition. Many cab drivers and hotel workers speak enough of five or six languages to get by.

Any costly signal one can send to donor agencies about being prepared to carry out fieldwork can matter at the margins, but there is no ceiling—there is always more to learn, and no one to tell you exactly when you've done enough. (The Middlebury College Russian language program has nine levels. Everyone in Level 9 has spent years in the classroom but is still not satisfactorily fluent to meet their personal or professional goals.) If you haven't started learning a language at all, what you can get from a crash course may not do much to move the needle, and the jump from 5 percent to 30 percent comprehension may not feel like an investment worth the effort to you.

Unlike other tools that are part of your graduate training, an attempt to learn a language prior to fieldwork is not just a cost-benefit strategic choice. It is about your idealized relationship with the field site, and its population, and the kind of distant future idealized self you want to cultivate. In the short term, between now and your dissertation, you *will* have a different set of experiences on your journey if you understand almost everything going on around you than if you understand 40 percent of what is going on around you and still more different than if you understand only 10 percent. Interpreting subtleties related to social cleavages, status, and relationships demands linguistic competence. Is this a language that you *want* to imagine yourself reading fluently thirty years from now? Are you flirting with the idea of "going native" even if it is not possible to switch nationalities fully? If you try to think of the research not as a quest with the goal of getting a tenure-track job, but rather as a quest with a higher personal goal, is fluency in a language part of your ideal self?

Do not get a local girlfriend or boyfriend, imagining "pillow talk" the best way to learn a language. That is a myth, and a dangerous one. It can yield serious complications and make fieldwork harder than it has to be (see FAQ #5). As an alternative, consider this program:

• Recognize that you are never going to "be yourself" in another language. Get used to the idea that across a language barrier, for the first few years, you will be a two-dimensional character based loosely on yourself. Create that character strategically. The material in chapter 3, "How to Think about Self-Presentation Once You Arrive," is meant to assist you.

• Begin by creating a vocabulary list for that character. It should not contain more than 1,500 words and 50 verbs. Strive for "active use words": the ones you *really* use, over and over again, in everyday life, going and coming, feeling and thinking. Memorize full sentences: "I don't understand that word," "I need you to repeat that again, please," etc. The good first- and second-year "how to" language books tend to put all of this stuff in easy-to-find places. Pick up a few used ones. Employ common sense. You need numbers. You need to order food. You need to manage the five feet around your body comfortably, to ask urgent directions ("That way? No, this way.")

• Verb conjugations can be maddening. A few ("I go/I went/I'm going") are necessary in the past, present, and future tenses in order to string a coherent set of ideas together.

• Supplement classwork with a private tutor a few times a week. Daily practice is obviously desirable but, like daily exercise, can become an unmanageable time-suck. A few good hours of practice a week are a lot better than nothing.

• Memorize entire strings of "stock questions" along with generic responses. ("Do you have children?" "Boys or girls?" "What is his/her name?" "Oh, that is a [strong/beautiful] name. How old is he/she?" . . .) Taxi rides are great times to indulge in your character—the stakes are low and there is an opportunity to repeat set-pieces over and over. It will boost your confidence, little by little. As you do this, develop twenty or thirty phrase-long pieces of "verbal static" that work as conversation-filler and keep them in the chamber for small talk. They buy you time while you search for words and are the easiest way to give the impression that you understand what is going on even if you do not: "That's not the point." "In my opinion . . ." "I can see what you mean, of course." "Yes, indeed, it is true, quite true." "That's a good one!" "If you don't mind my asking . . ."

• Revisit your flashcards. Keep them current. If you have not added two new sentences every week you are not working at this as hard as you could be.

• Once you have a working character, which will take six months to a year, you can add professional vocabulary. Begin with one hundred words that are necessary for your research. Words that are the same as those in English don't count. Add to this list as necessary. Do not over-load it. I do not recommend trying to add more than five words per week.

• If you are going to employ a standard questionnaire to keep track of data, or oversee a survey, make sure you run through all of the word-ings thoroughly with more than one native speaker. Only employ language you completely understand.

• Realize that this character is functionally illiterate beyond perhaps basic forms. You need other people to write short essays for you. The good news is that you can drop this character at any time and revert to being the hyperliterate English-language version of yourself, which is a very good thing to be able to do.

I've actually received several variants of this frequently asked question as an advisor. Here they are, along with the answers I wish I had provided at the time.

Q: *I'm a people person. How does charisma work if I can't express myself?*
A: I recall the same concern. I am certain, however, that my inability to express myself is why my data collection was so successful. It made me listen. It made me more aware of nonverbal communication. It made me slow down. All of this made the final product much more credible.

Q: *Look . . . life is short, right? I'm going be paying locals to collect data for me. I skipped ahead to chapter 5: That's me. Yeah, I'm going to have some privilege-based guilt for not working as hard as my colleagues in anthropology or comp lit . . . but I've listened hard in my methods classes and nobody believes that other stuff is our field's comparative advantage. It's misallocated resources to pretend it is. I'm going to the field to bring the data home efficiently.*
A: Life *is* short. It sounds as if you have a realistic view of some of the professional incentives and some of the trade-offs. There are lot of people in the world who are fluidly multilingual. If you were one of those people we wouldn't be having this conversation in this way. People who are really good at math are rarer—which is why, by the law of supply and demand, they are paid more. Spending energy on language acquisition may be a misallocation of resources. On the other hand, in my experience, locals appreciate the effort, even if the result is bad. Slowing down and living outside your comfort zone shows vulnerability. It can change the power dynamic when you struggle visibly with pronunciations, leave yourself open, even when it's clearly not in your self-interest. It can sometimes get interviews to places they would not otherwise go. If you act like a

distant manager, you won't get the most out of your labor. To many of us, discovering that we can invent a credible "new character" in our same body is itself very rewarding. And many careers in comparative politics are started by candidates promising to combine different things, all of which are "good enough" but none "great" in an original and compelling way.

But . . . I have to admit . . . You *are* on to something. Life *is* short.

———— ⊗⊗⊗ ————

Q: *Plenty of local sources speak English, or want to try to speak English and will make the effort to bridge to me. I'm putting money for a translator into my grant budget, too. Why isn't that enough?*
A: Maybe it is. It really depends on what you are trying to do. It is hard to claim you have studied a community with integrity if you have not made *any* attempt to understand the language, but you cannot make the perfect the enemy of the good in this job. Margaret Mead, the Franz Boas student who became the last century's most famous anthropologist, was not an expert in the language of her subjects when she arrived in the South Pacific.[15] No matter how far off the beaten path you go, you will be able to coast along on the efforts of the United States' primary cultural ambassadors—pop singers and rap artists. Many young people want to practice English.

The real question is whether you can discipline yourself to not over-claim your inferences based on data that only come to you through the filter of someone else's translation. Even through a filter you can still end up with an unmanageable amount of data. You will wreck your reputation, however, if you act as if you gleaned deep insights into another society based on interactions that your readers intuit you couldn't possibly have had. Some people arrive on a scene, can't understand a word of what is going on around them, and are conservative in reporting what they actually see and hear. Others give in to the temptation to exaggerate. You want to emulate the ethos of George Orwell in *Homage to Catalonia* or *The Road to Wigan Pier*, not of that fraudulent journalist from Season Five of *The Wire*. But presumably you already know that.

———— ⊗⊗⊗ ————

Q: *Since I don't have time to get fluent in time to go the field, why bother getting 10 percent fluent?*
A. Well . . .

1. Everything worth doing is worth doing badly at first. You start somewhere or you don't. If you don't start now, when you have so much unstructured time, when *will* you start?

2. A completed dissertation is not the final finish line. The academic market is based on calculated judgments of research potential, with your dissertation as a kind of "proof of concept" and calling card. Learning a language now can grease the skids for your second and third projects. You will need to continue to collect more data for later promotions.

3. The bar to sustain the claim that you are translating honestly is always moving. Google Translate is changing the landscape. (I personally doubt that we are more than a few years away from serviceable real-time universal translators for limited-use situations. These will be especially useful in multi-language archives.) Hitting the highest levels of the discipline, if you want to, will require that your readers trust your representation of your subjects' social reality. Language is a window into your subjects' country. Language reflects their reality. Acquisition of computer-enabled language scraping/analysis tools can complement traditional interpretative approaches, since as we all become more familiar with text-as-data tools we will see them as useful for analyzing what people write and say in the aggregate. Knowing what people *mean* requires interpretation, however. The "area studies" intuitions about woolly interpretative matters ("meaning," "code-switching," institutional or hegemonic structural constraints on speech, etc.) that have been devalued will eventually be repriced. At the more mundane level, nuances in question wording really do matter. The best predictor of a "don't know/refuse to answer" response on a survey is another "refuse to answer/don't know" earlier on. Yes, Geertzian winks are beyond what most of us expect to catch, document, or measure (see chapter 4), but no matter what, you *are* going to end up trading on your ability to make accurate psychological claims on behalf of your subjects. What separates the great fieldworkers from the herd is usually reducible to an intuition that what they are doing with their qualitative methods is functionally unique and that some people's work has higher (!) value to the discipline than replicable

cookie-cutter quantitative research, even if the latter is produced at scale. If you are not even 10 percent fluent in speaking the language, it is going to be harder to convince people that you employed active listening in the collection process.

———— ❦ ————

Q: *I'm just going to forget whatever I learn when I get back from the field and can't practice. And my students will never care whether or not I speak [insert exotic language], and, if they do, I can always trick them by throwing a few choice words into every lecture.*
A: That all may be true, if you decide you want it to be true. But . . . why drag the possibility of defrauding hypothetical future audiences into this? You have not earned the right to be up in front of students yet. Not even close. And with that attitude, you won't. Nobody wants to share authority with someone who is not trustworthy.

2

HOW TO PREPARE TO LEAVE
YOUR HOME INSTITUTION

This chapter is an attempt to distill the minimum requirements before you get on that plane. Many graduate students intuitively understand they need to *go* but do not know how to *leave*. This chapter is therefore divided into two sections: (1) a checklist of practical design considerations and (2) a checklist of practical logistical considerations. The advice provided in the second half of this chapter may seem basic, even pedantic, to a military veteran or other reader who has extensive pre–graduate school experience on a field site, but even experienced travelers may find useful tidbits.

In this work's spirit as a starter guide for a disoriented novice, I push a variable-based measurement approach as an entry point. I realize this may cause non-positivists and dedicated mechanism-based scientists to put the book down prematurely. As a teacher, I find that a first-draft measurement strategy helps graduate students make basic plans for what to do upon arrival. To demystify the process, I provide a short exposition of my own frustrations trying to implement the "codebook" approach advocated by Barbara Geddes in her seminal work on research design, *Paradigms and Sandcastles*.[1] I describe failing, persisting, adapting, and, eventually, finding indicators that were serviceable for my own first project.

DESIGN CHECKLIST

Upon your return, you must convince people that you had a well-thought-out rationale for leaving in the first place. Fieldwork, including justification for field site selection, begins with the process of translating research design into a series of site-specific tasks. Logistical planning follows.

PRE-PREPARATION AND A PRE-FIELDWORK TRIP

Because establishing an early-career publication pipeline is a multiyear process (submission, revision, rejection, resubmission, etc.), self-funding a preliminary scouting trip to a field site through RA work or squirreling away some savings can be a good investment in your future. Even a two- or three-day trip, if one treats it seriously and not as a vacation, allows you to get the lay of the land. A weeklong trip, perhaps paid for with the help of an exploratory grant, allows scouting for potential housing options, scheduling preliminary interviews (no IRB necessary!), comparing potential institutional affiliates, exploring regulatory regimes, conducting site visits to survey firms to acquire in-person price quotes, navigating public transportation, trying out your language skills by listening to radio and TV, and more. An exploratory trip is not enough time to uncover any cultural subtleties, but even brief exposure can provide a reality check.

A good time for this, if it can be managed, is the summer after your first year of coursework. Consider going to the country you suspect you want to work in under the auspices of intensive language training—often a well-institutionalized endeavor that is not difficult to get funded. Before you go, talk to everyone you can who has recent experience on location. Begin with academic researchers who have written papers or books in your field using data sourced from the site. If you reach out in a cordial and professional way, and especially if your introduction includes a question that evidences a reading of their works, they will likely extend you the courtesy of a preliminary conversation. Nonacademics (family friends, friends of friends, work friends) may be of help as well. You will have an advantage if you make contacts in advance with people who can make professional introductions on your behalf. Cold-emailing from a .edu address is not bad if you have no other options. A few hours of preparation in the weeks before an initial trip can fill a three-day schedule most efficiently. Scour the internet and the library for good up-to-date maps and basic travel tips. Academics often bristle at the idea that they should read *Fodor's*, *Rough Guide*, *Lonely Planet*, and similar beginner's travel books, but these contain all sorts of useful information if you actually take the time to read them: a country's baseline history, recently updated maps of the most well-traveled parts of the capital, and cuisine and travel advice.

The psychological benefits of a short trip vary. For some people, it is good to realize that the journey to "the field" does not require a rocket ship, just a few hours on a plane. As the field site becomes less exotic, your social-scientific voice becomes more credible. For others, to go and return can be a sugar rush, but also a valuable reminder that the grinding cogs and gears of university life keep turning without you. For others, the most daunting aspect of pre-fieldwork preparation is language triage in a place where they know they have insufficient language training. Classroom preparation is a good start (with caveats, laid out in the prior FAQ), but it does no good to worry abstractly when you could just take a trip and see how a place feels.

For still other people, even a short trip may force a personal confrontation with the nagging voice in your head telling you that this is not actually something you want to do. The focus of chapter 3 is adaptive self-presentation, and your persona is plastic in some respects, but at the "scouting" stage of fieldwork you may come to a personal realization that there are certain places that are just too hostile, too alien, or too uncomfortable for fieldwork to be a good idea. Perhaps you will realize that you cannot handle what you perceive to be endless unwanted sexual harassment, for example, or extreme poverty. The emotional toll of watching vulnerable children in acute need and not helping can be debilitating for many people. If you find you are one of those people, it will probably change your field experience and should very likely change your research design. The reality of the field site is often uncomfortable and even a short trip can yield unexpected (and unwanted) discoveries about yourself. Once site-specific constraints are less abstract, it is easier to assess what you are actually committing to. It may be better to pull the plug early on something you don't *really* want to do, rather than sinking months or years into a place that you won't ever want to go back to, for one reason or another.

One constraint that is rarely anticipated by first-time fieldworkers, but is a common contributor to exhaustion (see chapter 6), is the baseline expectation by your subjects that you have deep pockets. This does not necessitate exotic fieldwork, of course—Chicago residents a few blocks from his university saw Sudhir Venkatesh as a potential conduit for material resources.[2] In many places, however, you *are* relatively rich and there is going to be widespread expectation that you *should* be paying more for everything, tipping heavily, and paying bribes to subsidize the lives of people you come into contact with. At advanced stages of fieldwork, researchers working in these environments find ways to make peace with this reality, padding grants to carve out money for these kinds of transactions, hiring a fixer to pay critical bribes (only once), and the like. If you find yourself debilitated by the daily grind of constant corruption and extortion, perhaps the field site will not be a good fit.

One of the most important things that can be gleaned from a short trip is a "gut-level" response to the culture as it relates to gender-power relations, attitudes toward homosexuality, racial discrimination, and a variety of other things that may affect whether you *want* to spend long periods of time in a place. Racial and gender stereotypes open and close doors. Expectations of aggressive flirting are different around the world, as are norms related to touching strangers, alcohol and drug consumption, public displays of affection, overt discrimination, and much else. As you probe your own day-to-day comfort with a research site and develop personal strategies, remember that all of this is voluntary and you might not *want* to stay (even if you want to want to stay). Levels of harassment and danger for LGBTQ individuals differ between countries and cultures. Many aspects of queer culture (e.g., gender-nonconforming behaviors, gender fluidity/androgyny as choice, same-sex cohabitation, adoption or childbearing by same-sex couples, use of bathrooms) have changed more rapidly in the United States and Europe than in other parts of the world. Because laws against same-sex relations in many countries are enforced, sometimes by violent vigilantism, it may be prudent to change behaviors (e.g., avoiding public displays of affection) in order to avoid trouble in some field sites. The rubber hits the road on logistical planning for bedrooms and bathrooms. You may need to be prepared for a jarring recalibration of behaviors when you arrive in a place where prevailing public gender forms are more binary and traditional. Extra planning and spending may be necessary. Consult people who have worked in your area to find out what the norms and expectations are. Be honest about personal fit and which compromises are or are not endurable to you. If you or a member of your team want to bring a same-sex partner, before departure, consider consulting the International Lesbian, Gay, Bisexual, Trans and Intersex Association's State-Sponsored Homophobia index, which tracks repressive laws and behaviors against LGBTQ people, in order to help assess whether you (or your team) ought to prepare for higher-than-normal levels of anxiety.[4]

A preliminary trip can be useful to clarify the viable unit of analysis in the design stage. Journalists writing for the market "pitch" editors on the idea, having confidence that they have what it takes to go to a country, "get the story," come back, write it up, and push the product. The location sells the book. You need confidence in this job, and first- and second- year graduate students often get signatures from overworked advisors on pitches for scouting trips on a similar logic. Science writing is not about making that kind of sale (at least not exactly). It is often not clear until one arrives that "a country" is not "a case"—at least not for many interesting comparative questions. Treating it as such may even be a completely invalid way to think about the variation that one cares about, which is often between subnational groups.

Other questions of design specifics can be clarified. Rethinking the first draft of your design is often necessitated after a preliminary trip. You intuit that you are surprised something changed . . . but why, exactly? What is the *exact* sample you plan to observe change over time? Which city, village, or neighborhood? How can you compare units meaningfully? Do you have enough statistical power? What is the relevant population to oversample? Replacing romantic attraction to a research site with basic science problems ("*estimation strategies, how different causal mechanisms yield different hypotheses, testing in the face of measurement confounds, heterogeneous treatment effects, observer effects, sample attrition . . .* ") may sound like a step backward. This is completely wrong. Making your questions smaller has big advantages. You can

begin to take the design process more seriously, look for models to emulate, and seek advice. Even if the initial germ of a project no longer seems
feasible after a scouting trip, firsthand knowledge makes for more compelling grant applications and more credible IRB interactions.

Different benefits accrue to researchers working on societies that they
already know from a prior life. The hurdles faced by an Indian scholar
who realizes that when she returns to her home country she will be taken
less seriously than a white American graduate student are not ones that I
can comment on from my own life experience. I can say (from experience and from many conversations with colleagues) that "going home"
and trying to conduct research can bring special challenges. An especially difficult personal challenge awaits scholars considering work on
politically sensitive topics. They may begin to wonder if their local family
or friends are functionally pre-positioned hostages. Some of the most
inspiring unique research is conducted by individuals who can leverage
aspects of their background to gain access that no one else could imagine, such as Aisha Ahmad's ability to ask Pakistani businessmen directly
about their relationships with jihadis or Georgi Derluguian's to document the practical changes in behavior involved in transmogrifying oneself (unsuccessfully) from a sociology professor into a warlord in the
North Caucasus.[3] So do not give up prematurely. Think strategically
about how to make entrée (as described in the section below). If you have
work experience in the site from your pre-academic life, it can be a bit of
a challenge to interact with your former military, embassy, or other
social networks under the constraints imposed by your new role. The
most important considerations for academic audiences can sound twee,
abstract, or out of touch to old friends. Listen politely to what people who
know the site *think* the right questions are.

The best thing that can come out of these preliminary visits is a collaborative professional relationship with a local scholar. Because I am
writing this book anticipating the needs of a scholar who considers
"home" to be the United States, it is worth remembering that the academy is global and that many of your best potential collaborators are
academics just like you, doing more or less what you imagine you will
want to do someday, but housed in academic research universities in
the country where you plan to do fieldwork. If you can, find a trustworthy collaborator embedded in a reputable local institution with whom

you share rapport and research interests. Negotiate a coauthorship relationship with this person. You can write a local partner into your research grants to serve as your local interlocutor and translator, submit appropriate research paperwork, and troubleshoot friction on-site. A division of labor in which the local partner navigates the process of securing research clearance and the partner based in the United States secures IRB permission and funding from donors often has mutual benefits.

FROM CONCEPT TO VARIABLE OPERATIONALIZATION TO A "TO GET" LIST

Research often begins with outrage at how poorly the literature speaks to a specific case that the researcher already knows a lot about. What must follow, to create academic research and not amateur journalism, is a plan to contribute to the stock of case-specific knowledge with a peer-reviewed publication. For those of you who are anxious to get started, remember: the purpose of fieldwork for your project can often be clarified by figuring out what you cannot code using materials downloadable from the internet or available at the library. You should be heading to the field with a plan to fill in specific gaps that you have already established you cannot fill at home.

What data you need obviously depends on your particular research project. Translating your research question into a concrete set of rules that you will use to score indicators is one of the first steps of design. Once in the field you may find new indicators for the underlying concepts you care about, of course. Scoring indicators needs not involve any arcane quantitative methods—just systematic observation. Consider how Roger Petersen, in his study of Southeastern Europe before and after the NATO intervention in the Kosovo War, operationalizes ethnic status reversals. To assess his theory he must demonstrate that one group is visibly dominant over other groups in a society at a given time. To assess ethnic status hierarchies in multiethnic societies, Petersen proposes coding the following: "(1) The language of day-to-day government (2) The composition of the bureaucracy (3) The composition of the police (4) The composition of the officer corps (5) Symbols such as street names."[5] It can be helpful to begin to try to organize facts according to a transparent schema, a "codebook" making it possible for other members of the community to assess your empirics, even if they do not have the patience to follow all of the details embedded in your case study. In her research design text *Paradigms and Sand Castles*, Barbara Geddes makes the following case for a codebook (italics are hers):

- Most arguments involve complex *causes*, *outcomes*, and *limiting conditions*.
- The causes, outcomes, and limiting conditions must be *operationalized* and *measured* with great care if tests of the argument are to be persuasive. In quantitative research, *operationalization* refers to the observable indicators that can be used as proxies for abstract or unobservable concepts. In non-quantitative research, *operationalization* may not involve off-the-shelf indicators to use as proxies for a more complicated concept, but still requires that the research specify clear, concrete criteria for defining concepts.
- Once these criteria are defined, they serve as the basis for deciding which cases belong in the study, which time periods in the different cases can be appropriately compared, and how cases are classified by the researcher in an unambiguous and transparent way. *Measurement* involves the actual assignment of particular cases to particular values or categories of the operational concept.
- Classification criteria must be concrete, unambiguous, and public, so that other scholars can understand the basis for the analyst's judgments. As a means of disciplining oneself to stick to the same criteria across cases and over time, it is useful to produce an analogue of the kind of coding scheme used to code open-ended survey questions, as well as a *codebook* including a specific list of characteristics that will be "counted" as having a particular meaning. It should be sufficiently concrete and precise that if several analysts used it to classify the same phenomena in the same cases, the judgments as to the categories to which instances belonged would be very similar. The codebook is the report of the classification, categorization, or measurement of each potential case and the outcome in each case.
- These tools help the analyst maintain the same definitions of basic concepts throughout a study, make it possible for others to replicate or

extend the study, and enable the researcher herself to remember what she has done.

The discipline imposed by the codebook approach that Geddes advocates is calibrated to convince a skeptical audience, not present for the data collection, of the seriousness of your endeavor.[6] Defining tight coding rules is how late-night whiteboard 2 × 2s of "explanatory typologies" begin to give way to research design brass tacks (the universe of potential comparison cases, intercoder reliability measures, etc.).[7] The codebook approach allows you to move systematically to a predeparture list of specific things you want to measure. The researcher can thus prioritize logistical planning. Evan Lieberman employs the extended analogy between field research and a shopping expedition: You arrive at the grocery store and find certain items are out of stock and others are too expensive, and unexpected deals are available, but a shopping list ensures that a scarce budget covers the week's menu. This facilitates the march from generalities to specifics, up to and including specific names and times for interviews. Also, making a list "can help one to envision *actual completion* of one's research," and "if the 'to get' list appears truly overwhelming prior to departure for field research given available time and resources, then one's research design is clearly in need of revision."[8]

Once a design takes shape, a plan and finally a shopping list allow one to begin to bridge the practical implementation gap between the abstract ideas you pitch to a committee ("*I will conduct elite interviews with Uzbeks on post-9/11 security sector reform*") and the banalities of the day-to-day ("*At 11:30 a.m. on Tuesday, January 24, I plan to meet with Ibrahim at the station [Captain—do not use first name unless he invites it]; arrive early for security screening [no laptop]; bring passport and official letter of introduction from US military attaché and official introduction from Chief Librarian [reminder: bring official letterhead introduction].*")

There can be some tension between a philosophical approach that emphasizes planning and careful attention to design details and an approach that emphasizes searching and authentic first-person processes of discovery. While it would be a mistake to exaggerate the tension, the ethos of *improvisational pluralism* suggests a preference for researchers who favor the latter. Most of my students have gone to the field with plans to collect new evidence of something hinted at in the secondary literature but difficult to measure. Sometimes they find the new data exactly where they hoped to find it. They can then implement their plan to correct measurement error (by which I mean correcting others' miscoding of a case or tightening estimates forced by imperfect proxy variables or bad data in previous research) in the normal science mode. This is good when it works. What happens more often, however, is one of two things: (1) upon arrival it turns out that they had fundamental misunderstandings of the case, or (2) the fundamentals of their model are salvageable, but they realize that they will not be able to find the data they were looking for where they thought they would find it. In either case, tools for improvisation are needed. The emphasis on improvisational pluralism invites serendipity to play a role in your project as it matures. The temptation to "make good on a good plan"—essentially to go to the field, consult your "shopping list," find what you were looking for, and get home efficiently—feels over-rigid and makes many of us uncomfortable (for a variety of reasons discussed below).

The other extreme is to skip the planning completely and arrive with the confidence to improvise—to delay committing to design specifics until one gets to know a site. Striking out without any plan and then trying to back your arguments in the literature is time-consuming, even when it works. It risks squandering the goodwill of one's advising team, who may come to feel you are scattered or misrepresenting things to them or wasting time. All observation is theory-laden. If you are not explicit about your theory, or at least your question, you are probably not recording your observations in a way that will lend itself to a write-up. It is fine to hang out and drift for a while, but disciplined data collection and theory-building *are* what you are supposed to be doing. Too many false starts can have a deleterious psychological effect on the guild entrant, magnify impostor syndrome, lower morale, reduce the efficiency of time spent in the field, and make reentry into academic society more painful (see chapter 7).

A middle ground is desirable. While it is generically true that the planning stage of fieldwork is unlikely to survive contact with the field, if you are clever you will be able to cannibalize parts of an initial plan. The best-case scenario to muddle through with the theoretical framework intact is to network your way to original data that leverages unplanned, but theoretically well-justified measurement proxies (see chapters 4 and

5). If you are patient and dedicated to advancing the literature, you can allow the field to alter your theory fundamentally while keeping the literature contribution in clear view. The second path is not what is generally taught in research design classes, but in my experience it is preferred by more guild members than our second-year methods sequence syllabi let on. Revising your theory in light of discoveries and considering how to test the new research hypotheses that emerge from the theory in a compelling way *is* social science.

The "back-end" case for qualitative fieldwork research often rests on the claim that careful local measurement, especially collecting original data, was necessary for both high-quality induction and original theory-building. The claim that the theory only emerged because the researcher really knew a case intimately is often made explicitly (and not a little edgily). Committing to initial coding rules and being deliberate about the reasons that you modify those rules is a good strategy to keep yourself focused on your bottom line as you tell the story of "being there." The definitions and measurement strategies you set in place for yourself early often serve as a focal point once you begin to face constraints and improvise, and also help you identify the moment that you realize your previously held ideas were completely wrong.

Consider the experience of Will Reno. Throughout *Warlord Politics and African States*, he emphasizes that what he thought he knew about West Africa before fieldwork was just fundamentally wrongheaded.[9] Reno's deep commitment to fieldwork in graduate training is a reflection of his conviction that he could not have had the epiphany of the "shadow state" governance structure of West Africa—nor his detailed understanding of the role of Executive Outcomes—from the library. Some patterns are only visible from the ground. On the other hand, not everyone can be Will Reno (and most people would be foolish to try). Jonathan Rodden's first book, *Hamilton's Paradox*, is a study of fiscal federalism emerging from a decade of patient and careful observation. Quantitative analysis of administrative spending data leverages comparisons across many cases (Germany, pre–Civil War America, Brazil, the EU).[10] Rodden does not, in my reading, claim that in Brazil or Germany he had any special "eureka" moment analogous to Reno's, but the tight fit in the book between his empirical measurement strategy and his theory is surely the result of many previous ideas that did not make it into print and were left on the cutting room floor. So one kind of adaptation consistent with the ethos of improvisational pluralism is switching from the idealized sample envisioned vaguely in the prospectus (often the "magic dataset") to a more constrained and manageable (and really existing) sample. Sometimes more dramatic adaptations are needed. The indicators you are finding may not fit the theory. What you actually discover may not even fit well with the theoretical background concept that motivated your journey in the first place. If not, it may be that you need to return to your home library and start reading some different books to "sell" your new contribution to the relevant audiences. It may mean that you need to refocus. It may mean that you need to switch sites. Take these kinds of dramatic steps only after conversation with colleagues and advisors (see FAQ #4), to ensure that you are operationalizing concepts in a manner consistent with trending practices in the field.

A personal example may be useful to some readers. I selected Tajikistan as a field site because I had an intuition that the civil war settlement would provide many examples of side-switching across the "master cleavage" of the war (Islamists vs. secularists). I was especially inspired by the empirical work of Georgi Derluguian, Karen Barkey, and Olivier Roy, and was thinking theoretically about settlement dynamics in situations where the United Nations Peacekeepers were not perceived by locals as politically neutral. (*"And how could repurposed Russian troops in blue hats possibly be perceived as neutral?"*) I introduced myself to a lot of different kinds of social actors by saying, honestly, that I was studying how Tajikistan had settled its war so fast. This opened doors.

I began by trying to collect systematic biographical data on all the field commanders who had served in Tajikistan's civil war and by coding alliance patterns. The empirical project took months. It degenerated into incoherence. I could not articulate coding rules that made sense of the bargaining process. I couldn't even figure out who "the state" was. It seemed like a shifting coalition of warlords trading control of a few city blocks in the capital. I despaired.

I revised my conceptualization of the state based on this failed empirical exercise, however. I began to see the Tajik state in the 1990s as a fragile coalition of individuals and not as a corporate entity. The state was not a "principal": it was a semipermeable membrane allowing violence entrepreneurs ("warlords") to pass in and out of it. The project became richer when I saw dynamics in a different country—Georgia—through this new lens. By the time I returned to Tajikistan a few months later, a new indicator had suggested itself: How long, once a warlord joined the state (reinventing himself as a cop in a rural area, for example), did he *remain in* the state before he exited the coalition? This was a more straightforward question to answer with a dataset and regressions. It was hard to measure, and would have been impossible from my home institution, but in time I found it could be done. At first I tried to differentiate between different kinds of exits—being killed, being thrown in jail, retiring to another country, being encouraged to buy a one-way ticket to Dubai—but I found myself trying to chase down street-stories about shady drug addicts. The "how many years were they in the state?" question could be answered relatively objectively; "where are they now" was a source of innuendo and speculation.[11] With a less-ambitious indicator coded, I could crudely but systematically analyze the characteristics that predicted coalition survival, like warlord birthplace. Circling back to my initial motivation, this exercise made it clear that warlords often switched sides.

The process of doing empirical research in this way also upended my prior understanding and required that I jettison parts of the theory I had constructed before leaving for the field. I had to abandon theorizing about principal-agent problems and incomplete contracting between paramilitary agents and civilian principals. Once I admitted to myself that the governance authority of the state was a hollow shell, and thus there could be no domestic principal, there was no going back. In fact, I had had it all backward: The warlords were the ones installing and delegating choices to the head of state. The warlords were the ones who had the monitoring and enforcement problem. The figurehead president was the warlords' puppet—the "bad agent" serving multiple principals who would have to coordinate in order to punish him for defecting.

Was the progression linear? Of course not. The science article write-up fudges the process and makes things seem more linear than they really were—but this is a bit of an open trade secret.[12] If you read my work you'll find that I did many other things besides push through to a codable variable. It would be dishonest, moreover, to treat those other things I did as mere distractions before I got back to the "real work" of implementing a test with a large-n dataset. That is not how I remember the research process, nor is it how I describe my findings in *Warlords and Coalition Politics* (see chapter 4 of this book as well). I am still grateful, however, that I arrived with something I wanted to measure (side-switching in a way that mapped state-society relations, contra the oversimple predictions of the Islamist-vs.-secular-ex-Communist master cleavage of the war). In disoriented moments, I could remind myself what "my" story was.

No one advocates pounding the round peg of incoming insights into the square hole of an initial conceptual model. Often a journey to the field provides evidence that forces coding schema revisions or even a complete overhaul of the apparatus. In other cases, discoveries prompt useful (and original) modifications of the initial theory. Even a small shift in indicator interpretation can yield a picture that remains consistent with the overall goal of the research (i.e., still speak to a literature one has decided to write about), but is revealing of an initial lack of fit between the case and the theory. This is what social scientific progress sometimes looks like.

As an epilogue: About a decade after I started research for my first book, war broke out in Ukraine. I am learning that over the arc of a career, as a research agenda matures, new ideas for indicators conceptualized in one setting can be arbitraged to another. Because I investigated the processes by which self-formed militias "became" the state in Georgia and Tajikistan in the 1990s, it occurred to me in 2015 to ask Ukrainian militias to describe the symbolism on their battalion insignia. If you stay focused on the same outcome, there is an accumulating economy of scale to the collection of variable measurement strategies, even if not every idea pans out.

PLANNING TO USE ARCHIVES

If your research requires travel for archival work, put yourself in a position to make the most of your time on site by (1) developing your own archival methods in advance and (2) learning about the specific archives you will be visiting before departure. If you have not been to a special collections reading room before, practice using one in the low-stakes environment of your home institution or another one near you. Identify materials you would like to see—and then go to see them. Every archive will have its own quirks and idiosyncrasies about access. Going through the process with no time pressures, and in your native language, is a dry run. It will give you a general sense of what to expect elsewhere. Consider scheduling a conversation with the special collections librarians to get a comparative feel for the kind of help and knowledge archivists can provide. Also schedule a conversation with another scholar who has used the archive recently. This is unlikely to be a famous professor (who will have outdated war stories of what it was like fifteen years ago) and more likely a fellow graduate student, just a year or so ahead of you, who has recently returned home from a year of fieldwork.

Then leave your home institution and travel to another archive for a second dry run. Figure out your own archival methodology. Specifically, you need a system to keep a precise record of what you find as you find it, so that you can later search systematically (discussed in chapter 4). Begin with reliable scanning software. Most special collections do not permit the use of physical scanners, but may allow users to take photos or have their staff make photocopies for a fee, so check with the archive in advance. Many of my colleagues rely on apps attached to cameras or phones (TurboScan) but technology changes. Find a system and practice using it.

Once you have identified an archive with materials that you want to access for your work, find out everything you can about gaining access. Finding guides, or the lack thereof, can be a problem in some archives. A good starting point is to look at the citations that others use as a means of orienting. Learn the structure of the archive. You can come to develop an intuition about where your sources "ought to be" based on the institutional structure from which the archives are derived, as their structure will mimic the institutions that generated them. In time, you will gradually become aware of similarities across structures and be able to use other, similar archives (in different cities or provinces) faster. Facebook groups devoted to particular cities or archives are a good source. For example, for Soviet archival studies, the Foreign Historians Congress (FHC) Moscow is a remarkable source. When you are initially getting started, if you have no other leads, consult the institution's website to gather information about the archive's contents, requirements of access (e.g., arbitrary rules about how many files a single historian can see per day), and opening hours. Then get on the telephone and confirm the information with a live person. Schedule your visit with a telephone call to establish rapport. Be sure to write down the contact's name. Be sure to ask about preregistration.

Double-check which materials have been digitized and made available online so that you do not spend time on site looking at materials you could view at home. A Georgian colleague shared with me an anecdote about a graduate student in Persian studies from the University of Chicago. This student had heard about a particular document in the Georgian National Archive. Having gone through all kinds of exertions to get a grant to go to Tbilisi and see it as soon as possible, when the student arrived a Georgian professor showed it to him—on his blog. Even if the foreign archive has finding aids online, consult them thoroughly but do not expect them to be exhaustive. Be prepared to ask about uncatalogued or differently catalogued materials.

Finally, there is often a mistaken perception that because collecting data in archives involves documents, not people, preparation for social interactions can be ignored. This is wrong. In many cases, scholars considering archival work put even more thought, time, and effort into advance preparation, since so much of what they will need to "look the part" depends on official-looking props that prove they are a representative of their home institution. The people who find themselves working in archives are mostly very well-educated but extremely underpaid from their point of view. They spend most of their day being yelled at by frustrated and angry historians. Do not confirm their perception of you as a self-important foreigner (or perhaps a spy or something equally nefarious).[13] You must somehow overcome their presuppositions. Practice being nice. Introducing yourself humbly in the local language, smiling and showing respectful gratitude for being allowed to do research—all of this helps, and none of this comes naturally to some graduate students. Just remember, it can take days (or weeks) as files are moved in and out of off-site storage. If you do archival work for a long period of time, eventually there will be a critical juncture in the research process where one of these employees has total power over you. A great deal depends on human variables and you want that person on *your* side.

A customized letter of introduction from someone at your university is often absolutely critical. It shows that you are a subordinate in a formal academic hierarchy and that your superiors desire for you to be permitted to conduct research on their behalf. This kind of formal request must be in the local language, must be on department letterhead, and must look official: the more stamps and seals, the better. Ask a native speaker to write the letter for you to sound official. Frame your topic broadly and be aware of local barriers or sensitivities to the extent that they can be anticipated. Sarah Cameron framed her research on the Kazakh famine as an investigation of "the modernization of agriculture in Kazakhstan."[14] Be vague about the chronological boundaries of your study, as well, so that you do not artificially block your access to documents you want to see, but of course don't give such a broad range of dates that any serious person reading the letter would see it as absurd. Some archives may also require that the letter be addressed to a particular person (such as an archive director). Investigate these kinds of details in advance by telephone if you can, but also take a couple of extra copies of letters of introduction with you into the field and arrange to have a digital copy with you (in case you need to make edits so someone will accept it).

Finally: The book *Archival Research in Political Science* opens with a blunt observation: "In the discipline of history, archival research is common. In political science, it is not."[15] Later in that same edited volume, Linda Whitaker and Michael Lotstein go further, observing that "with the exception of an enterprising few, political scientists have been out of the archives for the past fifty years . . . three generations of archivists have had little or no contact with political scientists." Professional historians tend to believe that everyone else playing with history does so as an amateur.[16] This is not correct from my perspective, but the perception that political scientists use fancy math to play fast and loose with facts comes from somewhere. It is a barrier you must overcome if you want to rub elbows with historians and have your work receive wide attention. Consider taking a history or historiography class (or, better yet, an entire sequence) as part of graduate training. Also consider having a historian mentor you as a dissertation advisor.

PLANNING ENTRÉE FOR OBSERVATIONAL STUDIES

Schatzman and Strauss's classic *Field Research* describes the process of initial approach as "casing the joint": probing a particular site to determine its suitability, then devising tactics to get a foot in the door.[17] As you do, the same authors advise, "It is important for the researcher to get his 'story line' straight: he will probably have to repeat it again and again."[18] If you plan close observations, either in the context of ethnography or through day-to-day proximity to a research team, you can render an entire project unworkable by spoiling initial introductions. Begin by drafting a short (one-to-two-page) document in the local language describing your research. Begin this at your home institution in consultation with the IRB and your advisors. It can be complementary to institutional registration and the informed consent process. A friend fluent in the language can assist you if you are not fluent yourself. You can modify it later. The document is not binding in any way, in fact. It can always be revisited formally, if the terms are in question. There is no reason it cannot be vague or even a bit deceptive. What are the advantages of a document like this?

- It shows respect and deference.
- It identifies the researcher as a privileged observer who expects freedom of action (to come and go, but also to communicate thoughts afterward to her academic community).
- It gives you a focal point for certain phrases and sentences that you should rehearse, "in character," if you are working across a language barrier.
- It locks you into a particular story that you have ownership over (but can always edit).
- It gives you a reference point for how you hope people will discuss your research behind your back.
- It can assure respondents that their identities will be kept confidential, so that they can go about their daily routines (while you observe them) unencumbered.
- It gives your hosts explicit assurance that you are not attempting to disrupt or take sides in power struggles that exist among the group(s) that you are studying.
- It is a written statement that can be attached to an email and forwarded. Words on paper (or on a screen) can move faster than word of mouth and may be considered more reliable.
- It can commit the researcher to a timeline for research (with permission, of course).

- It assures would-be subjects that nothing is demanded of participants except time, access, and sharing opinions (on matters of common knowledge, of course) and perhaps some documents (harmless ones, of course).

Beyond these instrumental reasons to have the document, the act of writing and translating the information can be valuable. It forces you to think about your research from the perspective of the people who will come into contact with you. You will present that research to subjects in the field site as you introduce yourself, but by writing something like this and beginning to memorize parts of it (and thereby rehearsing for repetition), you begin the process of documenting the way you imagine your subjects understand your role in their social world. It is not sufficient to think of yourself in the context of your nationality (Norwegian, American, Chinese) or your place in the academic institutional maze (a graduate student/an assistant professor at/from X school), or your gender or your sexual orientation or your outward physical appearance. It is also necessary to consider systematically what your project and your habits convey about you. The next chapter provides advice on how to think about doing this.

GETTING IN-COUNTRY RESEARCH PERMISSION

Some countries have laws that require formal permission from the government to conduct any kind of academic research. Many publish clear formal procedures academics should follow to conduct their research legally. The rules are designed to slow you down and to incentivize collaboration with a local counterpart or institution. It can frustrate established researchers who try to play by these rules (and as a result move more slowly) when they are lapped by new students who act like cowboys, ignore local laws, spend money fast, leave, and then snag limited space in top journals publishing articles with the data they acquired.

Many US grant agencies, IRBs, and academic advisors consider the overall political acceptability of the research topic (in the eyes of the host government) a central issue related to proposal feasibility. Others do not. One can conduct research "under the nose" of the state by pretending to do one thing and actually doing something else, and there are many examples of successful careers that started this way. There is a growing awareness of the mismatch in incentives between researchers (who desire original data as quickly as possible so that they can publish and not perish) and governments (who feel they have a right to maintain control over the representation of politically sensitive matters in their countries). The tension is particularly acute for research questions that are sure to draw attention to the status of socially undesirable groups (e.g., religious or cultural minorities, rebels, drug addicts, or homeless populations).

To skirt the spirit of the law while adhering to the letter in this way carries risks. It blurs the lines among activist, academic, and agent of foreign espionage in a way that can put people other than you at risk. The most serious harms, at the time of this writing, come from states that are sufficiently high-capacity to track the movements and whereabouts of a researcher but are also "paranoid" about foreign (Western/American) influence: Iran, China, Russia, Uzbekistan, Azerbaijan, and a few others. Some of these countries have passed laws designed to limit the influence of "undesirable organizations" (Western-backed NGOs), and if your research is funded by one of these organizations there may be second- and third-tier implications for your assistants and respondents. The best thing to do, in general, is to act in an ethical manner, as transparently and aboveboard as possible, to be genuine about the research you plan to conduct, and to work with local collaborators to sculpt language that is pleasing to the local authorities. It often takes at least as much time to pretend to do something (as cover) as to actually apply for grants to do something you want to do. You are a representative of your profession. If you lie systematically, it betrays the trust of the people who make your work possible in your home institution and in the field. Bad behavior can spoil things for future guild researchers in the same site.

Paperwork for the research plans advocated in chapter 1 often requires fudging your uncertainty with little white lies. Acknowledging this adds an additional level of complexity. Students may get details (or fundamentals) about places wrong. Indeed, it is hard to see how this could not be the case if it is a site that, in fact, they, their advisors, and even the host university know very little about. Third- or fourth-year graduate student researchers often receive permission to do something that, upon actually arriving in the field, they realize is unworkable or riskier than previously understood. At the edge of the law, one tests one's own risk tolerance. It is almost always a bad idea to break the law in another country. While there is some truth to the adage that "some laws are meant to be broken," zones of contested sovereignty are especially high-risk places to play games of chicken. I will discuss these matters in more detail in chapter 6.

Any research design that depends on repeated association with criminal elements (especially drug dealers or users) carries special risks. It can start out as fun, but you are putting yourself in the presence of desperate populations. Some may see you as a conduit for resources. Some might be serial predators. You increase the probability of being scooped up as a result of police surveillance.[19]

A different set of ethical issues relates to researchers planning to work directly with the US military or in collaboration with foreign militaries. Advantages and disadvantages should be weighed. The advantage is often access to special datasets and supervised access to areas where you would otherwise not be permitted to go. The disadvantage is that the association will taint your research in the minds of many of your academic peers. One concern is that you will bias your write-up toward the point of view of the military in order to retain access to a flow of datasets. Many academic purists feel a little righteous about their work, and if they feel your career has resulted from leveraging your role as a co-opted intellectual, they may say so. Another concern may involve broad moral opposition to collusion with any national security apparatus or dislike for a particular state (including, for some, the United States). If the decision to observe a war up close is functionally a decision to embed oneself with one side or another in an ongoing conflict, this is outside the scope of much of what the standard IRB conversations about risk are calibrated to handle. Specifics of your identity, the identities of your subjects, the strategy of entrée, and the mode of self-presentation become life-and-death. Serious conversations with your advising team and trusted moral authorities are necessary. Chapters 3 and 6 revisit these matters.

GRANTS REDUX

Applying for scarce funding is a probabilistic enterprise. Assemble a list of possibilities using university research offices, the advice of faculty with relevant research interests, and Title VI area studies centers. Most research university libraries subscribe to databases containing thousands of prospective sponsors. Talk to a librarian to get started, then search the databases. Organize an Excel spreadsheet with addresses, typical grant sizes, exclusions, requirements, and submission deadlines. Follow all instructions to the letter.

There is an economy of scale to certain aspects of grant-writing. You can cut and paste well-honed paragraphs into different cover letters and into sections of grant templates (which often ask similar questions). There is an art to tailoring a generic work plan to a potential donor, however. Some interest groups want to fund research that affects public policy and have a theory of how to do it: the idea is to support the early careers of scholars whose research findings are likely to contribute to the group's ideological mission. Other interest groups may want methodological innovation (new kinds of measurement for hard-to-operationalize but important concepts) for its own sake—and would be skeptical of the ideological keywords the first donor prioritizes. If you can learn to package your competencies, you will be able to cast a broader net for seed money. A successful application involves reading between the lines, anticipating what the ideal project would look like from the point of view of the donor, and pitching the selective merits of your proposal.

If you are not sure how to get started, you have very little to lose by attempting to "cold call" an organization by reaching out directly prior to submission, unless the grants database instructs you not to. A direct, professional email from a .edu address conveying enthusiasm is more useful than a form letter. A phone call may be even better. Asking an earnest clarifying question about the grant competition may let you strike up a conversation or email thread. If you ask a question that is answered on their website or that reveals ignorance about what the group does, it sends the wrong signal, but a thoughtful question probing the fit of your framing pitch can open doors. In rare cases, it is possible to find oneself getting insider feedback about what exactly their funding priorities are. You can reference this correspondence in a tailored cover letter to help your application along.

Small grants may not seem worth your time, but especially if it's internal university money and applications are simple, given economies of scale they can be worth applying for. The money often comes with no strings attached. Multiple checks with zero reporting requirements can be "pooled" into a discretionary spending fund for high-cost start-up items (a preliminary scouting trip, a laptop, etc.). You should consider mentioning the previous grants in applications to other potential donors in order to suggest wide interest in your project.

Funding applications demand specifics combined with a forceful, confident voice. This is the biggest difference between science writing and grant writing. Often researchers make a mistake in being too honest about their lack of expertise. Your intent may be to "hang out" on a fishing expedition and to take advantage of a web of contacts that emerge organically. However, by saying so you can easily come across as an over-privileged, book-smart kid asking your school to fund a ten-week vacation. Donors demand confidence and the clear thinking of someone with a plan and strong intuitions about what they will find. Consult with experts who have just returned from the field site if you can. Fake it if you must. Start in the library. Recent dissertations are brimming with exactly the kinds of rich, field-specific detail that can be repurposed to the delight of grants managers (detail that will often "fall out" between the dissertation and the book version). For researchers who plan to work in archives, dissertations often provide specifics that cannot be found anywhere else. It is a myth that donor organizations will not fund "follow-up" studies. A project framed as a longitudinal study that builds on someone else's baseline research has the feel of normal science.

If you are *not* planning to measure something specific, but instead intend to use participant observation or non-representative interview techniques based on snowball sampling, be as specific as possible about where you will go, which population you are interested in representing, and why. Describe in detail how you plan to spend your days, how you will solicit members to your study, and how many interviews you plan to do. Be realistic and earnest. One barrier to getting work funded is convincing the donor that you are capable of transforming the experience into data and writing up something serious instead of just taking the money and going off the grid. Sending a signal that you are a good writer who is theoretically serious and committed to your subject matter is very important. Engage with interpretivist mentors in your department or a related discipline to get a sense of what proposals for first-person observational studies ought to look like. While ambition is important, any whiff of an applicant's ignorance of or unrealistic expectations about site-specific constraints is a killer. Preparation, attention to detail, and narrowly defined goals (timelines and budget specifics) are key. Prioritize feasibility.

I have three additional pieces of advice for preparing competitive proposals for overseas field research. First, securing a local institutional partner in the country where the fieldwork takes place sends a very strong positive signal. Even if grant agencies do not request them, assembling and scanning a few different letters of support and including them in a .zip file can help differentiate your proposal from others. It is possible to pitch past funding in cover letters as a subtle signal that others have had confidence in your project. Coaffiliations suggest that the researcher can frame theoretical research in a way that others understand. Get as many letters of support as you can. This kind of preparation can also yield more realistic and precise itemized budget estimates.

Second, the proposal should identify why this particular research site is the ideal setting to study an important social problem. A common "filter" for a busy reader is a lack of coherent fit between the site selection and the question. All proposals require internal coherence that facilitates a transparent linking of theory to research methodology in the shadow of discipline-specific evidentiary demands. To rise to the top of the pile, you must "hard-sell" case and site selection to convey confidence that you really believe a particular geographic location is the best place to answer an important question.

Third and finally, drafts completed at the last minute ("*because something is better than nothing*") are never good enough. Your submissions must be well-written and typo-free. They should signpost a viable and original plan in the abstract. The writing must convey a sense of authenticity, energy, and genuine enthusiasm. You are writing to a busy person, tasked with turning a pile of hundreds of applications into a select two or three. Present yourself as someone ready to write a polished book that is going to change the world and you are more likely to find a donor who wants you to thank them in the acknowledgments. Being a good writer comes first.

Some grants come with reporting expectations. Usually these are not onerous. Commonly, grantors require simple five-to-ten-page summaries of your research results and findings that they can repurpose in their own promotional materials to impress *their* donors. Think of this as a gift: They want to advertise your research for you and get your name out there. It is in your interest to help them. Repurpose a few paragraphs from writing you are doing anyway (emails back to advisors, preliminary drafts of working papers, etc.). Most grant agencies, after releasing the money, do not have much control over what you do with it, and even cranky government agencies are not likely to send a collection agent after you, but institutions providing seed money for researchers answer to someone, too, and reciprocal trust makes all this work. Be honest, report hiccups, and do your part. Researchers have obligations to the wider scholarly community to try to do what they said they were going to do when they applied for money and to be honest with donors about multiple sources of funding. It is poor form to quietly "sit on" two or three large grants, each of which could fund a year of someone else's research.

A few general rules about grant management are worth keeping in mind:

• Some funding comes in the form of a single check with no strings attached beyond a vague promise of future acknowledgment. Some arrives in sequential waves once milestones are met. Some is administered through your university and some comes to you directly. Given the stakes, and the stresses of being in a field site and unable to make payments, learn exactly how the grant will be administered. Whatever the reporting requirements are for this particular grant, adhere to them precisely, even if they seem burdensome. This may require receipts and a bit of amateur bookkeeping.

• The decision about whether to hold funds in a US bank (look for automated teller machines/Cashpoints with the CIRRUS logo) or a local one depends primarily on convenience and local banking regulations, which determine whether transfer fees are reasonable or exorbitant.

• Restrictions on foreign exchange regulations or swings in the exchange rate are a particular concern. A common "war story" for those who have conducted a lifetime of fieldwork involves navigation of unexpected exchange-rate fluctuations, causing a grant to essentially double in value ("I could hire three extra RAs!") or be halved ("I essentially stopped eating in order to make payroll."). Pots of money can grow and shrink due to events outside of anyone's control.

- Remember to acknowledge and thank all donors in your dissertation, the resulting book, and all relevant publications.

If funds run very low in the field, it may become necessary to explore short-term opportunities to supplement your income. The social network in many expatriate communities is tight and your background and training give you unusual human capital. It may be possible to ingratiate yourself with medium-sized charity providers or even large international organizations by leveraging your university credentials. Fluent English skills are an asset in grant writing on behalf of a local organization. If you have data management skills, you might seek consulting opportunities in which you receive more per diem than a local worker but less per diem than a midcareer European development professional, sufficient to live frugally and manage a few assistants. Arranging this with a group that does material related to your research (e.g., a survey firm or an NGO working on a related topic) may allow you to embed yourself with the organization temporarily. What is lost in this situation is a little bit of freedom of autonomy. What is gained is a more authentic sense of "giving back" to the community that you are studying by helping to build indigenous institutions. In a pinch, you may be able to attach yourself to a local university or even a church, teaching classes in exchange for a clean room.

If your funds risk running completely dry, and especially if this forces you to contemplate missing a payment to locals, it is your responsibility to resolve the matter in a way that keeps your professional reputation intact. You owe something to your subordinates and to every future researcher. You cannot "flee the jurisdiction" and imagine that you have gotten away with something. If you ever get to the point of considering taking out a loan, or reframing research work as advocacy or "action research" and asking if friends want to "contribute to the cause," or accruing credit card debt, the situation has become desperate. Return home and regroup.

Finally, if you plan multiple years of fieldwork, you will apply for continued funding from the field. It takes time, sometimes many months, between when a proposal is submitted and money actually appears in your bank account. For extended fieldwork, setting aside some time for grants is necessary. Applying from the field carries a costly signal of your

own seriousness and commitment to the project. From the field it is easier to arrange for local affiliation, including letters of support. Time spent
soliciting grants trades off with doing research, but a trade secret among
researchers is just how much time in the field is spent doing exactly what
they did back home: applying for more funding.

LOGISTICAL CHECKLIST

Up until this point, the advice in this chapter has blended conceptual
and professional matters. In order to use your time wisely in the field and
to represent your university and academic community faithfully, it is
also necessary to take care of many mundane logistical matters. Even if
you have secured grant money and your research plan feels mature, a few
weeks are usually the minimum required to manage all of the necessary
pre-fieldwork preparations. It can take longer to arrange certain visas,
put your finances in order, plan with a host family, or secure housing for
your pets.

HEALTH CARE AND INSURANCE

Getting sick in the field is unsettling. To minimize risks, there are ways
for all of us to improve our health habits. A candid conversation with a
physician on these matters is a good place to begin. You will be much
happier if you can fit exercise into your fieldwork routine.

Before any overseas trip for an extended period of time, contact your
health care provider and make an appointment with a physician for a
full basic physical. Explain in advance where you plan to go and how
long you will stay, allowing the physician time to assemble thoughts on
what advice to give. Ask what procedures the doctor recommends in case
of medical or dental emergencies and for any generic health tips. Some of
the same advice will apply to extended fieldwork as would to any physically demanding vacation. Travel will put your immune system under
stress (exposure to a new environment, jet lag, adjustments in diet, exposure to new diseases, etc.). Work fatigue will compound these problems.

Before leaving the office, make sure you have (1) telephone, email, and fax numbers (including after-hours numbers) so that your primary care physician can be reached in case of emergency, and (2) a physical copy of your clean bill of health, including a record that you are up to date on relevant immunizations. Border agents can demand the latter at any time, so have it on hand.

And if you do not get a clean bill of health? A serious preexisting condition, especially one that requires you to bring medication with you, may necessitate documentation of your condition and special needs or even revising the fieldwork plan. The risk of losing a supply of a needed medication, or having it stolen, requires special kinds of preparation. (On the other hand, arriving at a border with many pills can invite suspicion, and no one should want to visit the part of an airport or border police station reserved for suspects of drug trafficking.)

Investigate the health specifics of the site. Start with water. In certain parts of the world great care must be taken with the ingestion of water, including ice. Rely on bottled water and well-boiled tea no matter what. You are always taking a risk with street food, as well. Lightweight, commercially available camping filtration systems, boiling water, and soaking the fruits and vegetables you eat in bleach water are all options. If you are planning to be in certain places, be prepared to get a nonlethal parasite. Even if you are very careful, if you stay long enough, it is inevitable that you will be invited to someone's home and you will have to eat or drink to avoid humiliating your host. Carry toilet paper in your pocket for emergencies.

After determining whether or not you want to drink the water, think about other common illnesses. Advice varies greatly depending on field site, disease, and infection vector—malaria is different than MDR TB, neither of which has very much to do with HIV—but carelessness is potentially life-threatening. The Centers for Disease Control are a good source of basic information on required immunizations and disease vectors for all countries. Make sure that you have met all country requirements before you embark. Have documentation at the ready or else you may find yourself detained at a port of entry. As COVID-19 demonstrated in 2020, circumstances can occasionally change rapidly.

Once you have arrived and acquired local bearings, investigate emergency health care options. The likeliest scenario for a life-threatening emergency is a road accident. Rapid urbanization has brought large trucks onto small roads. A head-on collision between one of these trucks and your taxi is often a bigger risk of death than disease, an avalanche, or anything else. Embassy personnel or long-time NGO professionals can provide advice on which doctor at which local hospital is trustworthy, how to make emergency contact after hours, etc. If there is a local blood bank, identify it. It will be staffed by volunteers who are also first responders. Strike up a conversation while you discuss whether you can safely give blood (and then do so, especially if you have a rare type), and you may make a friend worth having in a pinch.

Emergency health insurance often feels like an unaffordable luxury to cash-strapped, risk-acceptant, basically healthy twenty- or thirty-somethings. Grant agencies tend to be administered by people with stable middle-class jobs, however, and appreciate the need to write health insurance into travel planning. Keep in mind that you are responsible not only for your own well-being, but that of your dependents and whatever field staff you plan to employ (see chapter 5). The main thing to prioritize for yourself is medical evacuation (medevac) and repatriation insurance. In the event of serious injury, you will want to go home immediately—but without insurance, the costs of last-minute plane tickets can be high. Even in-country emergency care can be quite expensive, and you may be morally obligated to backstop it out-of-pocket for your employees or research associates.

Depending on your field site, it may be worth considering life insurance or kidnapping insurance. Planning interviews with rebels or criminal entities especially justifies considering these options.

PREPARING YOUR FIELDWORK LAPTOP

Learning how to do anything involving coding or computer languages is much easier at home than in the field. In my experience, a big part of solo fieldwork involved merging and cleaning datasets, transforming string variables into numeric variables, and other tasks involving skills that were a little too specialized to be reliably outsourced. I was glad I knew how to do them before I arrived. In general, I advise political scientists going to the field—even self-described "qualitative" types who are "bad with computers"—to be able to merge found datasets reliably and quickly and display/interpret preliminary descriptive statistics. These are basic guild skills.

Technology becomes personal. Your machine will see a lot of use, and it will probably come to mean a lot to you. Remember that it is a tool for doing a set of fairly mundane jobs. You will want it to work everywhere and run everything efficiently and reliably. There is a good chance you will only use this computer for about two years. Spend less, not more. Low-end technology can comfortably accomplish everything this book advocates. The analogy is a reasonably priced bread knife that you do not plan to resharpen and can stand to throw away when the time comes. Specifically:

- You need a laptop with a sturdy, permanently attached keyboard, a trackpad, and a standard USB port, probably running Microsoft Windows. Your upper boundary, weight-wise, is 4.5 pounds; 13" or so is currently a bit of a magic number in terms of the cost/weight/usability/battery-life curves you want to optimize. Durable and lightweight 11"–12" laptops can run for a long time on a charge. I use Apple, and my old iBook still runs, but the money you don't spend on Apple's design premium will either get you a lighter, faster, more durable machine or a cheaper machine with comparable abilities so it will sting less if you spill water on it, drop it, or have it stolen. It will be easier to repair, too. If you need a large screen for tasks like spreadsheet management, you can buy a large external screen once you reach your field site for less than $100 and then leave it when you return home.

- Configure your machine to log out and require password reentry whenever the lid closes and reopens. Pick a non-obvious, reasonably long password (fourteen characters or more).

- Acquire a cheap wired USB mouse to be used if the trackpad fails and an extra power cord (a single point of machine failure). A portable laptop battery or a charger (a two-to-four-pound brick that can recharge as if it were plugged into a wall) can be worthwhile in rural areas or archives where many researchers are expected to share a single outlet.

- A new Windows PC usually comes preloaded with "onboarding" software. These programs run in the background, slow down your computer, and drain your battery. Delete them all. Convince a computer-savvy person to rip them all out at the root and create a restore point.

- Plan to back up data in two places. I recommend a compact, high-capacity external backup hard drive to complement subscription cloud storage (more about which in chapter 6).

PUTTING YOUR AFFAIRS IN ORDER

Begin by making a list of all the things you will need for your life to resume smoothly upon return. Paying taxes, parking your car, subletting your apartment, lodging your pet, deciding whether to turn your phone off or manage international charges, putting bills on auto-pay, setting up an "away" message on your home or work telephone, and a hundred other chores can be time-consuming. Consider giving a trusted friend or family member power of attorney if you anticipate anything complex (beyond routine bill-paying). Consider providing a few different kinds of people with your emergency contact information if you want different parts of your social network to be able to reach you.

Leaving your family behind for weeks or months at a time in order to do research is difficult. It is not uncommon to bring your spouse with you to the field. Because many academics have children, and because it is possible to conduct fieldwork with children in tow, there are many prominent professionally successful examples of "family fieldwork." I have even heard it said that travel with family can open unexpected doors. All around the world people love children and recognize that families appreciate extra help.

The other side of the ledger is that because discomfort and suffering will be externalized, fieldwork with children (like travel with children) changes what is feasible and enjoyable. The calculations of "acceptable risk" change. What happens, in practice, if family matters are prioritized in site selection and design is that a field site where the entire family could feasibly go is selected, *then* design questions are backward-inducted, until one finds oneself asking literature-advancing questions that are appropriate to that site. When triangulating questions related to health conditions (most obviously water and insurance) and physical security with the needs of childcare, certain field sites suddenly make a great deal less sense than others. Refugee camps are out of the question.

Rural village life may be manageable or too difficult. It depends a great deal on the family. A place with a critical mass of English-speaking families—with a vetted pediatrician and recommendations for local day care or a live-in domestic—may not even feel like all that much of a change. Spousal/partner considerations are also highly idiosyncratic. Depending on the ages of the children, the expectation that one spouse researches while the other does full-time childcare may or may not be sustainable or reasonable.

Suffice it to say that all families are different, but some families *do* do this. As a parent of two, I honestly don't know how people do it with infants. But some people do.

A PLAN FOR ARRIVAL

Break time down into small chunks in order to optimize a schedule for the first seventy-two hours. Everyone needs a plan for getting from the airport to wherever you will drop your bags, a walking map of the immediate surrounding area, a temporary SIM card (or a well-scoped plan for unlocking a smart phone), a prearranged office space, and a flexible work plan.

The most common short-term lodging preparation is reserving a room in a guest house or downtown hotel a comfortable drive from the airport. This is the most expensive way for a trip to start, but it has the advantage of predictability and centrality. If the arrangements are completely unsatisfactory, you can always switch hotels. The same is not necessarily true if a first point of contact in-country is a friend's prearranged homestay. If you can afford it, and especially if the bulk of your research will take place in the capital city, using the hotel for a few days in order to "get the lay of the land" and price various options is usually ideal. A pre-fieldwork scouting trip allows you to familiarize yourself with urban geography, public transportation, and the layout of the relevant parts of the city. A friend with whom you can stay for a day or so can be a good way to start, but can also be awkward if either party becomes uncomfortable. Take care not to overstay your welcome.

Temporary homestays often begin initially with idiosyncratic connections. Some "take." Some do not. You may need to move once or twice to find a place that is sufficiently comfortable, convenient, and affordable. Unwillingness to settle leads to long search times, even if one has local associates (met on previous "scouting" trips) running logistical interference. Just like anywhere else, you need to be local to scout promising leads on Craigslist, AirBnB, or the word-of-mouth spare-room market for people seeking dog-walkers and house-sitters. If you have to find a place sight unseen, you may be in for discomfort or compromise or surprising adventure. As a last resort, if you are passing through a town for a few days, you can usually spend a night or two on a church floor in exchange for a charitable donation. At a certain point in every journey, you will settle for anywhere.

There is no textbook path to finding a good place to sleep and use as a long-term base. In general, the best two medium- and long-term options for solo or dual/couple travelers on a tight budget tend to be homestays and private apartments. Private apartments maximize privacy and autonomy. It is useful to investigate what cultural associations people have with different housing options in advance. In parts of the Caucasus, for example, a single woman renting an apartment for a few nights has a very specific association with prostitution.[20] Homestays maximize security and allow the opportunity to practice your language skills. If you plan to conduct interviews in the homestay, this must be discussed explicitly with your hosts in advance (and it is not recommended—see chapter 4).

GETTING ON LOCAL TIME

Upon arrival, fight jet lag by staying awake for a "long day" so that you can get a full night's rest, wake up in the "new" morning at a regular time, and get on schedule. Fill up the first day with tasks that you can manage while running on very little sleep. Make your way to a grocery store or market and purchase some fruit and nonperishable snacks and bottled water to rehydrate. Purchase a cheap cellular phone and a local SIM card (a pay-as-you-go plan usually makes sense). Investigate short-term options for email and internet connectivity. Send a quick batch of emails home.

Keep your computer in your bag to the extent that you can on these trips, especially in the early phase. It can be tempting to fill gaps in your schedule with familiar tasks, and internet connectivity is ubiquitous in urban areas around the globe. There are clear opportunity costs, however. Instead, get out your map. Walk around. Take that empty notebook that you set aside for ethnographic observations with you. Find a place to sit. Write down what you see. You will never have the chance again to record your first impressions of this place, since it will never again be new to you. Take note especially of the unexpected. Try to describe smells. Discipline yourself, at least for the first long day, to minimize consumption of alcohol or caffeine to avoid dehydration and allow your body to exhaust itself naturally. Go to bed early and get a full night's sleep, wake up early, exercise (even just a jog or some push-ups), and begin prearranged interviews. Walk as much as you can as you make your way through the day. Expect to be tired in the afternoon, but do not nap. Then give yourself ten hours or more that night for deep sleep.

The opening days of a project are exciting for many reasons. For me, one of the most exciting parts of exploratory research is that a web of contacts can branch organically in unexpected directions. One never really knows where the branches will lead. There are many ways to proceed with integrity, depending on the specifics of what one wants to accomplish—and chapters 4 and 5 will present a variety of options in some depth. Before getting there, to introduce ethnography, the next chapter will detour into matters of strategic self-presentation.

FREQUENTLY ASKED QUESTION #2

What should I bring?

Rural mountains are different than deserts. Mumbai is not Moscow. Before departure, consult experts to determine what you need to bring and what you can procure on-site to save space. The following are essentials wherever you plan to go:

Five empty notebooks. You should begin to discipline yourself to keep five different kinds of notebooks:

- A diary. You must have a dedicated place to write things that you do not plan to share.
- A book for ethnographic field notes, hand-drawn maps, and/or pictures.
- An organizer book. If you are used to keeping track of a daily schedule using calendar software and your phone, by all means go ahead, but a place to quickly jot phone numbers is critical. In addition to serving as a place to keep track of logistics (e.g., the "key" for when/where interviews are held), consider this book a Rolodex—just tape other people's business cards straight into it, along with reminder notes.
- An interview book, organized by numeric identifiers. The ritual of opening a clean page in a dedicated book filled only with notes that will become data immediately transforms a conversation into a professional interview. Shorthand is always good; writing to yourself in code that only you understand can be bad. Avoid private cipher to the extent

possible. Developing shorthand (e.g., the use of different-colored pens to sort your ideas from theirs) is inevitable, but ideally a book of this sort will be the sort of thing you will want archived someday, with PDFs of its pages downloadable to meet transparency requirements while still keeping interviewees anonymous.

- A book to supplement your local language acquisition (e.g., homework words to study).

Most beginning researchers get a blank book or two and fill them up with a sequential mish-mash. This makes it harder to transform the writing into data upon your return home. If it should ever become necessary to destroy some notes or records or hand them over to authorities, you should be able to do so without losing your diary or your cheat-sheet of verb conjugations. It is also a useful exercise to begin to separate your public and private identities to some extent. Private writing (diary, emails) will cross-pollinate your academic writing (data), but keeping the books separate helps you remember that the work is not your life. It's just work.

Your passport. Memorize the number. You will need it on many forms and you should not constantly need to fish it out. Scan the passport and email a PDF to yourself and to a trusted friend as a point of contact (see chapter 6). Make a few high-quality photocopies, as well; you will occasionally need to hand your passport over to embassies for them to process a visa, but will still want some proof of citizenship at a hotel or police checkpoint. A useable backup passport has obvious utility for certain kinds of fieldwork and may be worth acquiring. Permission is rare, but not unheard of for professionals whose work requires constant travel between countries with visa regimes that routinely take and hold passports for a week at a time while they adhere visa stamps (e.g., semiauthoritarian states in Central Asia).

A good paper map with major cities and roads—printed from the internet or photocopied from a travel book—of where you are going to be. Fold it into a book you carry and pull it out from time to time, in a meal break, to brush up on proper nouns and remind yourself where places fit. An internet map isn't enough. In the event of an emergency loss of electricity or internet connectivity you will be glad you have the paper version.

A box of business cards. Professional business cards add a sense of seriousness to every interaction, so it is about as good a $100 investment as a graduate student can make. Before departing for the field, find the best local printer who can get the university seal on high-quality paper. Include your name (with the preferred spelling in the local alphabet), your title, and permanent contact information for your home institution. Especially if your plans involve dealing with business or military elites, do not go cheap. It is common to switch phone SIM cards if you go to the field many times over a few years, so it's best to hand-write a local cell-phone number on the back of the business card—in any case, it adds a personal touch. A box of five hundred may seem like overkill, but as your project evolves you may find opportunities to have your research assistants or survey enumerators hand them out on request.

"Dollar Store" gifts. You will often find yourself in a position where you want to pass along a small token of appreciation or give children something to make them smile and purchase a little goodwill. Stop by your university bookstore or a nearby thrift store and spend $25 on cheap keychains, lapel pins, pens, or stickers. I got a lot of mileage out of buying ten cheap but comfortable watches, wearing them, and then handing them to people at the end of long taxi rides or interviews. It sounds cheesy, but try it yourself. See if you aren't glad that you did.

An expandable ("slinky") folder to keep all of your official travel/health/insurance documents organized and hold receipts for grant reporting. These are readily available in office supply stores but often difficult to find in the field.

A pocket dictionary for spot translations. If you look up the same word more than twice, make a flashcard for it (e.g., memorize the word embedded in a short sentence).

A bank card that you plan to use regularly to access funds from an account at a large international bank. Before you leave home, make sure that the bank knows of your travel plans, that you know how to access your bank account electronically to monitor the inflow and outflow of funds, and that it contains enough money for you to get home in an emergency.

A credit card that you plan to use sparingly, with the company's fraud detection unit alerted to your travel plans. Spend a bit of time looking into the field services fine print (not just the lost cards and cancellation policies, but fees for currency exchange, options for accessing the card issuer from the field site, and offers of additional services) in case your wallet is stolen.

A universal adapter and a six-outlet power strip/surge protector to get the most out of one electric outlet, plus a few cell-phone charger "back-ups" too in case you lose them. (I often do.)

Three to five thumb-sized flash drives. One is just for you, others to show the RAs you trust them, another to have out on loan . . . Cheap and lightweight, these are the researcher equivalent of "Dollar Store" gifts.

At least one long genre-fiction book you have been meaning to read for inevitable downtime. E-readers can hold a lot of content, but an actual book is good barter/gift currency.

A single print copy of an academic field journal that you want to publish in—ideally one that includes several exemplars you hope to emulate someday. Absent the social classroom rewards of summarizing by reformulating an article's abstract or conclusion in your own words, you will have time to probe the real guts of an article, following closely the way evidence is used (including the model choice, the caveats buried in footnotes, etc.). You will have time, perhaps, to read some articles you otherwise would not, providing a wider sense of the subfield you want to join and the standards of evidence for publishing in it. It is an anchor for "why am I here?" moments. You are what you read, after all.

Whatever toiletries and personal gear you need to keep your routine. A lot can be purchased in-country, but we all have things for which the substitutes do not really substitute. If you rely on eyeglasses or contact lenses, bring an extra pair or two. You will almost certainly need high-SPF sunscreen or "your" skin cream or allergy tablets. Tampons and birth control devices are personal. If you anticipate the need, definitely bring your own contraceptives and Plan B. Again, get in the habit of keeping toilet paper in a jacket pocket.

Whatever clothing you need to look the part in a minimal way without going shopping. If you arrive with less than two to three days of formal "interview wear" and two to three days of normal "walking around" wear, plus exercise clothes, you are probably packing too light. If you bring much more, you are setting yourself up for a lot of laundry. Showing up for formal interviews dressed like a graduate student shows disrespect for the time of busy professionals; showing up in too-fancy clothes in a village may be seen as rubbing your wealth in others' faces. A local source for high-quality climate- and class-appropriate clothing is worth investigating on arrival. Bring more underwear than you think you need. It wears out fast if you are handwashing and can be awkward to buy.

A battery-powered short-wave radio. These are light, cheap, and useful in emergencies.

Backpacking/survivalist equipment. If you anticipate lengthy periods of time spent outside the urban core of the field site, set aside an afternoon to walk slowly around a backpacking specialty store such as REI. If you need inspiration, read Chris Blattman's "Field Work in the Tropics" blog post (see bibliography). Definitely purchase *Where There Is No Doctor*, the *Pocket Guide to Emergency First Aid*, or some similar guidebook meant as a complement to first responder training. Then notice that generations of industrious engineers have thought about how to optimize functionality in the utility-weight-cost space. Small flashlights. Antibiotics. A first-aid kit (always best to make your own so you know what's in it). Tweezers. Safety pins. A threaded needle. Nail clippers. Solar-powered space lanterns for night reading. Good waterproof boots. A water filter. Lightweight sleeping-bag liners to stay extra warm and keep the bedbugs away. Quick-dry no-chafe clothing and a towel. Engage in friendly conversation with a salesperson to solicit useful suggestions of things you can buy cheaply elsewhere ("*Ziploc bags, twist ties, multi-use heavy binder clips, non-melt hard candy . . .* ").

A labeled "Open in Case of Emergencies" folder. You leave this with a trusted local contact or in an easy-to-find place in your office. It should contain phone numbers and email addresses for a list of family contacts and local friends, your embassy contact, a photocopy of the front and back of your credit card, and a photocopy of your passport.

An "Open-Only-in-the-Event-of-an-Emergency" envelope. This one you'll carry with you. Families make "exit plans" to get everyone out of a house in the event of a fire, just for peace of mind. Specifics matter, but once you begin thinking systematically about an emergency exit plan for a vague crisis (e.g., no electricity, no time), you will quickly realize that who you know is much more important than what you have. Nothing in an envelope can be a substitute for trusted friends if you really need to hide, to flee, or to hunker down. Still, consider packing a sealed manila envelope containing:

- A cheap, fully charged local cell phone and a charger
- An emergency credit card with the company alerted to your travel plans
- A photocopy of your passport or passport card, or a backup passport.
- $50–100 in the local currency in small denominations.
- USD$600: three $100 bills, four $50 bills, and five $20 bills.

3

HOW TO THINK ABOUT SELF-PRESENTATION
ONCE YOU ARRIVE

I f you opt to write up findings a certain way, you will become the main character in a work of nonfiction. Alternatively, you may opt to hide your voice and keep yourself in the background. Which is the "real" you—the silhouette of the silent outsider, or the well-defined participant? In the field, you are inevitably going to be playing a part in others' social theater—so who is your main character going to be? It would be a waste to go so far from home, meet so many interesting people, and not think about how ethnography (formal or informal) can change you and your writing.

"Habitus," as employed by Pierre Bourdieu, was operationalized for me early in my training as "how you occupy your immediate space."[1] Most people do not consciously control the way that they walk, talk, or hold their posture when they sit at a restaurant table and think no one is watching. (If you doubt this, notice that you can spot friends in a crowd from a blurry distance by their walk.) We all adopt slightly different roles at different times, subconsciously modifying our behaviors for parents, teachers, competitors at the poker table, friends on a recreational soccer field, or police officers who pull us over for speeding. Some of our habituated behaviors are even more pronounced when we are socially uncomfortable, disoriented, or isolated—as is often the case living abroad in a new place. Travel presents an opportunity to cultivate awareness of social habits. With care, you can alter your role strategically.

Begin by thinking systematically about what theory you believe your subjects are using to explain your presence. Table 3.1 is a tool to assist you in doing so. It organizes some of the roles fieldworkers play. Much of the diversity represented is distorted or obscured by the scripted "quantitative vs. qualitative," "positivist vs. interpretivist" debates usually used to introduce students to design choices on graduate syllabi. Rather than take sides, I deliberately constructed this table to reveal how much these normal bifurcations omit that may be relevant to the collection of one's data. The nine fieldworker archetypes can aid in reacting constructively and perhaps adapting flexibly to the reality of your field site. Improvisational pluralism sometimes requires changing your character.

The advice in this chapter, and the typology in table 3.1 in particular, is geared toward the experience of scholars doing research in a country that is not their own. Making conscious and consistent choices about self-presentation is important wherever you are, however, and it can benefit everyone to spend a bit of time thinking systematically about how daily habits overlap with your personal theories of social change. It may help you to see yourself as others do. Inconsistency in discussing our motivations may confuse our subjects and research associates. It can even occasionally be dangerous. At a minimum, consider how your presence is being perceived from the vantage point of your informants, your host family, state security forces that may observe your daily habits, other academics, and other interlocutors. Critical self-reflection as the project matures, including self-correction mid-project, is desirable as well. A carefully cultivated habitus balances your project's needs, your hosts' expectations, and, just as importantly, your values and perception of yourself.

BEING YOURSELF: OBSERVER EFFECTS IN SOCIAL INQUIRY

It is best to be honest. If you are going to ignore this book's advice and attempt to employ deception of any kind, be strategic and deliberate. You must position yourself between sources of local knowledge (research subjects, native academic specialists, journalists, embassy personnel,

NGO workers, new friends, key informants, and the like) and the imagined readers of your final research product. Why are you are collecting data? Who do you want to read whatever it is you hope to produce? Most of us write for a hybridization of commercial, policy, and academic audiences. What is your optimal mix? If you have never really thought about this before, honest reflection is overdue. You cannot fully control what other people think that you are doing, and misperceptions are inevitable, but there are a few instrumental reasons to devote energy to deliberately curating the role you will play in the field.

It is never too early to begin a first-draft written account of key fieldworker–informant relationships, even those that grow out of chance encounters. First drafts can begin in a diary, but eventually you will need public versions of them to circulate. Providing an account of why you believe your most trusted sources should be part of every write-up. Some people are sure to doubt your integrity, your training, or your qualifications as a cross-cultural translator. Being tagged with voyeurism or Orientalist fabrication can sting, and there is no way to get untagged. Nor, perhaps, should there be.[2] We are a fragmented guild. As apprentice scholars, we are often told that our understandings should change in the field. We intuit that *we* should change as well. Yet we are also constantly reminded that, when it comes time to write up our findings, it is not supposed to be all about us. Dealing with rejection at the write-up stage after years spent collecting data because "you're writing it up wrong" is genuinely disorienting. The simple truth is that our aesthetic tastes do not converge. Some social scientists value a style of writing that expresses discoveries as a process of recoding or reconceptualizing variables. Others value an embodied style of narrative presentation. You choose. Table 3.1 may assist you in making a more informed choice. No matter what you choose, however, certain key informants *will* be part of your story. It is incumbent on you, the author, to figure out how you want to write about them.

I am sympathetic to the idea that our personalities are constructed through processes of iterative role-playing. One mechanism is that our academic advisors, sometimes unconsciously, take on parent archetypes in the minds of advisees. Writing for someone who is playing the role of a surrogate parent can sometimes be constitutive in ways neither party appreciates. In an appendix to this book, I combine a conceptual map of

TABLE 3.1 A Typology of Roles Often Played in the Field

		Underlying theory of social change		
		Statist	**Liberal**	**Critical**
		Believes in states, because they actually get things done	Believes in progress, because people everywhere are basically all the same	Believes in the epistemological primacy of place, because exposing contradictions is how local power relations are unmasked
Daily routines, habits, and general disposition toward chosen field site	**Missionary** — Believes in effecting change and trying to make life better for one's study population (who are not free to come and go)	**Health and Security NGO** — Believes in assisting state agents by providing them the best possible training and advice	**Progressive Optimist** — Believes in linking academic structures to slow-moving social processes (by transforming people's values, a little bit at a time)	**Roving Activist** — Believes in empowering local activists as they confront injustice
	Ascetic Drifter — Believes in the value of seeking learning for its own sake	**Roving Ombudsman** — Believes in crafting a compelling original argument employing careful measurement and designing tests	**Roving Experimentalist** — Believes in crafting a compelling original argument employing experimental techniques	**Roving Interpretavist** — Believes in crafting a compelling original argument employing patient observations and use of interpretative techniques
	Tourist — Believes in the importance of acquiring academic credentials as a practical aid to his or her career	**Beltway Bandit** — Believes in generating a portfolio of research to make him- or herself attractive as an employee or subcontractor to a state bureaucracy	**Trade Press Author** — Believes in supplying the market with a compelling commercial product	**Roving Blogger** — Believes in sharing a great story

measurement validity with the monomyth of the hero's journey, showing the march from "conceptualization" to "revisiting the background concept" as a quest. Many graduate students, in my experience, are thoroughly self-aware about fieldwork as a kind of rite of passage, a recognizably Jungian hero's journey to deliberately change themselves. The imagined readers at the finish can help you create a version of yourself that you can be proud of. You should be conscious of your patterns of thought. As Kurt Vonnegut put it, "We are what we pretend to be, so we must be careful about what we pretend to be."[3]

Instrumentally, consistency in self-presentation aids data collection in concrete ways. When we work with our human subjects to produce the evidence that we rely upon as data, we engage in a process of collaboration. Sometimes we find our data like shells on a beach. More often, processes of interpretation and collection are influenced by the relationships that we form with our various key informants, research participants, fixers, collaborators, hosts, translators, and enablers. These people may come to feel confused or betrayed if they decide that you are deceiving them by playing different roles at different times. If you explain your research one way to one community and a different way to another, this risk is magnified.

The table's vertical columns are a map of *internal theories of social change*. Each column is a theory of how political change and social progress occur, an account of why the work we do as researchers might matter. The rows represent *external perceptions of our dominant motivation*. Each row contains a different account of why we are there—to effect change, to learn new things, or to gain credentials back home. Combining rows and columns, each cell contains an analytically distinct set of habituated dispositions and behaviors adopted by different researchers as they go about their routines. Think of each as an archetypical protagonist fieldworker.

The *Statist* approach anchors faith in perfected applications of bureaucratic capacity. Better thinking by better-trained state agents can produce better-targeted policies. Whether the goal is reducing poverty, reducing the prevalence of corruption, improving the quality of social provision (e.g., as the delivery of critical medical care or reduction of measurement error on the census), or the professionalization of military and police forces for competent counterinsurgency, there is often a common solution: more research, more outreach, more basic science, more conferences to translate findings into policy. Your research might provide a useful push.

The *Liberal* approach diagnoses the same social ills, but tends to favor different prescriptions. Liberals believe that *people* are the font of change, not states. They often see themselves in solidarity with civil society and partner willingly with law associations, election monitors, and sometimes even special-interest groups and activists. Compared to the Statists, they are more likely to celebrate regime change (so long as the methods are nonviolent) and to be skeptical of the state's ability to reform itself in fundamental ways without sustained pressure from society. Nonstate actors slowly transform social values. Again, your research might provide a useful push.

Note that both of these paradigms presuppose that a push is desirable. A *Critical* paradigm, by contrast, embraces an epistemology that favors local validity over universalist value claims. The critical paradigm sometimes seeks to facilitate social change at home, in the metropole, by exposing the hidden power structures behind the impulse to push in the first place. The Critical approach shares with Liberals an inclination to see people as the source of change, but confronts the implicit or explicit attitude by Liberals (often tagged as "neoliberals") that people are basically the same everywhere. The Critical theory of social change is harder to pin down than the other two, and can be criticized as abstract and oversubtle, but it involves changing minds in the academy by exposing tensions and contradictions in hegemonic discourses. Critical disrupters imagine themselves as the speakers of truth to power, willing to criticize the motives of those inclined towards pushing (whether Liberal or Statist).

Columns represent laterally insulated communities of thought that dominate political science. No normative judgement is implied. There is only so much time, however, so scholars tend to settle comfortably into one column over a career. We are more prone to accept invitations to appear on panels or in edited volumes with vetted sparring partners who share core assumptions, and we cease tracking the details of conversations occurring across columns. It also makes sense for a discipline with scientific pretensions to cultivate a kind of zeal on the part of its junior members. Every guild must fix incentives to drive out the unserious, leaving only the high-quality elite apprentices (self-imagined artist-scholars, throwing themselves fully into their craft, ready to dedicate the tens of thousands of hours necessary to advance to the journeyman stage). Zealous novices, observing divisions, may imagine themselves as rivals locked in zero-sum competition. The reality, at senior guild levels, is more-than-occasional complementarity.

What of the rows? Imagine that a local observer in the field began to pay very close attention to you and your routines. No matter who you are, or who you imagine yourself to be, they would probably be able to intuit a few things about you: for example, that you are a privileged observer, an aspiring writer, "good at school," writing a specialized travel memoir for an elite audience. Who is the readership for your memoir? Consider the different kinds of life-choices that inform the writing of three different market-tested genres of nonfiction travel memoirs, all of which are found in airport bookstores: those written by *Missionaries*, by *Ascetic Drifters*, and by *Tourists*. Missionaries journey in order to change things. Ascetic Drifters journey in order to learn things. Tourists journey in order to document having a good time.

The Missionaries want to document a time when they spread the good word and helped produce good works. The readers for their books already agree that the outcome is desirable, and buy their stories of hard-working travelers who sacrifice for the common good. At the other extreme, memoirs written by Tourists want to let readers know what great trips they went on, what exciting adventures they had, all the great people they met while doing something that was a bit self-indulgent. The Ascetic Drifters want to convey an intense personal experience of hardship spliced with rarely noticed beauty—mindful journeys for their own sake. The ethos that produced *On the Road* is not a missionary spirit. Nor does its author take the path of comfort.

While orienting oneself along rows and columns can be disorienting, and overlap between the templates is inevitable, you can probably situate some authors of books or articles whose designs you admire. Try to fit the experiences of your mentors and your heroes—as well as frenemies or intellectual adversaries—into various cells. Be aware of which role models you are imitating and which you imagine yourself to be writing against. As you do, note that neither gender nor class performances are perfectly predictive of placement in either rows or columns.

Identity traits influence a researcher's perception and ability to navigate the "insider/outsider" relationships, to be sure, but substantial variation exists within the well-analyzed bins of identity politics. The field experience *is* different for different people, but table 3.1 reorients the positionality conversation in a way that may help you apply constructivist insights productively. You can hold ascriptive identity characteristics (such as sex or skin color) constant and still have many variants. A queer Black man who believes strongly that strengthening local state capacity is the solution to urgent social ills is likely to collect different kinds of data than a queer Black man who is out to expose hitherto hidden dimensions in USAID's imperial overtones. Just as a skilled actor can subtly alter a character to subvert audience expectation and get the most out of a performance, a skilled ethnographer can alter a research question or framing to get the most out of a research site. For a concrete example of what I mean, consider Christian Davenport's reflections on code-switching across field sites in "Researching while Black":

[W]ho I was seemed to impact how the participants in earlier conflictual interactions viewed me. In [Rwanda], both sides saw me as sympathetic and sought an association to not only secure an ally, but also someone who would carry their message to others throughout the world by going back to America with my "mind right." International perceptions of blackness are not uniformly ones of anti-Americanism and hostility. Researching untouchability in India, it was presumed that I was more Martin Luther King(ish) than Malcolm X(ish), and I tapped that other element of black culture—the one with the deep moral authority to discuss struggle amidst seemingly insurmountable forces and the strong association with non-violent direct action. Here, I discussed restraint, chess-like strategic dynamics, and a hint of religiosity/spirituality, and basically the rest was filled in. My blackness served as the beginning or sometimes end/middle of conversations, and in the context of a prolonged discriminatory situation where I was hanging out with the outcasts—or as they prefer, the "dalits" (those who are oppressed)—I fit right in. . . . individuals' stereotypes regarding African Americans, women, or whatever does some of the work which "greases" the social science wheel of familiarity that, in turn, leads to everything we could possibly want to get access to in a conflict situation: conversations, lists, documents and the like.[4]

We are all also destined to be defined, in this business, by the fights that other people decide to pick with us based on what we write. To preview material from chapters 5 and 6, the rhetorical high ground in methodological and ethical debates turns primarily on audience and context. Even in the abstract, some tensions are predictable. Missionaries critique Tourists as frivolous and fault the Ascetics for being too lost in disciplinary debates about self-referential esoterica. Tourists critique Ascetics for taking the life of the mind a bit too seriously. Ascetics critique both Missionaries and Tourists for being disingenuous, demanding academic validation for the research programs that are (arguably) just platforms for showcasing their own righteousness or excuses to travel the world. Sometimes these charges are expressed openly, in the spirit of friendly banter. Sometimes they come out cloaked and anonymized in the peer review process. The Liberal column invites go-along-to-get-along, "let a thousand flowers bloom" attitudes. The Ascetic row counts on reciprocal, respectful dialectic exchanges and long-term reputations, so courtesy rules. Cutting observations designed to draw blood, which can yield personal animus, can fly between Critical-Missionaries (*Roving Activists*) and Statist-Tourists (*Beltway Bandits*) ("*social justice warriors*" vs. "*co-opted intellectuals*") or Statist-Missionaries (*Surrogate State Capacity NGO Workers*) and Critical-Tourists (*Roving Bloggers*) ("*savior complex, much?*" vs. "*those who can't do, comment.*").

"Being Yourself," then, is not meant to be about picking a cell and sticking in it. It means understanding the conflicting pulls that you feel from several cells, as well as being conscious of the cells that you find either morally objectionable or epistemologically unsupportable. For consistency in presentation, to assess your own progress as you adapt to macro-level changes in your prospects and your priorities, keep a ready answer to explain which of the cells you are *not* in. Some drift is necessary and inevitable, and a diary can be a valuable tool to track it over time. There is diversity among academics who conduct field research. Conversations with your co-travelers will gradually change you.

THREE KINDS OF ASCETIC PROFESSIONALS

All observation is mediated by theory. As Thomas Kuhn put it: "what a man sees depends upon both what he looks at (observations) and also upon what his previous visual-conceptual experience has taught him to see."[5] Systematizing our observations requires close attention to theories that inform our biases—but how do we learn these habits of mind? In my understanding of Kuhn's conceptual framework, science is a social practice first and an intellectual endeavor only secondarily. Thinking of academic disciplines as flexible social communities is a useful entry point to the middle row of table 3.1. When you imitate the kinds of speech that you imagine your professors and mentors want to hear, or write the sorts of things you imagine they want to read, you are likely performing one of the three "middle row" archetypes.

Few people realize that the decision to attend graduate school begins a long process of embedding yourself in a community. At first it can seem that you are just hanging around school—as if you won the computer game of the undergraduate experience and now, as a prize, you get to "camp out" and explore the hidden level. What you are actually doing, if Kuhn is correct, is volunteering to be exposed to practices. You begin to appreciate characteristics of the kinds of articles you admire. You also learn other things you may not appreciate at the time. You learn how to behave in a relatively flat hierarchy. You learn norms of mutual intellectual respect. You learn strategies for living a life of dignity in a middle-class milieu. In political science in particular, you learn how to listen carefully for people to overstep with rhetoric and how certain arguments fit together to "block progress" by your opponent. As a practical matter, you will also acquire friends and associates who form links in a network reinforcing your perception of yourself. Every year at our annual meeting you will see many of the same people. Within this selective community, an Ascetic ethos can send a signal of seriousness. I cannot improve on the prose of Anne Norton in her essay "Political Science as a Vocation":

> The ethic in which I was trained suggested that if we were careful, if we were responsible, if we took certain precautions, if we confined politics to a carefully demarcated sector (rather like the ghetto or the West

Bank) we could do science honestly and honorably. The ethical conduct of political science required discipline. The ethical conduct of political science required the evacuation of politics or rather, that politics came into political science only as an object, never as a source of imperatives. . . . This ethic directed us to science as a discipline, science as a duty. We were required to subordinate our political to our scientific ideals. . . . Method was discipline, an asceticism of the intellect, a means of maintaining a strict suppression of longing, of desire. Whether that desire was for a higher salary or a better world, it was corrupting. Discipline would make us neutral, and in that neutrality we could fulfill our duty.[6]

A dedicated focus on professionalization and academic production unites the three archetypes in the middle row. A dissertation-length project teaches a set of habits that will serve the scholar through an early career. The dissertation is the calling card on the job market, but as soon as one finds oneself on the tenure track at an R1 university, advising *others'* research becomes part of the job. The clock is punishing. Post-tenure, you continue to read and write and try to publish and keep high standards. You will have to get somewhat lucky, in any case, but at a certain point you will also have to get serious about your comparative advantage, double down, then quadruple down.

All of the Ascetic archetypes aim to produce artisanal works for a specialized readership. Our books and articles are, ostensibly, meant to guide intellectual debates and to impart erudition. Ascetics are united in agreement that as trusted, neutral observers, we must put a high value on normal science. Many argue that if our enterprise comes to be seen as a Trojan horse for partisan goals, it will erode our authority.[7] All distrust the impulse to write for the mass market and are aware that biases are introduced by treating "the state" as a client. With those caveats stipulated, Ascetic researchers can still be fundamentally Statist, Liberal, or Critical in their orientation. All recognize that there are economies of scale to developing a research pipeline in a particular cell. This is in part because of the high start-up costs necessary to establish a research program, in part because reputations are sticky, and in part because of simple path dependence as certain habits, even if grandfathered in haphazardly, prove durable.

ROVING OMBUDSMEN

Ian Shapiro asserts that the goal of political scientists should be "to embellish political argument with political reality. We should be roving ombudsmen for the truth rather than partisans of any particular message."[8] Cautiously conservative, but also not likely to avoid pointing out when people say things that contradict the evidence, the archetype is a *Roving Ombudsman*. In the field, these are meticulous curators of data who meet all of the standards of transparency and replicability valued by top journals.

These actors are likely to treat the validity of the data collected as the paramount goal. In the grant-writing stage, the research is often motivated by appeals that well-informed state interventions can help alleviate social ills best if supported by rigorous scientific evaluation. Roving Ombudsmen always take care to maintain formal neutrality as much as possible, however, for their power is interwoven with their claims to be impartial scientists, not hacks. Strengthening state capacity is an ancillary externality of some of their research, perhaps, but this is only a coincidence. The state that a Roving Ombudsman serves is an ideal one. She often does not try to perfect the law of any particular country (or see the laws as legitimate), but always hopes to illuminate the higher ("*different?*") laws—the moving shadow of scientific findings with law-like regularities. Perhaps she imagines her publications are contributing, if only marginally, to the development of a better Platonic ideal polity in the future. Perhaps not.

This is a densely populated cell. Most graduate students, fresh from comprehensive exams, like to imagine they will be judged by standards of excellence that they have some ability to predict. Once physically in the field, there are many ways to proceed consistent with the march of normal science, but deviating from the standards established by confident purists can be caricatured as lowering one's own and settling for second- and third-tier publications. Some ambitious apprentices are only in the field in the first place because they expect more of themselves. ("*Publishing is a tournament, friend. Tournaments need fair rules.*") There is no single best approach for managing a high-integrity observational study, but multivariate analysis with a goal of identifying cause-and-effect relationships (e.g., measuring and quantifying purported relationships with econometric tests) is a time-tested way to proceed as a purist. Qualitatively describing the mechanisms that link causes to effects in a normal-science mode is also a widely respected practice. If the author cannot sustain the claim that the work is high-integrity, however—because of a haphazard or slipshod feel to the collection process or the interpretation, or the final write-up—this research enterprise could be criticized as being politically motivated. That would endanger the distanced neutrality that gives the enterprise its power and authority. That would not do.

ROVING EXPERIMENTALISTS

The Experimental ethos promises better traction on certain kinds of causal processes. Because social systems are complicated, controlled perturbations are a recognized way to estimate the magnitude of a single-variable change.[9] Armed with confidence in their ability to generate unimpeachable "gold standard" causal evidence for narrow claims, the archetype is the *Roving Experimentalist*. This scholar arrives at a deliberately chosen field site armed with a well-thought-out plan to generate evidence. In exchange for total control over all of the relevant confounding variables and an ability to confidently quantify the magnitude of treatment effects, this scholar self-relegates to studying comparatively small questions using well-worn manipulations (e.g., changes to names on otherwise identical job applications, varying just one component of a conditional cash transfer, use of different pamphlets to mobilize voters in an election campaign). Careful planning allows the claim of laboratory-like control of confounds. The ethos that motivates this type of purist, contra the Critical ethos of the *Roving Interpretivist*, is fundamentally optimistic and liberal: since people are basically the same everywhere, if we can be certain to randomize the high-integrity randomization application of a treatment, and measure the effect, we may try to improve the world by improving our understanding of it. Questions of external validity have not been resolved to anyone's full satisfaction, but controlled experimentation may be the most straightforward way for social science findings to accumulate.

Accumulating scientific findings may or may not have anything to do with directly improving policy, of course. The possibility of gathering high-integrity evidence that politically popular programs are *not working* the way they are advertised, however, is one reason why these techniques have gained attention. Dedication to them sends a signal that the researcher is interested in actually answering a question, not altering the answer to fit the preferences of politically powerful interests (contrasted with *Beltway Bandits*, below).

Many argue that the field understands certain causal processes with more clarity as a result of gradual experimentation. Indeed, deliberate randomization of activities occurring in the real world is attractive to scholars interested in measuring causal impact for many reasons, among them avoiding Hawthorne effects, as subjects are not aware they are being experimented on, and controlling for confounds even if they are unobserved or non-theorized. A great deal of prestige is attached to findings produced by experiments, as well, as evidenced by the fact that they "seem to receive greater than average attention . . . [with] an expected citation rate approximately 47 per cent higher than their non-experimental counterparts."[10] They are also attractive because they reward careful planning at the design stage. Even intrepid scholars who value time in the field, at a stage of their career, begin to desire turning out clean papers at intervals and not tainting their reputations by submitting papers that have the feel of ad-hoc improvisation. The philosophical certainty that the experimental ethos brings to the conversation is very attractive. Preregistration of designs allows early vetting.

There is also a logic of interdisciplinary pragmatism supporting this cell. The most successful and visible Experimental purists are well-funded, since they can broker collaboration with World Bank constituencies (Missionary Liberals) at the same time they generate findings ready-made for donors as TED Talks (Tourist Liberals), all the while ducking or avoiding rhetorical shells that fly, in predictable and well-rehearsed lines of fire, between entrenched Critical and Statist positions.

ROVING INTERPRETIVISTS

Some political scientists care more deeply than most of their peers about getting the description of a place, or the people who live there, as correct as possible. While area studies has gradually ebbed in prestige, there is still an interdisciplinary audience for interpretative approaches.

Members of our sister disciplines do not care much about the march of our theory or our measurement fads, but sometimes share an interest in describing the same real estate. They do not always pretend excitement (or patience) for the impulse toward reductionism that comes from the rational-choice approaches that currently dominate our field, and tend to be skeptical, in particular, of claims that Roving Ombudsmen and Roving Experimentalists make in the first few pages of their empirical papers, which is that they "have a simple model." Instead, one is more likely to find a statement of what their work is going to "problematize." In contemporary political science, interpretivists often understand themselves to be a counter-hegemonic force, committed to writing that demonstrates that what is omitted from the dominant approaches has intrinsic value.

Self-defined *Roving Interpretivists* often favor the solo methods of chapter 4. These methods make explicit the central position of the researcher in the collection, interpretation, and curation of data. An Interpretivist is often fluent in the vernacular of constructivism, making common cause with other disciplines whose practitioners listen very hard to people and extract meaning from words (anthropologists, sociologists, historians, and many other scholars in the humanities). Our subjects probably would not recognize themselves in the reductionist models that are the coin of the realm in our top journals. When values clash, on balance our profession should privilege the values, beliefs, and lived experience of our subjects, it is said. The claim is often made in a somewhat edgy way. Roving Interpretivists are acutely aware of power disparities, willing to advocate in faculty meetings for the epistemological primacy of local knowledge, willing to endure hardship in order to engage in close observations, and infusing their writings with an appreciation of how language is deployed (to ensure nothing of importance is lost in translation across cultural barriers).[11]

The reason these political scientists are in the "Critical" column is that, by making common cause with other disciplines, they are the most likely to come into contact with, and be influenced by, Critical traditions. Other fields are genuinely concerned that tainting the purity of a scientific enterprise with outcome-based policy goals is not only vulgar, but also likely to backfire. These Ascetic Interpretivists take issue with both Liberals and Statists, especially in their Missionary variants, as being too confident that they know what kinds of changes are desirable, too certain that they know how to control the uses of their work, too eager to make change happen. In one summary, they are too "confident (in defiance of Foucault, Derrida, history, and common sense) that their acts will follow their will."[12] Interpretative approaches tend to reward the memorably Critical voice and writing tempered by hard-won wisdom.

None of this, incidentally, needs to have anything to do with postmodernism. Social history and macro-historical sociology, to pick just two examples, are buttressed by claims that description for its own sake is valuable. I have heard three different colleagues in the discipline of history, none of whom have met each other, refer to their time in the archives as "chasing ghosts" or "communing with ghosts." Grounding their narratives in archives fixes a geographic space and a specific point in time. They, as authors, gradually acquire a different point of view than if they had allowed their minds to wander. Consider Karen Barkey's *Bandits and Bureaucrats*. It tells the history of rural taxation, patrimonial institutions, and banditry in the Ottoman Empire in the seventeenth century. It is empirically rich, fully consistent with Turkish historiography, and legible to our field because it suggests that the Tilly thesis ("war makes the state and the state makes war") may not be universally applicable. The Tilly thesis may not even travel far beyond France's borders.

It is important for a graduate student holding this book to pause and reflect on the diversity contained in our discipline. It is also important to remember that we are a readers guild, not a fieldworkers' guild. Each cell contains hundreds (arguably thousands) of professional political scientists, scattered across many colleges and universities. Each conducted fieldwork at some point in the past. Now they teach, read, publish, and write referee reports. They hope to curate a section of the literature with work that reminds "the field" of their contribution, even though the *physical* field may be far behind them. Different readers expect different things in a paper, value different methodologies, are impressed by different kinds of evidence, and celebrate different archetypal heroes in their footnotes.

You may get very lucky, but you probably cannot please all of them at the same time with the same book or paper, no matter how hard you work. Calibrating the presentation of data to a fractured discipline like political science is therefore difficult. For one thing, scholars early in their careers get contradictory advice on what to do with insights gleaned from immersion. Some in our field privilege testing, for a variety of reasons. These voices are quick to slander their fellow-travelers as "storytellers," insist that as a discipline we ought not "settle for mere description," and the like.[13] Others disagree forcefully, arguing that crafting a credible narrative requires being situated, not pretending to take oneself out of the story in the name of chimerical objectivity. Table 3.1 is there to remind you that it is hard to write in a way that pleases both sides. Your early career will be spent doing what all journeymen have done in craftsmen guilds from time immemorial: you will acquaint yourself gradually with what the taste-makers expect, establish your own brand, and work as hard as you can to distinguish yourself by the excellence of your niche product. Not in the field, but sometime before tenure, if it comes, you will need to decide what "your" lane is. Eventually you will find that you want to stay in it.

That being said, there are other audiences for our writing than journal referees. It is not hard to sustain the argument that a typology of ideal-type purists is navel-gazing of the most useless kind. The truth is that there are so very many things to value in life other than pure academic discourses, which are (admittedly) driven by fads and fashions as much as anything else. This implies that there are many *other* ways to do the job. You can go to the field to affect social change. You can also use the field to try to break free of the rigid structures that the purists have built to organize debates in the academy. I thus sketch six alternative archetypes.

THREE KINDS OF MISSIONARIES

Missionaries want to change things. Many researchers indulge in the possibility of maintaining dual- or hybrid-practitioner/academic careers. They make arguments in the vernacular of science to appease referees, but often as cover for work in the service of political goals (*"even higher goals, friend"*). These goals may involve not higher salaries or fame, but rather the potential to play a heroic role in a bigger story. These researchers use their time in graduate school to find a war to fight, a movement to assist, or a community to help. The source of internal motivation is personal and idiosyncratic, but there is no denying that the motivation that sends some people to the field is bigger than the careerist impulses that inform the professionalized Ascetic academic mindset.

SURROGATE STATE-CAPACITY NGO WORKERS

Maybe you want to help a state provide public goods to its citizens. Cleaner water. Safer streets.

Many political scientists have normative agendas that are unapologetically Statist. Winning the Cold War was important. It brought the Department of Defense into conversation with the academy over how to map non-Western societies and how to translate academic findings into local languages. In recent decades, analogous research programs have justified themselves by (purportedly) building state capacity. Police and military clients will continue support for the work of scholars who presuppose a role for careful science and empirical measurement in sorting the terrorist wheat from the neck-bearded chaff. These scholars, many of whom have military backgrounds, are positive that they are providing public goods to their fellow citizens and to the world. They are often not ashamed to say so.

Many non-security research agendas assume the normative desirability of a strong state as well. Data collection to increase the efficiency of aid provision by parastatal humanitarian relief NGOs or government agencies holding the line against the COVID-19 epidemic, research agendas aimed at helping United Nations Missions function more effectively to provide public goods, and medical outreach are all examples of research programs that blur the line between positive and normative goals and prescribe state action. The simple truth is that some academic practitioners feel a need to "give back," putting tangible good into the world beyond inward-looking guild-work. Even well-funded government agencies may need help that we, with our training and interests, are well-qualified to provide. Assisting in public goods provision changes lives more directly than writing papers for cloistered scientists. Some think it is important to act directly. (*"Life is short, friend—what are you doing with yours?"*)

Any researcher who has imagined "research impact" in the form of a deck of PowerPoint slides for a government agency to use in a training module has felt the pull of this mindset.

PROGRESSIVE OPTIMISTS

Maybe you want to help your subjects access the liberal donor community funding your work.

There is no consensus on what policies ensure high levels of prosperity or well-functioning democracy.[14] The gap between good intentions and outputs is wide. State interventions designed by and implemented with assistance from the World Bank or the IMF do not have an unimpeachable track record of success. Some people just want to give up and retreat from the responsibility of improving the quality of life for the world's worst-off. Missionary Liberals want to keep trying. William Easterly, in his celebrated 2006 book *The White Man's Burden*, advocates for a philosophy based on searching: observing the world with an open mind, documenting what works, and trying to theorize why certain policies work and others fail.[15]

Liberals are often drawn to the field because they want to try to help the most people at a time, and some of them decide that writing papers is part of how they are going to do it. Especially if the fieldwork goes on for a long time, some productive researchers *can* uncover original social facts at a fast enough clip to keep the bean-counters happy. Along the way, in the ideal form of the thought experiment, there will be both research opportunities and chances to alter the balance of power in one's site. Institutionalizing linkages between donors in the West and social actors living in desperate conditions is a conduit that only a few people are lucky enough to try to construct. By shouldering some of the costs of collective action, *Progressive Optimist* scholars go so far as to write grants for NGOs, start companies, volunteer with lawyers' organizations, assist judges or political parties, and other activities to make elites more accountable to constituents.

Any researcher who imagines starting an NGO, trying to improve the material quality of life for research subjects (with better-designed aid policies or more effective redistribution), or trying to pass life opportunities along to her subjects or their families, has felt the pull of this mindset.

ROVING ACTIVISTS

Maybe you want to help local activists confront oppression or injustice.

Many scholars are drawn to the canon of political science because it promises to explain how political systems change. For many of us, the choice to be in the field feels overdetermined. Many personal goals and values can blend with youthful optimism and wanderlust. The convergence of values can release great energy. We often arrive on site with the potential to see things, to change things, *and* to acquire an academic credential, all on the same journey. Many researchers also intuit that fieldwork is the best opportunity they will have at any point in life to experience political extremes, such as living in an authoritarian regime or working in a refugee camp.

A confrontationist political ethos can emerge while observing abusive governance at close range. If political science is the study of constraints on political change, and the scientist thinks change is normatively desirable, perhaps it should be no surprise that an activist often lurks quietly beneath so many carefully curated professional veneers. Researchers often experience things that emotionally invest them in the plights of their human subjects. Sadness is common, often followed by anger. That anger has been known to leak into academic labor. At some point, some researchers intuit their ability to go further and to actually effect social change. Once they feel that they *can* cause change, some feel guilty if they do not try.

Any researcher interested in processes of social mobilization, who thinks about radical politics, and who struggles and wonders whether he or she ought to do more, has felt the pull of the *Roving Activist* mindset.

THREE KINDS OF TOURISTS

If you cannot enjoy yourself while in the field, friend, perhaps you miss something important about what draws many of us to the life of the mind: *otium cum dignitate* (leisure with dignity). The life of the mind involves huge amounts of unstructured time and Tourists, in this context, are distinguished by having made peace with baser goals. They want an educational credential, all right, but are also self-aware about the fact that knowledge and expertise generated by research can be repurposed. Many researchers, having noticed how capricious the academic market is, approach site and topic selection with an eye on a back-up plan—a second-best thing to do once a PhD is in hand. Perhaps prudence demands nothing less.

BELTWAY BANDITS

Maybe you want to write something that will help you get a job working for a government.

Many of us are drawn to the canon of political science because it brings us closer to power. Over time, as grant-writing processes teach us that money is the lifeblood of academic progress, one comes to suspect that powerful constituencies basically buy findings. Over time, we acquire a mature sense of just how much bad work our journals publish and, just as important, how many findings are not submitted in the first place because it is hard to get negative results accepted or because the paper doesn't mesh with disciplinary fads. Over time, we learn of a large professional class that has mastered the art of talking like Missionaries while also padding their retirement portfolios. Over time, research brings us into contact with a panoply of state and nonstate agents working in development assistance, democracy promotion, post-conflict reconstruction. Many in this social milieu of embassy workers, academics, and subcontractors have impressive academic credentials but, for whatever reason, are no longer prostrate to the higher mind.[16] These observations are not meant to encourage cynicism, nor to imply that we in political science are all hacks and quacks—only that lines drawn by young purists blur over time.

Anyone who has noticed a salary differential between successful academics and many other pretty sympathetic people doing pretty good work has felt the pull of this mindset.

TRADE PRESS AUTHORS

Maybe you want to write something for which there is market demand outside the guild.

It can be easy to forget that until just a few decades ago higher education was, quite deliberately and unapologetically, a gentleman's club. Our top schools are research institutions built atop what used to be finishing schools. Children of the upper classes would attend to meet and marry each other. Alumni donors in this environment appreciate the ability to rub elbows with erudition, to buy books and put them on their shelves. They like to know their children are being taught by worldly intellectuals. In *A Culture of Fact*, a history of intellectual life in sixteenth-century England, Barbara Shapiro described a familiar-sounding market for what we today call "fieldwork":

> Travel experience was considered desirable particularly for gentlemen, but many were unable to do anything more than armchair traveling, benefiting vicariously from the experiences of others. Travel accounts were . . . written with an eye to public policy, as contributions to natural philosophy grounded on 'matters of fact,' or as a means of enhancing the educational opportunities of the political class.[17]

This may, in part, explain the well-documented tendency to "graduate" after tenure from writing books with a disciplinary audience to writing "big think" books that are aggressively marketed on Amazon and promoted by TED Talks. If you want to try to participate in a broader conversation, or to write for a wider audience, or to give a book talk at Google, that ambition is actually natural, healthy, and not mysterious. Many of us got into this business before we really understood what the guild was, thinking naïvely that *that would be the job*. Might it be possible, some ask, to skip a few steps, do what many of the journalists and novelists who are our heroes did, and just begin to publish things that a mass audience might actually read, enjoy, and pay to have on their book-shelves? By living a great story someone might pay to read about?

Anyone who has thought about ways to hybridize a career with com-mercial endeavors, or who has put serious thought into crafting research pitches that might appeal to a wide audience of potential donors ("*without compromising my liberal values . . .*") has felt the pull of this mindset. Note well that even for someone careful to curate the CV of a self-styled professional purist, nothing about the guild necessitates poverty. Some of my colleagues have tenure and also drive pretty nice cars. They crafted research agendas to qualify themselves to provide expert testimony for corporate interests. I also have colleagues who have nurtured a love of amateur photography while rubbing elbows with powerful people, col-leagues who have produced quite good films, colleagues who will some-day act as tour guides on cruise liners.

ROVING BLOGGERS

Maybe you just want to write something cool that you can share with friends back home.

Stephen King claims that he doesn't write for the money but rather "for the buzz."[18] There has to be more to life than pleasing referees. Net-worked computers and smartphones have completely transformed some aspects of "the field" in the last two decades. The ability to curate one's personal stream of data using social media to follow journalists and other academics is another game-changer. There may be alternatives emerging to the standard academic publishing route. The Critical col-umn contains three archetypes of people who care the most about places. When this care comes from a normative desire to change things, the Roving Activist takes up the cross of beleaguered locals. When the care is intellectually driven, the Roving Interpretivist makes common cause with rigorous academic anthropology or history. When the care is laced with desire for instant gratification—comments and likes—Instagram and Twitter present a very real temptation for the *Roving Blogger*.[19]

Many of the people holding this book are young, directionless, and honest about the fact that they do not actually know what they want to do. They aren't Missionaries. They aren't sure they even want to set themselves up strategically for a career in the ivory tower, having had time to observe that life in the ivory tower is perhaps not as much fun as they thought it would be. What they are doing is less dramatic than the master narrative implied by any of the other cells, in fact. They are improvising. They are living out a script that they wrote themselves a few months ago. They got some donors and advisors to buy into it, and now they're doing the graduate school equivalent of skydiving and taking selfies. Because of a combination of factors—differential standards of living, international exchange rates, romance, exoticism, the fact that they like the attention—they find that their quality of life improves. It is an intoxicating stage of life, even if it is doomed to be temporary. Much in this book presupposes a desire, and ability, to delay gratification for decades. Self-publishing on social media offers instant gratification. These young scholars *are* good writers. They *are* living a great story. They *care.* And *they're there.*

Anyone who has felt a temptation to humblebrag about fieldwork on social media, or wonder whether it might be a good idea to skip a multi-year delay after sending something to a good journal and instead just post something to plant a memetic flag, has felt the pull of this mindset.

RECAP: REFLECTIVE PERCEPTION DILEMMAS

Experienced researchers will surely recognize something of themselves in more than one archetype. Identities are complicated. A commitment to maintaining a single archetypal role will probably never be credible—it is not only the Roving Blogger who uses Instagram, for instance—but figuring out for yourself how social media fits into your research is important and personal. Everyone knows that curating a stream of content for your followers can mean a lot of time staring at computer pixels, which trades off with doing other things (your research, face-time with loved ones, etc.). Everyone also knows that these devices are part of our lives now.

Recognize that certain kinds of fieldwork, especially the sort that puts you in contact with state security agents, will require careful curation of your online persona. Presenting yourself one way to donors at home and a different way to respondents in the field is impossible if you are "blasting" a real-time unfiltered narrative from your phone. I suspect that my coauthor and I could not have safely conducted our survey in Mogadishu if we had been live-blogging at the same time, given that so many different kinds of suspicious social actors were second-guessing our motives.

More broadly, anyone can inadvertently damage his or her professional reputation by oversharing at vulnerable moments. Consider two caricatured ideal-type voices on academic social media. The first is the happy warrior, a strategically branded Roving Activist, unapologetic and edgy. The second is the angry graduate student, frustrated by the whole system and ready to let everyone know it. Either might hit "send" on ideas they later regret.

Regardless of which cell represents your ideal self or which you abhor, issues of dependency and power are inevitable—and genuinely tricky. It can be instrumentally useful to think about which cells we hope to inhabit based on our own values and goals, and with a strategic eye toward people we want to meet. Some common issues that occur in face-to-face interviews will be discussed in the next chapter, but a researcher's immutable characteristics (race, gender, and arguably class) are often the biggest practical site-related and personal barriers to doing the kind of research that one imagines in idealized form from the ivory tower. The power issues involved are sufficiently diverse and multifaceted to defy easy categorization. In some cases, local elites—archive managers, high-ranking military or police officers, elected representatives, warlords, criminal bosses, religious figures, important people in a community—are functionally gatekeepers to the entire research project, which means the researcher needs their goodwill. They have the upper hand and they know it. Conversely, vulnerable subjects, especially those who have lived through violence, may reasonably perceive a researcher, even a lowly graduate student, as "important, official, or having power over them."[20] The official letterheads, business cards, letters of introduction, and other access tricks employed to bypass gatekeepers can, at the same time, increase your social distance from powerless people.

You may also not be able to credibly "act" outside of certain cells if you engage in certain activities. A Russian officer accused me of being a spy with the following observation: "Of course I believe you are a Stanford graduate student. That just means you'll go in as a G-13." (Translation:

When you eventually join the Western intelligence community, you will be well-compensated for your time.) Around the same time, I had a genial conversation with a Western ambassador who told me, pointedly, that a reason I was getting access was that "everyone assumes you'll someday be a [CIA] station chief. It's the Stanford thing, but also . . . how you carry yourself, your early morning runs, something about the way you talk." Much would be different about the data I collected on that trip if I were female, tall, fluent in Russian, and capable of projecting the authority of the Russian Academy of Sciences (like Anastasia Shesterinina). I would also have had different kinds of access if I had shown less interest in the war and more authentic interest in religious-social relations (like Egor Lazarev).[21]

Thinking about your behavior in the field as a deliberate process of "character creation" does not, it bears reemphasizing, necessarily require dissimulation of any kind. The advice in the last chapter insert suggested that you "create a character" to navigate on the other side of the language barrier. This character *is you* to your subjects. They will remember it. Better that they remember the character who is in an authentically good mood and not sulking in front of computer pixels. The character likes the same things you like, regardless of whether it is cooking, or going to bars and watching football, or listening to live music and clapping, or playing pick-up games of soccer or Frisbee.

Finally, remember that the perfect cannot be the enemy of the good. Immersion is hard. Working across a language barrier is daunting. Start small. If you can find them, read a few novels (in English) that take place in the field site. Cruise some travel websites. Educate yourself about local food, music, and sports. This can seem like a gauche affect if you overdo it, but it gives you more opportunities to practice language scripts on topics of friendly conversation other than your research. See if you can become genuinely interested in what is interesting to people there, especially if they are not your subjects. Stretching yourself can be rewarding. The culture of your host country, and the fabric of your host community, is worth observing.

FREQUENTLY ASKED QUESTION #3

I feel overwhelmed. Going to the field has made me aware of
my racial/class privilege in a way that is less abstract than
before. I want to do more than watch people suffer, then go
home and write about them. Shouldn't I try to help?

Big questions, friend. I don't really know what you've seen, or what you're
loading into "help."

*If you are asking whether or not the feeling of guilt over privilege goes
away, my sense is "No."*

It's a strange calling, writing about people from across a language-
class-cultural boundary. It is confusing. It is not "weird" to feel empathy
for your subjects. It is not "weird" to want to help. It is, in a real sense,
"weird" to just watch, record others' experiences as data, analyze it, and
write up results as nonfiction for a narrow readership (in a vernacular
that your subjects could never themselves read). The normal thing to say
next is something sanctimonious like, "If you engage directly you're giving up your objectivity," but I am not actually convinced objectivity is
possible or desirable. I witnessed acute suffering in the field. I still have
some bad dreams.

I am also rarely confident that I *know* how to help. At certain times in
my life I listened hard and I gradually organized my research with an eye
toward helping. For the most part, this made it more emotionally painful
when circumstances changed and I had to stop.

If you are asking whether it is OK to pursue academic work overseas and also try to help people (missionary/policy motivations), my sense is "Absolutely." Just keep three things in mind.

1.   It is hard to manage two careers at the same time. Some scholars do manage what seem to be enviable hybrid careers as policymakers and academics. Even for exceptionally prominent models of success, however, there is always tension. Michael McFaul observed: "You're always the stinky kid in the room." Academics think your ability to engage in dispassionate analysis is warped by proximity to power, plus part-time readers fall out of rhythm with fads. Policymakers think you think you're smarter than they are. It is hard to be a well-published academic as well as a soldier, an NGO administrator, the founder of a company or a charity, or anything else. There aren't enough hours in a day. For most people, something eventually gives.

2.   You can't believe everything you hear when it comes to support for what you do. There is a tremendous amount of cheap talk inside the ivory tower. With so many liberals and so few ladder jobs, how could it be otherwise? The feedback you get from sympathetic *individual* academics is distinct from the market. It is not one person who hires or promotes: it is always a political coalition, and coalition membership is always changing. Everyone answers to someone who uses Google Scholar. The median voter in the coalition rarely sympathizes with the ideals embedded in extracurricular missionary work. Missionary science is distrusted by different purists for different reasons (e.g., *"telling only part of the story," "hiding the error term," "crusading"*).

3.   There is always quite a lot to do at home. "Home comes first" tends to be good advice.

4

HOW TO THINK ABOUT SOLO
DATA COLLECTION

One of your primary goals is to convince professional readers—journal referees, series editors, search committees—to invest time in reading your work. You need to be a credible empiricist. Interview quotes, carefully curated and deployed with care at critical points in the manuscript, are the most common method used to signal seriousness to busy readers with limited attention spans.

The highest professional rewards in social science go to scholars capable of demonstrating that they are three things simultaneously: (1) experts in a place who know how its proper nouns fit together; (2) good teachers, capable of explaining a well-calibrated working model of how they believe important political phenomena work (so that they can explain politics to nonexperts *without* falling back on proper nouns and draw general lessons across cases); and (3) detail-oriented scientists who have thought carefully about research design, measurement, construct validity, and other relevant concepts. It is not uncommon for social scientists to "parachute in" to the field, bringing with them a precrafted theory and a well-funded, theoretically sophisticated measurement plan—but these people are sometimes faking (1), even if they have (2) and (3).

Having a good plan and sticking to it is consistent with the march of normal science. People who spend a lot of time in the field, breathing the air and building a model from the ground up based on what they discovered talking to people, can also, sometimes, find themselves occupying prime real estate in the ivory tower. What is the secret? The previous chapter discussed external perceptions of your internal character. This chapter and the next consider the nuts and bolts of data collection. The techniques discussed in this chapter—*participant observation, semistructured interviews, group interviews*, and *archival work*—all represent strategies for managing solo observational studies. The methods in this chapter are meant to help you decide what you believe to be true about a relevant facet of a case.

HOW TO POKE AROUND

One neglected aspect of entrée at a prospective field site is a set of "starter" conversations. If you have prepared by reading the academic literature before arriving, you will perhaps have an easier time of it, but it is important to initiate conversations with low-stakes interlocutors to begin to bridge your "book smarts" with the real case. There is no good alternative to a little bruising and humility when it comes to learning how to pronounce names correctly, for instance, or how to tell the story of the last election without emphasizing the wrong parts to the wrong audiences. For the first few weeks in the field it is a good idea to initiate conversations with anyone you can. Listen in a way that subordinates you, the foreigner, to their local expertise. When you have a question, do not interrupt, but raise your hand (or a finger) to signal that you need them to slow down, then repeat the exact sentence back with the intonation altered to transform the statement into a question. Take notes if you must, but do not let it interrupt the flow of these conversations. The goal is to practice pronunciation and harvest background data. Resist the temptation to ask questions that could be perceived as showing off. Ideally select people you do not plan to speak to again.

Then begin to branch out. As mentioned in chapter 2, a bit of preparatory planning can easily yield a full schedule. Carry your scheduling book with you to the interview. At the end of every interview, get a business card. Place each one on its own page and let them see you write the name and time of the interview, then ask the person to suggest someone else for you to talk to. Between meetings, use Scotch tape to adhere the cards to the pages so they don't fall out. These contacts may pass along people from their personal networks, or you will be able to show them that you already have that person's contact information in your book (credentialing yourself by showing you did your homework). These informational interviews can even begin before you reach the field site. Leveraging academic networks and haphazard introductions is not a good strategy for convincing survey methodologists that you understand population-representative sampling, but this method is nonetheless a very good way to begin getting to know a place. One of the best reasons to attend area studies conferences is academic networking with researchers who have just returned from the field and can tell you how to say names right. Pre-fieldwork introductions can speed on-site entrée, too. Even if you have nothing to present, the benefits of networking at the annual meetings of area studies associations and their various conferences (LASA, MESA, CESS, etc.) can save you weeks or months.

If one transitions to the investigation of taboo or politically sensitive topics, it may become necessary to renegotiate access. Sometimes you can prepare in advance from your home institution, but sometimes you do not really discover the most interesting facet of the case until you arrive—and then find that proceeding invites political scrutiny. Seek advice and proceed with care. Attempts at access reward patience and improvisation. It may be good to try a few strategies to gain access, treating each like venture capital, and seeing which investments pay off. Be open to random opportunities if they present themselves.

Especially if your research is taking place in the capital city of a small country, it may be possible to quickly make contacts at different social strata. (Getting thirty minutes on short notice to meet with mayors or ministers is not likely at home.) The risk is that an unprepared researcher may be perceived as unserious. If your first contact with someone who turns out to be a gatekeeper leads them to perceive you in a negative light, it can render an entire site unworkable. Basic rules of courtesy are even more necessary once gatekeepers are identified. Always be polite. Introduce yourself and your research. Inquire authentically about whether any other people in the government, the NGO community, or the business community might be interested in the research and talking with you. Answer any questions. Always leave a card.

If you know in advance that you will be working on something politically sensitive, especially in a war zone, strategies for access may require planning introductions from your country's embassy representatives or other brokers who live in the country and can trade favors to get you access and candor. This all takes time and lends itself to the perception by locals that you are working with your home government. Consult chapter 6 before you begin poking.

HOW TO OBSERVE AS A PARTICIPANT

Participant observation means treating everything as data. This can be quite exhausting, as you will find if you discipline yourself to try and do it. Much of this work quite explicitly leverages charisma, wisdom, streetsmarts, people skills, and other things neither classrooms nor books reliably instill and must be learned by doing. Since this is difficult to teach, it is rarely given pride of place on graduate training methods syllabi. Many graduate students therefore conclude that these methods have somehow become obsolete, or that there are no professional payoffs for employing them. This is wrong. It is closer to the truth to say that the payoffs for using these methods are nonlinear, that it is hard to "churn" papers with them, that their data tend to end up in books, and that the sunk costs involved in employing them are relatively high.

Political scientists who employ participant observation do so because of a theory that, by doing so, they will acquire robust data of a certain kind.[1] If the goal is to understand the values of the subjects that you claim to care about, authentic attempts to get to know your subjects intimately is obviously not a bad way to start. "Getting to know your subjects intimately" is not something that comes with a standard guidebook, since subject pools are so diverse. But if you want to know what people are thinking, you sometimes need to spend a lot of time listening. Indeed, the most persuasive justification for doing immersive fieldwork is the claim that something about it assists us in uncovering and understanding how people experience, think about, and live politics. All models of human behavior make psychological claims, often implicitly. Different people have different things in mind when they say "participating in the culture": everything from working in a slaughterhouse to reading the Qu'ran with religious students to participating in religious rituals as a friendly observer to "just talking" to people at diners or train stations to living for long periods of time in difficult rural conditions to making daily visits to Roma communities to working at the United Nations.[2]

Qualitative researchers, especially ethnographers, are often slandered with the same well-rehearsed charges: a lack of rigor, an absence of transparency and replicability, an embrace of the inductive and abductive, a willingness to update theory based on field observations, primacy given to the embodied-ness of observational experience, the privileging of intersubjectivity over objectivity, and a writing style that emphasizes the first person. Most of these charges are either matters of aesthetic taste or are malicious and false.[3] Perhaps some stem from a lack of understanding of what ethnography is or a lack of aesthetic appreciation of interpretative methods. Lisa Wedeen observed that ethnography tends to be "subordinated" in the status hierarchy political scientists construct, "deployed in the service of the very sorts of objectivist aims that current ethnographic approaches in anthropology undermine," but it is a rare political scientist who cares very much about what anthropologists think of their work.[4]

When I began doing fieldwork in my twenties, I was one of those few. I remember viewing my time in the field as an instrumental exercise at first. I talked to my subjects in order to understand how they remembered the past, what strategic games they were playing, and what unrealized solution set might be possible. I was also living at the fringe of the development and reconstruction aid community that provides a critical source of employment and social mobility for Georgians and Tajiks. At some point, I realized that this was a variable I was well-positioned to measure (as a material inducement to side-switching). But how was this source of future rents viewed by Georgian and Tajik militia members? I spent days rereading interview notes and trying very hard to decide whether the stories I was hearing ought to coalesce into a stag hunt or a hawk–dove game. I had a sense that evidence for both claims was there for the taking. If one wanted to be harsh, this could be described as exactly what Wedeen was critiquing in the quote above. If one were more forgiving, you could say that I was trying to see the whole picture, observing connections between everyday life and politics that could not occur to me otherwise.

As described in chapter 2 of this book, I had to change my measurement strategy and my coding rules in order to score the indicator for the variable I wanted (side-switching). The same story could be told differently. I could say that by listening to my subjects, I began to realize that my erudition had led me to the wrong questions. Proceeding inductively or abductively is difficult. It can involve throwing away work that one did back home—a whole dissertation prospectus, in fact. If you are like me, however, and you find, as Tariq Thachil and countless others have, that the dominant theoretical frames used to study your problem both in the Western ivory tower *and* in the Global South are misleading, then your objectives change because of experience in the field. What you really come to want is a sense that you are not wasting your subjects' time or misrepresenting their lived experience.[5] There is no sure way to guarantee that you are asking "the right questions" or "getting the real story," of course, but ethnography and other immersive approaches incentivize listening. Actually listening is a skill.

After listening, what comes next? As an improvisational pluralist, in my own work and as a referee I try to stake out a neutral middle ground. Rather than resign ourselves to being second-rate ethnographers, incapable of sorting Geertzian winks from blinks, in my view we should aspire to be researchers who possess a special sensitivity to institutions (structural power), social position, and the role of violence (applied and threatened). What this might mean, if everyone wanted to do a little more of everything, is that more of us would explicitly deploy what the late Lee Ann Fujii called "accidental ethnography" in our writing: drawing ideas, potential trajectories, and even data from unintentional, everyday encounters in the field over the course of a project.[6] This often happens as a line or two in a job talk but it rarely transforms into publications that are submitted. Perhaps this could be changed. We can also deepen our comparisons by engaging with an ethnographic sensibility, which would highlight our field's advantage in moving between levels of analysis.[7]

I also believe that writing good descriptions is an important part of what a craftsmen's guild like ours should be expected to teach and incentivize. If we fail, we are failing our subjects. I find a lot to like in powerful ethnographic writing. It can be difficult to read Mitchell Duneier's descriptions of homeless men discussing urinating or Begoña Aretxaga's accounts of resistance tactics by prison inmates. (When I say "difficult," I mean something different than when I admit that it is difficult for me to read formal theory.[8]) This difficulty suggests that what the authors are doing with language transcends "mere description." They labor in their prose to make you feel discomfort, including the literal physical discomfort associated with disgust, in order to teach you something important about their subjects. This is powerful. It is (arguably) not science writing. It is powerful nonetheless. It is closer to magic.

My strong advice, then, is that if you are seriously considering this kind of work, you begin by doing a lot of your own reading and listening. Consider interdisciplinary coursework in an anthropology or sociology department beforehand—if only to see how other people who are just as smart as political scientists (!), but with different professional incentives and different canons, think about evidence and testing. You must also befriend political scientists who value (and do) ethnographic work. Purchase *Writing Ethnographic Fieldnotes*, 2nd edition, by Emerson et al. and Ed Schatz's edited volume *Political Ethnography: What Immersion Contributes to the Study of Power.*[9] Actually read them. Carry them into the field with you. Try to meet up with some of the authors over email or perhaps in person in the interpretative methods group at the American Political Science Association conference, and get them to read your drafts. Begin to be specific, in writing, about how you are using immersive methods. Be aware of what constitutes ethnography for those trained in it.

In my experience people do not, as a rule, like to be studied. And as Jarvis Cocker observed, "everybody hates a tourist." People do, as a rule, like to talk about themselves, like to be listened to as if their life experiences matter, and like the idea that their stories will be recorded for posterity. Ethnographers—by their deliberate presence—force these two decision heuristics into conflict. As the line between researcher and subject blurs, what occasionally emerges is a crucible for creative, cooperative theory-building. People can tell when their words are being received with empathy (i.e., when they are being treated as subjects) and when their words are being clinically recorded for some other purpose (i.e., when they are being treated as objects). Once a person decides that the researcher is actually listening, the researcher gets better data.

HOW TO THINK SYSTEMATICALLY
ABOUT SAMPLE BIAS

Sampling considerations should ideally occur in the design phase of dissertation prospectus planning at your home institution, since sampling issues are logically prior to the logistics of data collection. Many designs on political science topics require oversampling populations that have expert knowledge of a subject. Some of these populations have reason to mistrust the intentions of a well-funded social science researcher. This can be an insoluble problem, as enumerators employed by census bureaucracies worldwide discover each year. Consider five different research designs to study patterns of gang recruitment in Central American cities: (1) a study that solicits the beliefs of gang members on the streets; (2) a study that solicits beliefs of gang members in jail; (3) a study that solicits beliefs from the families of gang members; (4) a study that solicits beliefs from the victims of gang members; and (5) a study that solicits beliefs from the police units that have been tasked for years with dismembering the gangs. Each of these five designs would have to identify and correct for different biases and would yield completely different frames of reference for the phenomenon. Each of the five studies would potentially be of great interest. It is easy to imagine ways in which any of them could be more informative than embedding questions about gangs in a nationally representative USAID household survey.

After deciding upon the population, the next step is usually to commit to a procedure for selecting individuals to interview. Because no one wants to be lied to, or to invest resources collecting a large dataset of uninformed speculations, you may want to prioritize the credibility of the sources at the time you solicit their participation, maximizing the validity of the results and the reliability of the inferences from the data.[10] Getting university research permissions forces precommitment on the question of how to recruit individuals into the study. Broad consensus exists that claims made at the level of a population require some defense of representativeness, but any kind of centralized list can be used to draw a random sample.

Uncovering a list like this in pre-fieldwork is the equivalent of "striking it rich" on your first trip to pan for gold. Recalling the five sample sets from above, it is unlikely one would ever acquire a centralized list of gang members on the street. A list of police officers assigned to task forces might be feasible, but their names would likely be classified. A list of victims could be assembled, since presumably the identities of murdered citizens are published in local papers. One might be able to acquire a list of gang members in jail, but special Institutional Review Board considerations would apply to a sample of prisoners (to account for the background level of coercion). Some of these studies lend themselves to getting started with lower start-up costs than others.

Sometimes serendipity opens doors. This becomes more common, in my experience, the more one's research draws on the perspectives of local social actors. Sometimes one's human subjects begin to recognize themselves in your theory and offer helpful emendations. In other cases, they actually befriend us and open up their social networks to us. This allows access to different interview subjects than you would have thought possible. In some cases, making friends can yield complete datasets that can be repurposed. State bureaucracies run on metrics, after all, and spreadsheets can float around. If they find their way into your possession by some happy accident, they can sometimes anchor an entire chapter, stand-alone paper, or dissertation.

If one discovers a new source of data, it may perfectly validate a well-laid plan—or it may be a disorienting moment. It may necessitate winding the process backward, asking for what this new data source could serve as an indicator. Begin by considering a short modular paper. You will eventually want to be managing a portfolio of projects, so the experience of treating a special dataset like venture capital is not necessarily a premature thought experiment. If you find a special sample on site that is just too good to pass up, but that requires you to collect the data in a way that you know will feel like flying by the seat of your pants, it may come at the expense of the better-planned research that brought you to the field site in the first place. Minimally, take breaks to think about what the paper is supposed to look like at the end, as a finished product. You may eventually need to take time to learn an entirely new literature, or bring in a coauthor who knows it already. Also remember that the best practice—the other papers to which yours will be compared—is to think first about what population you want the study to represent, then about a strategy that can be used to defend your procedures of recruitment and sampling. If you go the other way and try to "fit" the part of the library to the data you find, that is fine—but the written product will have to be very compelling.

If you are casting a wide net and collecting your own data when something unexpected happens, sometimes you will have a flash of insight that what is taking place is actually a defensible instrument to anchor a natural experiment. If you can tell the story correctly, you will get credit for having put yourself in a position to observe something rare in the first place; then you can credibly claim you made your own luck by being prepared, patient, insightful, and entrepreneurial. Ever since Steven Levitt popularized the concept of the natural experiment, there have been many attempts by social scientists to lay claim to this mode of discovery that do not quite pass the sniff test. Telling the story of discovering an instrument is its own art, and the best dissemination platforms for the narrative may not be the academic journal article where the paper eventually lands.[11] Pivoting from a high-integrity observational study to a treatment effect based on an exogenous shock is consistent with the ethos of *improvisational pluralism*.

If you can be systematic about the assumptions that you use to generate a representative sample, or at least be specific about what biases you believe might make your interview sample systematically different from the rest of the population, it sends a very strong positive signal about the seriousness of the research enterprise. Acting as if your interviews are representative when they clearly are not sends the opposite signal. Even if you do not plan to do a survey, you will benefit from familiarizing yourself with an accessible book on statistical sampling procedures so that you can learn the lingo that is expected. Most studies do not demand national-level representativeness. You should be able to put together some descriptive statistics from the most recent government census data (or a recently conducted survey) and explain to a lay reader where your sample fits into the national distribution. Sometimes a census is not available, however, even if the population you are trying to represent is large. When I was considering a survey of Abkhazia, the breakaway portion of Georgia, the most recent census had been conducted in Soviet times, prior to a war and demographic displacement. After living in Sukhumi for a few weeks, I concluded that a DIY survey, sampling off of the energy grid, would give a good picture of where people were living de facto. A few years later, planning a survey in Mogadishu, my coauthor and I leveraged the fact that decades of artillery shelling had reduced most two- and three-story buildings to a single floor, and most used their own generators. Families would squat inside buildings for basic shelter and protection, however, so we purchased a commercial satellite image, trained a computer to count pixels that were buildings (not streets, trees, grass, or markets), and used buildings to make assumptions about inhabitable spaces.[12]

What if, despite your best efforts, systematic data collection efforts fall apart and all you have left at the end of your time in the field is interviews? Having stuck stubbornly with snowball sampling methods for long enough, a researcher may decide that the inferences emerging from the sample are sufficiently representative to meet a personal threshold of integrity. A survey statistician or purist may not accept this strategy, but a great deal of published qualitative work relies on responsibly qualified probabilistic statements of validity. Many serious people[13] recognize the importance of the haphazard and emphasize that access and establishing enduring personal rapport with some people (while making no connection whatsoever with others) is part of the process. Yes, this creates selection bias, but if the alternative is not having any data at all, honestly—who cares? The procedures by which the information was collected change the content of social data, but that just means it is incumbent on you to be as transparent as possible about the practical social boundaries that you were aware of, and aware of the limitations of the inferences that you can draw from your data. Many books and dissertations contain thoughtful methodological appendices that can serve as models.

If you intuit that you will depend on in-depth interview data for inferences, you should make peace early with the epistemological constraints implied by a small number of interviewees and embrace the advantages and constraints of the "depth" end of the "depth vs. breadth" trade-off. Accept that the design choice means grappling with the problems of selection bias, since each voice will weigh more heavily in the researcher's understanding. The design choice can be sensitive to outliers, to unreliable interlocutors, and to social desirability bias. It demands that the reader take a lot about you on faith. Persuasive observational studies are deliberate and explicit in the write-up about the trade-offs in the choices that were made. The problem of non-representativeness is

most acute if one has reason to believe characteristics of the study population that make for good interviews would make respondents systematically different from the overall study population.

HOW TO CONDUCT A
SEMISTRUCTURED INTERVIEW

The in-depth, semistructured interview is the method best calibrated to
soliciting individual perspectives on a few narrowly defined themes.
When it works, a researcher "gently guides a conversational partner in
an extended discussion."[14] It is incumbent on the researcher to ensure
that the interview environment is professional and the procedure is scientific. This means a well-prepared system of taking notes, a standard-
ized set of thoughtfully designed questions, and a willingness to allow
the interview to drift.

Semistructured interviews are organized around a questionnaire
cleared through your university's IRB in advance. This structures the
arc of the interview. Strive to ask each person the same questions, to
allow controlled comparison across interviewees. A major distinction
between semistructured interviews and surveys is that both researchers
and subjects have the freedom to diverge from the structure at any
point. Nothing stops you from following up on a related theme raised by
an interlocutor; nothing stops the subject from speaking extemporaneously about something you did not ask about. After following an improvisational path as far as you decide that it is useful, you return to the
structure of the prepared set of core questions. You take responsibility
for encouraging the interviewees to speak freely at some times and wrap
it up at others, often with subtle nonverbal cues. There is nothing wrong
with asking unscripted follow-up questions and engaging with probes.
Exert judgement over when it is appropriate—or not—to cut things off.
In unusual circumstances it can make sense to allow a thread of conversation to continue unraveling for hours, only concluding with a promise
to meet again at a later time for additional follow-up. Guiding the questions to closure after two hours or so is common practice.

The quality of in-depth interviews usually depends on three things: (1) preparation by the researcher; (2) the skill of active listening; and (3) haphazard luck. When these come together, the value of the methodology will become clear. The subjects will surprise you. Some will open up and volunteer things you did not think to ask about. If this happens, and they strike you as trustworthy, your project can be transformed. You will take notes, then revise your next set of questions and begin to triangulate facts in a way that would not—could not—have occurred to you if you were analyzing data from your desk. It can be a methodology that allows you to gain access to processes of strategic decision-making directly, to discard models that locals themselves think are inappropriate, that can provide a deeper understanding of which theoretical concepts that were lurking inert in case background ought to be brought to the fore.[15] It is a reliable methodology to determine which structural variables locals believe are relevant and causal. These locals may be incorrect about their beliefs, but accurately recording what the beliefs are anyway can be a valuable exercise.

PREPARATION

The purpose of these interviews is *not* basic information-seeking. You are not a journalist, nor do you engage in descriptive essay-writing: you have come to this place to answer a narrow question to advance an academic field of knowledge. If you can, prepare interview questions that demonstrate familiarity with the relevant background history of the country through secondary sources and preliminary interviews (see "How to Poke Around," earlier). This makes it easier to establish rapport with interview subjects. If you can construct questions that literally pick up where other sources leave off, you can quickly convey to your readers that you have done your homework. This makes it easier to transform your data into an academic publication at the end of the study.

Constructing an interview that feels effortless often takes quite a lot of preparatory work. As you design questions, prioritize theory. Formulating interview questions, translating them, clustering questions by topic to create natural flow that simulates an organic conversation, doing a few "test run" interviews on friends or colleagues to allow you to gauge the time it takes to answer questions—do not underestimate how long it takes to do this part of the job.

Make the core questions very simple at first. Do not show off. Use basic language to convey that you did your homework on the case, but your interlocutor must feel she is the subject-matter expert (which is why you are talking to her). Ask simple questions. If you can satisfy your genuine curiosity, improvising follow-ups on the fly is easy. It is often necessary to revise the instrument while in the field: some questions that seemed like a good idea to you (or the IRB) will not be the right ones. Improvise if you must. Even if you do not ultimately make revisions, spend thoughtful time at multiple stages of the research process considering alternative question wordings. You will have to revisit the core research question again and again, no matter what, as you decide which meandering branches of your conversation are worth allowing to blossom and which to prune.

Aim for an interview somewhere in the twenty-to-forty-minute range if your interlocutor is nonresponsive. An awkward meeting is not useful for either of you, so you should not waste a large part of a day. If the gears mesh and the subject is invested in telling you things that he or she thinks you want to know, a twenty-minute skeletal framework can easily expand to fill two hours. Begin the interview with basic background, then move to emotional or cognitively demanding topic matter, then, as the interview winds toward a close, tone it down again, ending finally with a summary. End on a good note so that, even if the conversation was difficult, the interviewee does not feel betrayed or used.

ACTIVE LISTENING

Listening reflectively is a skill. The most important tools are empathy and a situational judgment of when it is time to stop. In this context, empathy means the ability to imagine how someone else feels and what they are experiencing, to try to see things from someone else's perspective. Empathy is most difficult when we do not agree with what is being said, when we are afraid, or when we are disgusted by either the speaker or the ideas being expressed.[16] Most people think they do this naturally, but researchers can train to improve their ability to be empathetic.

Practicable techniques to build rapport involve communication of understanding (or attempts to understand), engagement with the feelings and perspective of the speaker, and subtle signals of investment in the subject matter. The most useful techniques involve increasing awareness of body language (serious nodding vs. rigid body language but soft eye contact), verbal cues (*"tell me more"* vs. *"yeah, I get it"*), and nonverbal cues (*"huh"* vs. *"hmmmm"*) that are part of your communication process.[17] A simple technique is to restate an answer in your own language in order to confirm that your understanding is correct. This can be especially meaningful (and efficacious) when you attempt to do this across a language barrier, because of the forced intimacy created by demonstrating your vulnerability as a nonnative speaker and stumbling over words. The native speaker is invited and empowered to state the sentiment again, her expertise having been subtly validated. When these techniques are mastered, you will better understand what the interviewee is trying to say and acquire confidence that your intuitions of the significance of this information (as well as misinformation or silence) are valid.

LUCK

Sometimes people just "click," even across a language barrier. It is hard to say why. Perhaps this methodology rewards researchers with innate "people skills" or those who remain open to haphazard possibilities that present themselves, but it may be the case that sometimes everyone just gets lucky, managing to put themselves in the right place at the right time.

By coincidence, I learned a great deal about urban racketeering in Eduard Shevardnadze's Georgia in the 1990s from the proprietor of a guest house who had been a fire inspector at that period. We were talking over tea as a part of standard introductions. The conversation turned to my work. I quickly realized that the best possible use of the next five hours of time was to collect my notebook, retreat to the living room, and use my structured interview questions to allow him to tell me his life story. He proceeded to draw a set of maps for me, which I still have, of who was permitted (by law) to knock on doors and inform people that their homes were not up to code in which parts of the city—along with the name of the militia commanders embedded in the security sector infrastructure and drawing their share of these rents. The maps served as icebreakers in subsequent interviews. That interview changed how I thought about what Shevardnadze was doing as he consolidated the state in postwar Georgia.

STEP 1: INITIATING THE INTERVIEW

Before anything begins, ideally before your subject arrives, take responsibility for securing the location for the interview. If the subject is already on location, I often find it useful to engage in a conspicuous ritual of professionalization. You can sometimes take control of the situation by doing something as simple as deciding where you will sit and suggesting where the other person will sit. Make sure you have privacy if there is any chance that the matters that will be discussed demand it. The goal is to create an encouraging atmosphere in which the interviewee feels safe and respected, but also an atmosphere in which your role is clear. Once you conduct a few interviews, you will establish a routine, including a few props that allow you to quickly set the stage, transforming a room in the respondent's home or a neutral public location into a workspace.

My critical props include a book in which to take interview notes (with no names), a scheduling book (in which I take no notes but keep the names of interviewees), a table with two comfortable chairs that allow eye contact, two glasses of water, three pens of different colors (part of my process),[18] a bathroom nearby (to allow a break with no questions asked), and a clock that all parties can see. Some of my colleagues like to record interviews and, in some cases, I have badly wished that I had, but because my initial field interviews were with people who made it clear that they did not want to be recorded, I never integrated the "recording device" into my setup ritual when I was younger. There is compelling evidence that the presence of recording devices, or even consumer electronics, alters the survey ritual—which is part of why I advise keeping your cell phone turned off rather than using it as a timer.[19] Begin the interview by letting the subject observe you powering it off. Put the inert object down on the table in front of both of you or in your bag. This is the first signal that the interview has begun. If they had a suspicion that you were recording them with electronic devices, you have sent a small signal to assure them you are not. It also precommits you to not check in with your data stream during the interview. You commit to face-to-face interaction at the beginning of the ritual. Shift your posture, open your notebook, establish eye contact, and record the date and time of the interview.

Thank the interviewee for volunteering his or her time. Even if you have met before, reintroduce yourself as if it were the first meeting. Explain where you are from. Answer questions. Describe the aims of the research in broad terms. If your interlocutor is literate, and you have written a short research statement (see chapter 2), provide a copy. Even if you have not, it is important to state up front what you believe the practical implications of the work are so that the person can assess your seriousness. (Canned language includes "to better understand . . ." or "in order to help improve . . .") Disclose relevant local affiliations. Provide a business card with your local cellular phone number handwritten on the back so that respondents know that they can contact you again if they want to, or pass your information on to third parties. Embossed business cards can give the affair a heightened sense of seriousness, in addition to establishing a mechanism for permanent contact through your home .edu email address.

Next, introduce the protocol for informed consent that you agreed upon with your university's IRB. When possible, I favor reading it aloud to the interviewee and asking for his or her approval to participate. In low-risk settings with literate subjects, there are few disadvantages to employing a written form. Subjects can then read and keep a copy and provide a signature as evidence of consent. In potentially high-risk settings things are different. If the data collected may be politically sensitive, and if anonymity for respondents is valued, university IRBs can often be persuaded that signed forms are a bad idea, the "smoking gun" linking the participant to a study that is retroactively defined as foreign espionage. Oral consent maximizes the security of the respondent. If you are recruiting your sample from populations that are illiterate, or if many languages are in play, being asked to sign something he or she cannot read may shame the subject and spoil things from the start (a clear case for preferring oral to written consent).

The next step is to explain to the subject what is going to occur. If the interview data will only be used anonymously, stating the reason that you are keeping the interview anonymous at the outset is almost always a good idea. This strategy attenuates some of the inherent power dynamics, especially if interviewees arrive hoping to be quoted or expecting you to record their names for posterity. Explaining why you are declining to do so helps them gauge the seriousness of your academic enterprise. On the other hand, if you plan to record the interview using a digital device, say so. Ask explicitly for permission before you turn the device on. Make it clear that the purpose of recording is to transcribe the full text for the purpose of analysis by future generations to ensure no information was missed or misinterpreted.

If the interviewee does not feel comfortable with recording, but does not mind the interview, this is a good sign. As with the cellular phone, show her that you are powering down your recording device and putting it away. You have formally introduced the possibility of a permanent record but then credibly demonstrated a willingness to eliminate that record, taking what small steps you can to create a safe space.

At the close of preliminaries, always remind the subject that she may stop at any time. Ask if she has any other questions. Ask if she is ready to begin.

STEP 2: CONFEDERATION

The formality and process-based professionalism of the introduction sets the stage for interactions that can be clinical and detached. The goal of initial questions is to (re-)establish a human connection. The main goal of the introduction is to reassure the interviewee that you are sincerely interested in the narrative and not passing judgment.

The secondary goal is to broadcast, clearly and consistently, your goals. Your introduction script and the follow-up questions you ask should cumulatively convey to the subject that you have a clear research question. You made a decision about what gaps in the academic literature your research was going to fill, which led you to this country, this sample, and ultimately to this interview table. There is nothing up your sleeve. You do not need to explain all of this explicitly, but allow a peek behind the curtain. Ask a few spontaneous questions to set your interlocutor at ease, but also ask a few with your eyes on the prize. What do you actually want to learn? Why is this important, really? Signpost. The questions that you ask in the first fifteen minutes of the interview have the potential to bring a person into your research as a confederate.

Begin with easy, factual questions that can be answered in a sentence or two, allowing the subject space to introduce important introductions and context relevant to her life conditions. Later in the interview you will take notes haphazardly depending on what strikes you as important, but, at this stage, record absolutely everything said. All of her story is important to you. If you are conducting the interview in a language other than your native tongue, you should practice asking these initial questions to strangers. Practice asking the question (and following-up on answers) in non-interview settings. Basic inquiries into a respondent's background—age, marital status, children, religion, ethnicity, occupation, etc.—are useful icebreakers that make your interviewee feel confident.

STEP 3: DIALOGUE

Asking too many irrelevant questions (including follow-ups) spoils an otherwise good interview by conveying to a subject that you do not understand what matters. The meat of an interview is usually a few well-crafted emotionally and intellectually demanding questions. (If these questions never appear, the subject is going to naturally wonder what all of the fuss about giving consent was about.) Such questions should never be improvised. They ought to be written iteratively, vetted by your university, firmly anchored in theory, tested, translated, and arranged in an order that makes sense, with follow-up questions carefully tailored to the answer.

Keeping the interview on track while also allowing the subject to meander productively is a skill that can improve with practice. A well-rehearsed and well-constructed semistructured interview questionnaire can be your best tool to guide the conversation away from topics that are "going too deep" without breaking character, interrupting, or ending the interview prematurely. Listen respectfully, but look for opportunities to guide the subject back. If the next questions flow in the same direction as her digression, this mitigates the risk of negative side effects by signpost-ing that you as a researcher had anticipated her experiences, analogous to other experiences you have heard. If, on the other hand, she has veered completely off course, a good strategy is to provide a short summary, in your own words, of what the interviewee has said, inviting corrections. If you have lost eye contact, reestablish it. Nod affirmatively. Thank the interviewee sincerely for sharing so much important information. Vali-date her as an authority once again as you close the subject and move on with the instrument.

It may be a good idea to literally close your book and take a short break (water/bathroom)—but before you do, ask if it would be possible, upon your return, to ask a few more questions. Convey that the inter-viewee's perspective would be valuable.

Let the subject understand that, as a scientist, you are bound by a duty to your questionnaire. Consider some variant of this script: "*I want to thank you sincerely for sharing with me in the way that you just did. It is very helpful for me to understand these important matters in the same way that you do. I want to be respectful of your time, however, and there are a few more matters that I need to inquire about. Can we proceed?*"

STEP 4: CLOSURE

A focused researcher can, with skill, improvise around the structure of a questionnaire. Everyone's time is valuable, including yours, and the boundaries of a conversation are defined by their utility to the research agenda. Use the clock to signal when to draw a topic to a close. Some-times ending an interview is easy. Sometimes it is one of the hardest parts of a researcher's job. If you have established rapport and the inter-view is branching, and the interviewee intuits that you have the author-ity to allow her to keep talking but you do not want to listen to her answers any more, the emotional response can be explosive. There are different contexts and different norms that are salient, mediated by class, gender, and other variables. Use common sense and go with the flow. If you sense that taking charge at a particular moment in the interview might embarrass a host, for instance, you are likely right. Trust yourself, and wait until things wind to a natural-feeling conclusion.

A few easy questions should bring the interview in for a soft landing and salve any wounds reopened by revisiting difficult subjects from the past. Have a few boilerplate questions on hand—"big think" normative questions about the research subject, or philosophical questions that do not have wrong answers—and ask whichever of them feels right at the time. Often these are not really questions, but rather reminders to the subject that you both care about the same things. Give the interviewee one more chance to say anything else she would like to clarify or share. Then end by thanking her again for taking the time to participate. Reinforce the value of these answers to your research. Consider shaking hands for ceremonial closure. When you turn your phone back on, she will intuit that the interview is officially over.

If you can, take a few minutes while everything is very fresh in your head to write a few more notes about the interview. Once you are reasonably sure that there is nothing else to add to your notebook, you are finished. Stand up. Take a short walk or use the restroom. Clear your head.

STEP 5: WRITE-UP

Your fieldwork laptop ought to be left in your bag or your room during the interview. Later the same day, however, while the interview is relatively fresh in your head, go back to your notes and transcribe them. Writing about the interview quickly is the best way to avoid losing data. Memories are fallible. We know that if we wait too long, our minds will fill in gaps with fictions.[20] If you find you cannot type fast enough, explore speech-to-text software.

In some cases, it will be obvious to you that you should also use this time to construct a first draft of the "hidden transcript"—an attempt to decode meanings behind the interview (along with warrants for specific inferential claims). Do this in italics or a different font, of course, to avoid your interpretative voice co-mingling with your subject's actual voice.

It is useful to create a separate document of new questions raised by the interview. You do not necessarily need to rush to revise the semistructured interview form; you may discover upon further reflection that the interaction was a one-off. Do notice, however, when you are told things that surprise you or contradict your previous understandings. If new information has been shared that challenges your assumptions, do not let the opportunity to correct yourself slip away.

Once the notes exist in digital form, they are much easier to review. They also become easier to alter or steal. For this reason, among others, it is crucial that you not include the name of the respondent anywhere in the document you create on your computer. If no signed consent document exists, a third party would need to take the time to read your "appointment book" (not on your computer) and your interview notes (also not on your computer) to know who gave you that piece of information. This offers your subjects basic protections. The procedure is fallible, but it gives you the option of permanently closing the circuit at any time by destroying the appointment book. Usually this is not necessary, but knowing that you have this power should put your mind at rest vis-à-vis certain kinds of paranoia (see chapter 6). There are many additional options for those who feel that their notes contain politically sensitive data. As a general rule, if one is working on a question where the importance of keeping certain material from the eyes of authorities causes paranoia, transcribing notes into electronic form (for example, encrypting a document and emailing it as an attachment to a trusted source back home) may cause risks to human subjects (again, see chapter 6). Paper and pencil presents fewer risks of exposure, but even if great care is taken, this method tends to yield data that is less organized and less transparent. This is a particularly salient problem for researchers working in the shadow of the host country's national security state.[21] Weigh the pros and cons carefully.

TROUBLESHOOTING COMMON CONCERNS

A few problems often present themselves when collecting and interpreting semistructured interview data. First, people have genuinely different points of view and different causal theories about events in their world. Responsibility falls on you, the researcher, to sort through differences of opinion. Second, people are not always reliable. In fact, they lie all the time, consciously and unconsciously. Responsibility falls on you to not reproduce others' fictions in documents that purport to be factual. Third, people often tell a story in a way that they believe that the listener wants to hear it. Responsibility falls on you to not lead subjects to predetermined conclusions by the way you solicit opinions. You must also report honestly whether a sample is systematically unrepresentative or basically good enough to be informative in the researcher's expert judgment, where it may be vulnerable to bias, and in what ways it might be misleading to extrapolate too far. Taken cumulatively, a great deal of responsibility falls on the shoulders of a researcher at both the design and interpretation stage.

Interpreting data in a way that does not reproduce strategic falsehoods your subjects may wish to plant in the historical record poses site-specific and study-specific challenges. When subjects look us in the eye and attempt to deceive us, how to proceed with integrity is not always obvious. Get in the habit of noticing which lies are rehearsed (part of a cumulative structure of myths) and which are improvised (designed to switch topics and quickly guide the conversation away from something the subject would rather avoid).[22] When people bother to construct elaborate lies, you may be catching a glimpse through a window into something operating in their culture that deserves attention. If you can do so without appearing condescending or incredulous, rather than directly challenging a falsehood, consider asking the subject to elaborate. This allows you to probe, gently but firmly, whether people are lying to you in order to pull the wool over your eyes or lying without meaning to. In the latter case, the best interpretive move is still not clear. On balance, the greater good is probably served by discarding interview data rather than validating false claims shared in the hope that the researcher will promulgate them widely, but I struggle personally with this ethical gray area.[23]

Particularly for scholars who anticipate working in post-conflict settings on sensitive political questions, two additional ethical concerns specific to this research methodology bear consideration: revisiting trauma and strategic deception.

Because a respondent may steer the conversation toward the things that he feels the researcher most needs to know, an in-depth semistructured interview can easily take on the feel of a confession or a therapy session. When you do your job well, repressed feelings can emerge. A respondent may surprise themselves and tell more than intended.[24] You are committing to remembering, writing things down, and curating facts into a form that serious people will later read. For a subject who is not normally listened to and unused to talking about trauma, this makes you an authority figure. Revisiting difficult memories with an authority figure can yield unpredictable emotions. There can be tears, followed quickly by shame at the tears and intense anger at the researcher for causing the shame. Maintaining professional distance in these delicate moments is important. Do not interrupt. Do not touch your subject until the moment has passed and you are concluding the interview.

Remember also, however, that you are not a counselor and you did not initiate this conversation in order to provide therapeutic healing. You may harbor a personal theory that the subject needs someone to listen, but it is important that you remember you are probably not qualified to make that judgment, since therapeutic professionals have special training[25] When questions involve emotionally intense subject matter, including personal tragedy and trauma, researchers have a primary responsibility to try to hold interviewees on the interview track. *Do not* to allow them to explore depths of trauma with you. For someone practicing reflective listening, determining when the thread of conversation begins to broach sensitive issues is not difficult: physiological signs of discomfort are usually observable.[26] How to reverse or alter the direction of the interview is not always obvious. The interviewee has made an internal decision to speak out loud about a traumatic event. This may be only tangentially related to the topic at hand and, from your perspective, completely unrelated to the topic of the interview—but it is clearly what he wants you to understand about his experience. As a privileged observer, however, you have created this situation, and you are now under obligation to hold eye contact and listen with empathy. The interviewee may begin to go into vivid detail about tragic events or be overcome by unexpected emotion, etc. This can be followed by sudden emotional awareness that the psychic harm *to him* is real, that the intended result is *not* therapeutic, and that the benefits of the information flow are one-sided. In this moment, the respondent can feel shame, often quickly repressed and replaced by explosive anger. More than once I felt I was in physical danger due to this sort of cascade. In both cases, I became afraid, the respondent noticed, and the interview ended shortly afterward.

Deception is also tricky. Keith Darden observes: "Always remember that in the field, the subjects of your research are not your friends, they are the gatekeepers to the information that you need. To get them to open up, you need to find a set of keys that are specific to that context . . . [T]he two things that you have the most control over in the field are the image of yourself that you present and the settings in which you present it."[27] On the other hand, an in-depth interview ideally starts a process of building trust. If your subjects are building trust with a character you have constructed strategically in order to engender it, you *are* engaging in deception—just not the kind of deception that the IRB (or anyone else) can prevent. Some degree of deception is inevitable in fieldwork on matters of human security or high-salience politicized memories. You are flirting with power, however, and the language of the "seduction of espionage" is surely appropriate.[28] Remember that afterward most subjects will try to reverse-engineer "what you were really up to." Consider which questions might systematically give the wrong impression.

HOW TO CONDUCT A GROUP INTERVIEW

A group interaction obviously differs from a one-on-one interaction. Group interviews, often called focus groups, are a commonplace tool in the study of attitudes and opinions. Dynamic social energy, including the give-and-take of contrasting and competing views, is to focus groups what empathy and intimacy are to semistructured interviews. The format encourages participants to vet their perspectives, share their experiences, and try to explain the motivations behind their behavioral choices. The researcher plays the role of facilitator and ringmaster and must be prepared to share the microphone. Subjects play off each other, developing and redefining opinions in real time. A skilled researcher can calibrate the control knobs of a one-on-one structured interview with precision. With group interviews, letting go of the steering wheel and losing control completely is often the point.

Group interviews can be especially useful when the research probes topics on which not everyone has a ready-formed opinion. For one thing, no participant is forced to voice an opinion on anything—a profound contrast with one-on-one data collection. In a one-on-one structured interview, if you ask a question of this sort, you will be able to observe your interlocutor struggling to understand what it is you really want to know, and sometimes feeling embarrassment at not being the expert you apparently thought he was. If the question is strange, one that participants do not pose to themselves every day, the respondent may make up an answer without thinking about it very much (to move on with the exercise) or, depending on the amount of rapport with the interviewer, report "I don't know" or refuse to answer. Participants in a focus group feel less social pressure to say something, no matter what, if they do not have a real response; someone else who has something to say can fill the silence.[29] The dynamics of the interaction also allow participants to define their own position vis-à-vis each other. Sometimes they will comment on each other's responses. (*"I completely concur, the exact same thing happened to me,"* or *"For me it was a little different, and here's how . . . ,"* or *"I strongly disagree, especially when it comes to . . ."*). Anyone who has had experience running a classroom discussion seminar knows that when this works well, meaningful organic answers emerge. Group interviews validate, or invalidate, initial poorly formed suppositions about collective meaning in the minds of a particular subject pool.

Focus groups can track a line of argument, as well, capturing specific language used to describe a controversial phenomenon. While there are many ways to study the production of meaning, the controlled environment of a focus group is a defensible middle ground between an observational study and a behavioral laboratory. Despite its absence of control and many well-rehearsed flaws (non-representativeness, susceptibility to groupthink, social desirability bias, etc.), the group interview is useful to scholars trying to move efficiently through the exploratory stage of research prior to survey design. If the researcher is not entirely sure what questions are the right ones, which is common in the initial stages of research, focus groups can be a good way to solicit ideas that can be explored later in semistructured interviews. Focus groups are widespread among commercial advertising firms and political consultants prior to costly roll-out of a product because they reliably yield relatively straightforward data that is easier for nonspecialists to interpret.[30]

Focus groups do not allow information to be shared anonymously. For sensitive questions, especially if the opinions are being solicited in authoritarian regimes or post-conflict settings, the inability to make credible promises of anonymity may make group interviews a non-starter. For other kinds of research, an open conversation format is a great way to get started and can be integrated into a calculated strategy of entrée (see chapter 2).

The group interview format can also sometimes be used strategically to modify an underlying balance of power between the researcher and the study participants. The simple fact that interviewees outnumber the moderator can completely change the power differential. Safety in numbers can make sharing in a group setting attractive to people who are at a social disadvantage from the researcher and don't think their voices matter: it can make them feel more in control over the extent and timing of their interjections and allow their voices to be included without their feeling interrogated. Specific circumstances matter, of course, but the researcher essentially free-rides on whatever trust already exists in the peer group.

The logistical challenges associated with gaining access to a study-appropriate "peer group" are too varied and idiosyncratic to be summarized in this chapter, but as often as not, access begins without even a semblance of a nod to representativeness, as an impromptu "snowball" from a key informant. If someone wants to help you out by gathering a bunch of old friends in one place, you should at least consider taking up the offer. The obvious caveat here involves safety considerations idiosyncratic to the research. There are numerous scenarios (kidnapping and sexual assault most prominently) in which an offer to meet up with a large group of unfamiliar men on their home turf may be a terrible idea. Use common sense.

The advantages of these methods really shine when talking to groups about a past shared experience such as participation in a political activist group, a government workplace, or a militia. By cooperatively explaining something, an in-group consensus can emerge on the important turning points. Members can fact-check each other's accounts, increasing confidence that one individual's idiosyncratic perception of events does not drive a factual interpretation.

There are many easy-to-use guides to organizing group interviews, because it is the kind of thing that corporate middle-managers must be trained in all of the time in the business world. Browse through a few books, run a plan past your university IRB, and plan to improvise. This methodology is a complement to introductory information-seeking but is unlikely to ultimately anchor a dissertation or book.[31] Since psychological risks to either your subjects or to you are lower than in semistructured interviews, a learning-by-doing approach tends to be low-risk. Some basic tips that worked for me:

- Control the environment by arranging for a "public" private location such as a restaurant or bakery after hours. It should be a room that comfortably seats everyone. Fit it out with beverages or snacks.
- As with a semistructured interview, you will need to clear your list of inquiries with your IRB. Unlike a semistructured interview, you will probably not use the "script" as a tool to reestablish control of the interview narrative. Instead, bring a bell that you can use to ceremonially "call everyone to order" if there is cacophony. Ring it once so they can hear what it sounds like. Plan to never ring it except at the beginning—but it helps everyone to know it's there.
- Begin by introducing yourself and thanking everyone for their time. Explain the research project in two minutes or less, then lay out the ground rules.
- Ask everyone to introduce themselves to you and to each other, even if they know each other already. Ask them to give their full names and, in a few sentences, to briefly describe their experience with the topic of the research. Take notes.
- Make sure there is a clock nearby that everyone can see. An hour or two is fine. Three hours is most likely too long.
- You have probably had the opportunity to run a few discussion seminars in your native language back home and have a sense of your classroom style. This is not a classroom, however. No one is there to listen to you. Listen and observe. Take notes as you go, with pen and paper. Resist the urge to act as a guide.
- Don't check your phone or open your laptop under any circumstances.
- If you get lemons, make lemonade. If a dominant voice monopolizes the session, suggest a follow-up semistructured interview with that individual. This will buy the person off temporarily and give you a leg up in establishing rapport for a great in-depth interview.

- If you get silence, don't feel bad. It happens. Try a few subjects. Go lighter. Call it quits after thirty to forty-five minutes, which is about the minimum amount of time these sessions should last. Even if there is no energy or buy-in, given the amount of time it took to get everyone in one room, people expect you to try to coax and listen.
- Remember: these exercises yield data that are informative, not representative.

HOW TO USE ARCHIVES

Just as all fieldworkers traffic in war stories about the trials of data collection, social scientists who work in archives compile horror stories of terrible experiences in deliberately hard-to-use collections.[32] Archives often have severely restricted working hours. Files are often stored in different buildings that happen to be locked. Sometimes it can take hours or even several days for files to be delivered once they're ordered. One of the most common variables in these war stories, however, is the personalities of the archivists. These people are, by definition, gatekeepers. They know you need what they have and often expect to be shown deference. They determine the speed at which your documents will arrive and can make your life easier. You will also have no recourse if they opt to make it harder. You have to manage the relationship.

Do as much prep work as possible before you arrive. You do not want to spend valuable time on site figuring out how an archive works. All archives have idiosyncrasies, their own rules and restrictions that you must abide by or learn to finesse. In this spirit, good archivists can be your most important resources. Treat your first interaction with an archivist ceremonially. Consider presenting an official letter of introduction from your home institution with the embossed seal of the university. If you know in advance which archive you will be visiting, or can identify the name of the head archivist, a customized letter is a good idea. Carry an uncreased copy of this letter with you in a special folder. Frame your topic in a way that the librarian will understand, even if that means being cagey. (*Talk less. Smile more.*) Archivists typically have good intuition about the materials that will be useful to you, and they will always know their holdings better than you do. Be open to their suggestions and nudges. On the other hand, if an archivist stonewalls you, be persistent and professional. Few things spark rage like an officious yet resolutely useless librarian, but you must never lose your temper. Persist politely and remember that these are underpaid people used to being berated by cranky historians. If you are brushing up against one particular person and cannot charm him or her with whatever human touch you can bring to the problem, seek assistance.

If, despite all your preplanning, you show up on a work holiday, or if the materials you specifically requested are randomly unavailable, ask when you can expect access. Proceed with your backup plan for the day. Think in advance about how to best make use of waiting time doing other research-related tasks, such as transcribing the information you have already gathered, or doing oral interviews, or using periodicals or other primary sources at libraries with longer hours. At many modern archives, it is possible and typically necessary to set up an advance account online. There, the first question you will be asked when you show up is, "Did you preregister?" If the answer is no, then you have failed to take your own research seriously. Preregistration can allow you to begin calling for materials before you are on site (a time-saver). If there is no online option, inquire about preordering when you call ahead. If someone is willing to prepare documents for you, you could have boxes of them waiting for you on arrival. Even if this is not an option, there is no disadvantage to letting the archive know ahead of time what you think you need based on the finding aids that are available, confirming with a person (whose name you should record in your notebook) what the policy is for photos and scans of materials. If you have to negotiate, repeatedly make it clear that your images are for research purposes only, i.e., that you are not going to publish them, only refer to them in your writing. You may be required to keep a running list of which materials you have scanned or to ask permission in advance of each image. Ask fellow scholars about ways to make the procedure less tedious.

The collection process rewards organization and focus. Time in archives is limited. It is not uncommon for them to open an hour or more after normal business hours start, close for a full hour at lunch, and shoo out researchers before 5:00 p.m. so the employees have time to shut everything down. This leaves only six to seven hours in which to work.

Arrive early and prepare to hit the ground running. If you find good material, the days go by quickly. Get in a rhythm. Find a good chair and plan to swallow a sandwich quickly on the way to the bathroom. Go through as many documents as possible, skimming as you go. Take brief notes. Scan, jot notes, scan, jot notes, repeat, repeat.

There are many archives where bringing your own computer or scanner is forbidden. You may only have access to a single copy machine or microfiche reader and prices may be exorbitant (and also require coins). Even if you are allowed to bring a computer, there is often a lot of competition for a single power outlet, so extra battery packs are helpful. Do not question the strange rules regarding technology—learn them (in advance) and develop a system that allows you to collect data in a way that will make it easy to process once you get home. Back up everything periodically a few different ways (to the cloud, but also on an external drive).

We have a natural tendency to want to read from beginning to end. Having traveled a great distance with plans to use a particular archive, one has the urge to dive in deep at the chronological beginning and begin to read in detail. Often archival files aren't arranged front to back, however, which means there will not be enough time to see everything you might want. You need to focus ruthlessly on collection while on site. Discovery usually comes later, at home, when you have vast quantities of unstructured time to pore over the documents you have collected.

Many of the materials you read or scan, if not most of them, will be less useful to you than you hope. You will likely become distracted. You might allow drift to occur at times, however. Stay open to surprises and discoveries. For instance, you may encounter redacted items. If you can be specific about why you need information not available in the existing documents, you may be justified in making an appeal or filing Freedom of Information Act requests (or the in-country equivalent process to formally request declassification of documents into the public record). You will soon realize that this process is designed to slow researchers like you down. You must learn to ask and frame the request in an acceptable way (or else give up, which is the point). Professional rewards accrue to the persistent. This is frustrating, but also, perhaps, a tantalizing hint that you are on the right track.

Once you have a strong sense of how the archive is organized and what you want in it—and, as importantly, once you become a known quantity to the archivists—it may be possible to arrange for a research assistant or a team to take your place. Circumstances matter. It is difficult to rush the process. Archivists commonly privilege high-profile scholars (you) and refuse access to students (your RAs) due to perceived matters of status. Working elsewhere while someone else uploads materials to the cloud for you to view later might be efficient from your perspective. However, do not be too surprised if it turns out to be impossible.

The process of archival discovery is rarely romantic, especially if you are under stress or looming deadlines. The mundane obstructions and distractions sometimes feel like a waste of time. Sit with that feeling. Is the particular social fact you are documenting worth it to you? As with conducting interviews or experiments that do not pay off directly, this is the real work of scholarship. If you do not enjoy it or find peace with it, you are not going to be able to do this job in a sustainable way—at least not in a way that privileges these kinds of methods. Thankless archival work does not reward people skills as directly as other methodologies. It is lonelier.

RECAP: WHAT IS THE VALUE OF "GETTING THE STORY YOURSELF"?

The qualitative methods described in this chapter are a means to an end. They help you, the author, discover facts that you will assemble into a causal narrative and present to the guild as an original work of nonfiction. In some circumstances, the enterprise is better described as theory-building. If you use these methods in your first dissertation-length research project, as you get to know a place and discover which alternative hypotheses are the most meaningful ones, theory-building and empirical testing occur hand in hand. In a sense, barefoot empiricism of the sort being advocated here—interviews, ethnography, and observational research designs that are not fully fleshed out—represents a high-risk professional strategy. You are gambling on your ability to slow down, to find the right story, to revise the measurement strategy concocted back home to "sell" the project to advisors and donors, and then to write the story of the new research discoveries in a compelling way. Those of you who identify as quantitative scholars can benefit from these methods, too. High-integrity longitudinal observational studies generate compelling identification strategies, with compelling instruments, for patient observers who know how to look for them.

Many of us rotate back to ethnographic methods. Perhaps it is the case that we lack the technical prowess, or the desire, to compete on the frontier with the young hot-shots. This is probably not the whole story, however. If research engages a political problem that is real and important to our subjects, and these subjects actually help us find solutions (because they understand that the prescriptions derived from the conventional theory are incomplete or flawed, or just not working for them), the narrative is likely to make a more important contribution. The people you are studying can also pass judgment on the validity of whatever observations you make about their lives. If you reach the point where your subjects' opinions come to mean more to you than that of an advisor or journal referee, you may begin playing a high-level translation game. The fact that my Georgian and Tajik subjects certified the validity of my theory helped to give it much-needed legitimacy to the scholar who mattered the most, in the end—myself.

FREQUENTLY ASKED QUESTION #4

What do I do if I discover that things I told my advisors in writing, in my prospectus, or in my preanalysis plan were completely wrong? How do I know when I am supposed to start over? How long do I pursue a failing project?

- From one scientist to another: How did you think this was going to work? Triangulating methods, based either on discovery or constraints, is the arc of every project. We sometimes pivot, change questions, and explain why we did what we did—what *specifically* we learned in the field that changed our original point of view. This is the process of scientific discovery in practice: *improvisational pluralism*. (To quote Alfred the butler in Christopher Nolan's 2005 film *Batman Begins*, "Why do we fall down, Mr. Wayne?")
- Preanalysis plans are meant to be community tools, not suicide pacts. Maybe future editors at some outlets will want one as a condition of publication, but the regime is new and contested and (at the time of this writing) still a bit buggy. You should not want to confuse (or defraud) the discipline by writing a paper you know is wrong or misleading, even if it is based on a pre-analysis plan that you filed earlier in good faith. Now you have more experience. Act on it.
- Also, don't feel guilty about little white lies you felt you needed to tell to get paperwork stamps. If you have made it this far, your advisor won't disown you for being honest. Own the mistakes.
- You may think you need the dissertation equivalent of open-heart surgery, but before doing anything rash, consider that you may really

TABLE 4.1 Repairing Your Ship at Sea, or Jumping Ship?

	"I can't get the data I need to answer my question!"	"I'm surprised by what my data are telling me!"	"I'm testing the wrong hypothesis!"	"My research question is the wrong question to be asking!"
What seems to be the problem?				
Why is this happening?	You've asked an unanswerable question—check for falsifiability of all key hypotheses *before* you leave for the field. You've run into problems with access to people or documents; there are records of what you're looking for.	Your original guesses and hunches are wrong. Your respondents or other sources are not giving you the full story.	The theoretical literature was out of date, not attuned to the realities on the ground in your corner of the world, or otherwise inapplicable.	(1) You're bored of your topic, and something else looks more appealing. (2) Too much time has elapsed between conceiving the project and getting into the field, and your issue no longer seems important. (3) Your time in the field has convinced you that life on the ground does not reflect the theoretical issues your question relates to.
Possible fixes	Try multiple sources and methods. Triangulate different kinds of information. Come back later if you can. Do without that piece of information.	Find a way to make this into a "good" surprise; something that illuminates a larger theoretical debate. Is this a case of someone else's hypotheses holding up under unexpected circumstances? Of the common wisdom not prevailing? Of an unexpected application of a different literature from the one you relied on in constructing your project?	Come up with new hypotheses and ways to test them.	If (1): go back to your research design and remind yourself why you picked this project: what is its import for political science theory, what attracted you to it personally? If (2): Link up to a different theoretical literature that seems even more relevant given what you've learned about your topic. If (3): take a historical view.

What seems to be the problem?	"I can't get the data I need to answer my question!"	"I'm surprised by what my data are telling me!"	"I'm testing the wrong hypothesis!"	"My research question is the wrong question to be asking!"
When to jump ship	If *multiple, central hypotheses* are untestable given the limits of the data you can get your hands on, you may need to consider changing your emphasis or your topic.	If what you've learned tells you that you were so mistaken in your framing of your research question that there's simply nothing to be gained from pursuing it further, consider retooling.	This shouldn't be a deal-breaker unless you have discovered the problem at the last possible moment and there is no way for you to go back to the field or get more information remotely.	Better to shift the emphasis than to abandon your project altogether. Major changes only you and your network of feedback-givers agree.

Source: Julia Lynch, "Tracking Progress while in the Field," *Qualitative Methods* 2, no. 1 (2004): 10–15.

only need the dissertation equivalent of a different exercise routine or a haircut. Julia Lynch, in *Tracking Progress While in the Field*,[33] tackled this head-on, so (with permission) I am reprinting, word for word, her "jumping ship" conversation diagram (table 4.1).

5

HOW TO THINK LIKE A MANAGER

The previous chapter spoke to the role of the solo fieldworker as a craftsperson. This is a natural perspective. We labor alone when we write. The burden of collecting one's own data is a disciplinary rite of passage. Dissertations produced after years of unstructured time in graduate school have traditionally been an opportunity to show what you can do. Quietly laboring alone is not the only way to demonstrate why one would be a valuable academic colleague, however, and perspectives change if we conceptualize a solo fieldworker's role as an aggregator of human capital—as management rather than as labor. This chapter addresses the concerns of readers who desire practical advice about how to get the most out of paid labor. While the previous chapter provided advice on trying to get the story oneself by acquiring credentials as a credible narrator, this chapter provides advice to someone considering a role as a team manager directing a group effort to collect data.

Some graduate students adapt quite quickly to what they see as a natural division of labor. The scholar takes responsibility for design, grant-writing, managing Institutional Review Board permissions, and doing the bulk of the write-up (including the literature review, constructing and interpreting figures, framing the findings, and handling submission logistics and referee reports), while others take responsibility for actually collecting and cleaning the data. For some, treating fieldwork as an individuated heroic journey is a delay tactic (maybe self-aware, maybe not) to stave off the real work, which is a professional transition to the management class. The skills they learn on the job will serve them as academic advisors and field leaders. They learn to oversee a pipeline and organize the outputs from overlapping and often redundant workflows across many assistants (survey firms, NGO employees, graduate student research assistants, and the like). The most valued skill sets are those of the general contractor (not the artisan finished carpenter), the seasoned campaign manager (not the zealous volunteer), the field commander (not the advance scout), the hospital manager (not the therapist). It can be an unapologetically corporate view of knowledge production. I do not fully endorse this perspective. I do understand it.

HOW TO GIVE YOURSELF LICENSE TO THINK LIKE A MANAGER

Epistemological tension between quantitative and qualitative research traditions (especially ethnography, participant observation, focus groups, and the use of long-form semistructured interviews, all of which are discussed in previous chapters) often makes graduate students feel that they have to take sides, in which "qualitative" researchers claim one kind of high ground (relying on inductive logic that privileges the researcher's ability to synthesize multiple streams of information) and "quantitative" researchers claim another (relying on careful measurement and conservative claims about what a large number of respondents say they believe). In the end, however, the reality of the field, the demands of the market, and the ethos of improvisational pluralism all push toward multimethod investigation. Some of the tension between the two traditions has been backgrounded in this book already. The virtues of "sticking to the shopping list" (chapter 2) do not fully fit the "let your subjects' stories change you" advice (chapter 4). Still, there seem to be more and more graduate students arriving on site prepared to take charge, spend money, and issue orders to subordinates than there were two decades ago.

One reason is globalization and growing awareness of wage differentials. Graduate students in some settings can employ research assistants for pennies on the dollar, sometimes without having secured dedicated funding in a grant. Skilled labor comes so cheap in some places that it can be paid for from repurposing a modest living stipend, which suggests far more complementarity between qualitative and quantitative research designs than oppositional caricatures suggest. Even as you earnestly attempt the methods advocated in the last chapter, you will naturally make friends. There are many other trained social scientists—some graduate students like you, others working in NGOs, at embassies, and in the government—and many more students and enthusiastic amateurs. In time, water seeks its own level. Unique data collection opportunities come from leveraging social capital in the field, bartering one's skills (as a grant-writer, data analyst, etc.) in exchange for access and data.

The second reason is that development and civil society NGOs are more common and confident in the twenty-first century than in previous eras. This means that, even for Missionary idealists hoping to conduct research that changes the world, the realization often strikes unexpectedly that one can do more for people in urgent need with one's comparative advantage in grant-writing and management. Not everyone has what it takes to hold eye contact with sociopaths or convert ethnographic field notes into prose worth reading, just as not everyone is equally talented at the "people skills" necessary to excel at many of the tasks described in the previous chapter. Not everyone is a talented writer fluent in English, either. Whatever their other skills, most graduate students arrive on site well-positioned to assist an NGO in capacity-building by submitting grants to donors or helping with data management. Again, local volunteer labor is often in excess supply.

A third reason is that technology is reducing the costs of remote management and increases opportunities for remote data collection. It is possible to leverage telephone connectivity and the proliferation of cheap cell phones to solicit samples of displaced Somalis squatting in Mogadishu. This would have been science fiction not very long ago. Lowering the costs of travel has a similar effect. In principle, it has long been possible to parachute into a country for a few days, fight jet lag, and do a little bit of work, but now one can Skype in remotely a few times a week in order to oversee aspects of a survey or engage in analysis of an experiment. Dropbox never sleeps. The edge of the map is simply not as distant as it once was.

A more speculative reason is that our discipline may be changing. There are more good departments granting PhDs today than there were in the past. Some departments have been aggressively pushing a transition from a "book guild" to a "paper guild" in their training sequences. More apprentices seem to be competing for journeyman ladder jobs. The incentive structure seems to be pushing toward "going on the market" with multiple publications in hand. With more to read than ever, it is tempting to measure productivity with citation indices rather than take the time to read. There is a lot of market pressure on young guild members. I do not think it was necessarily easier in previous generations, but I am certain it was different.

Put all of these trends together, and it is common for scholars to approach the task of fieldwork with a careerist eye, aiming to create a flow of modular small papers, each of which contains a tightly identified single-measurement contribution. This approach rewards investments in pre-fieldwork planning and design. It assumes that scholars will not actually be involved (hands-on) in collecting all the data that is destined to appear in their pipelines of publications. Strategic graduate students often come to desire two things: (1) in the short term, a research design that allows them predictability in the form of a manageable shopping list of variables so that hypotheses can be tested, and (2) in the medium term, a local network or laboratory, manageable at a distance, to keep a flow of data coming for many independent contributions to maximize the probability of tenure and upward job mobility.

HOW TO CHOOSE A FIXER AND RECRUIT RESEARCH ASSISTANTS

What parts of the data collection one can delegate to untrained laborers, what parts can be done remotely, what parts require hands-on attention by someone trusted and with specialized training (but not necessarily you), and what parts require investigation that you want to do yourself? Graduate students often make these design decisions implicitly through coursework choices. If you find yourself taking classes on sampling and analysis, it may be because you intuit that you want to run surveys.

If you are disoriented, perhaps start at the library. Read through the methods appendices of the books that you imagine you might someday want to emulate. Books and papers that appear in journals are presented as polished laboratory write-ups and rarely go into vital detail on the nitty-gritty of data collection. If a book or paper emerged from a dissertation, there is often a detailed methods appendix explaining exactly what was done, and what the hurdles were, preserved in the hope that someone just like you will benefit from it. At the planning stage, you might consider reaching out directly by email or telephone to the authors of studies whose designs you admire, but only once you have taken the time to thoroughly familiarize yourself with published materials (including methods papers and appendices). Careful readings of many first books provide a relatively clear picture of how field discoveries forced adaptations to initial plans. You can read between the lines of their acknowledgments section for useful hints, too.

Most researchers solicit research assistance of one form or another for a book-length project. No practical alternative exists if research takes place across a language barrier. Even if translation is not an issue and one does not need a local guide, there is often a need for a fixer, a driver, a personal assistant, and, once one begins to acquire momentum, a subordinate for many workflow-related tasks that will free up time for the researcher to do other things. Advance planning, including writing grants that include budget items for paying local research assistants and translators, obviously helps. A do-it-yourself approach is more tempting to graduate students short on funds. It is a hassle to try to coax high-quality labor outputs out of local agents who are poorly compensated. Sometimes, however, even on a shoestring budget, you just need more temporary hands. You can only be in one place at one time. Locals are fluent in the language.

Whatever the anticipated duration of employment, hiring a "fixer," or someone to assist with a variety of research tasks, is a very big step. You have only a few carrots and fewer sticks to induce high-quality participation in your project, yet the quality of the research itself comes to depend vitally on the integrity of a subordinate. If your fixer or research assistant (RA) fabricates data, you have participated because of your misplaced trust. Because your reputation will be tied to the performance and professionalism of the people conducting research in your name, training and supervision are required. Screening to find the right person can be time-consuming, but there is often no good alternative to providing a full explanation of the project's objectives, the methods you plan to use, and other details.

Set aside a full day for interviews and training. Think carefully about how to frame the research project for the study community. The moment that one begins to pitch the project with the hope of eventually delegating research tasks is often the one at which the researcher irrevocably "loses control of the story" of her research. Curious third parties no longer have to speculate about your goals—they can just ask the person you interviewed but did not hire for an RA position who you really are and what you actually want. With this in mind, carefully consider if you want to reveal measurement tricks that involve deception if you are unsure about long-term fit. Take time to answer whatever questions your applicants might have. Listen. Use the opportunity to solicit advice on design modifications.

There is a huge upside if you can foster a collaborative relationship from the beginning, giving associates a sense of ownership over the research product. In situations where your research collaborators view themselves as partners, not subordinate employees, everything can go more smoothly. Conversely, the risks involved with mishandling this relationship are potentially quite serious, since many people's interaction with your research will be with these interlocutors. On one hand, if they are unhappy with you, the information will not remain private. If you establish rapport and trust, on the other hand, you could potentially stay in touch for years afterward, providing you with a trustworthy set of eyes, ears, and hands on site long after you return home.

Make sure that you establish expectations early about "quotidian bribery" (colloquially called *baksheesh* in many countries). Be aware that regular "costs of doing business" are imposed on people who are seen as doing favors for a rich foreigner. In some places, a certain amount of money must be spread around in order to get anything done, and it is naïve to pretend otherwise. It is important to set time aside for a frank conversation establishing your expectations up front with the fixer who will be negotiating on your behalf. How will accounting take place? Where will money for the side payments that are needed in order to make the research possible come from? The fixer will almost certainly *not* expect to pay them out of the share of the salary you are paying him. This book does not advocate that you "buy datasets" directly, and it is almost never a good idea for a researcher to attempt to use financial inducements to bypass state security checkpoints (see FAQ #6), but delegating to a trusted associate to find the optimal price to smooth transactions can be a cost of doing business.

Vetted research assistants are sometimes recommendations from other researchers who are familiar with your site. If you have never hired an RA before, screen candidates using the same characteristics essential in any professional setting: signals showing the ability to follow instructions and improvise when solving problems, attention to detail, computer literacy, legible handwriting, a professional personal demeanor, a strong work ethic, and basic personality fit. For many kinds of sensitive work, an ability to keep intimate interview materials confidential is vital. Especially if you are planning to work closely with an assistant in a research design that involves deception, periods of extended discomfort (such as overland travel on bad roads or across checkpoints), or real-time translation on sensitive topics, it is a good idea to "try each other out" on a paid basis for a few days, then a week. Commit to a longer professional relationship only if it is mutually agreeable once both sides have had the opportunity to assess each other's style.

Depending on the topic of your research and your design needs, you may have a preference for a male or female assistant with particular identity characteristics (ethnicity, religion, language skills, etc.). Certain class and identity markers may be socially relevant but invisible to you as an outsider, so be aware that there are limits to your ability to predict which assistants will be best able to assist in tasks related to interviews and translation. It is generically preferable to employ older, married research assistants rather than undergraduates. Older people tend to be more mature, more disciplined, and more likely to treat the relationship as a professional job. These individuals may be difficult to locate or lure away from their current employment opportunities, and are more expensive due to their likely family obligations.

If you have no alternative plan but need to get started, leverage contacts at a local university to introduce yourself to a large group of students. Describe your research, allow them to ask you questions, and ask if anyone is interested in working with you. You will likely get some volunteers. Establish a deadline and have them submit writing samples and résumés. Select a promising few. Isolate some simple tasks with short-term deliverables and allow the students to compete with one another. Everyone ought to be compensated for their initial labor regardless of quality, but gradually winnowing down the labor pool eventually leaves you with a smaller set of more trusted subordinates whose work product you have screened. This process will also yield contact information for a pool of back-up individuals who can be used for short-term spot research (as enumerators, short-term labor for an archival expedition, to translate or check translations into a tertiary language, etc.).

Keep professional and personal boundaries clear. Just as in any manager–labor relations, symbolic acts of appreciation and joint commitment to the project (in this case, knowledge advancement) are always appreciated. Your assistants will likely take pride in their country and be honored to be part of teaching the world about their home, and often they will see you as a celebrity because of your credentials and your exoticism. You should also go out of your way to buy cold drinks on hot days, to always pay for group dinners, and the like. Above all, invest time in writing personal formal letters of recommendation, written on your university letterhead, that your assistants can use for social mobility. Except in special circumstances (e.g., writing on sensitive security-related topics) you can never go wrong providing research acknowledgment in the first footnote of scholarly books or articles and then sending them copies of the final published products as a memento of the experience. This can also be a highly useful tool for them to land future research assistantships. Pay it forward.

Before paying local researchers, make sure you have done due diligence on whether there is any possibility that employing them might run afoul of foreign agent laws. The specific statutes I have in mind are designed to curtail the activities of Western-funded NGOs but can be repurposed to target academic research, essentially charging local RAs with espionage. These laws are increasingly common in some parts of the world.[1]

HOW TO TRAIN A PERSONAL TRANSLATOR

In many cases, your resource constraints will necessitate working with a multilingual student rather than a professional translator. Especially if this student is socially distant from your interview subjects, it is up to you to enforce procedures that will minimize the probability of your subjects feeling belittled by the presence of this translator. If they come to feel their voices are being lost, they will not share their experiences.[2] During preliminary screening, practice an interview situation with the interpreter and a local colleague as an imagined interviewee. This is an opportunity for both of you to practice using the questionnaire. The ideal setup is when the interpreter who facilitates the interview is completely removed otherwise.

- Discipline yourself to speak in very small sequences. Speaking in manageable clusters of short sentences takes practice. This is the best way to make sure that your prospective interpreter understands your meaning exactly. It has the additional benefit of signaling to your subject that it is socially appropriate to respond in short sentences that your translator can convey perfectly to you, as well. Stopping after each sentence is not necessary, but if more than four sentences go by without a pause for the interpreter to translate, information is likely being lost.

- Give the interpreter time to interpret in a way that conveys identical meaning, using the same wording and pronouns that you do. Specifically, pay attention to the use of pronouns. If you say, "I would like to ask you . . . ," the interpreter ought to repeat in his or her language, "I would like to ask you . . . ," not "He/she wants to ask you . . ." Explain to the interpreter that you also want them to use exactly the same words and pronouns as the interviewee when translating. The interpreter ought not to say, "He [the subject] is saying that he has always lived in his village . . . ," but instead translate exactly: "I have always lived in my village . . ." If exactly the same pronouns and words are being used on both sides of the translation filter, intimacy can be maintained even through a third party.

- As the interviewer, take special care to keep eye contact with the interviewee as the interpreter speaks. This is especially important if the interview becomes emotionally or intellectually charged. The translations will naturally slow things down, allowing you to use your eyes, your breath cues, and your body language to reassure the interviewee. You, not the translator, should be the focal point.

HOW TO MONITOR REMOTE PERSONNEL

A vast literature in management science considers managing horizontal and vertical relationships and the use of incentives to get the most out of workers. If monitoring the quantity or quality of inputs presents insoluble problems, their levels of compensation should be tied to outputs.[3] The physical context of the work matters a lot. If you are running a virtual call center on Skype, calling respondents on cellular phones, the simplest thing to do is put all of the callers in one room where they can be directly monitored. Paying people by the work hour is then straightforward. If work takes place remotely, such as hand-coding Tweets in a foreign language, how hard someone works cannot be verified. Output-based pay ("*$5 per twenty accounts coded, once we check your work*") should dominate.

Various information management technologies, such as Dropbox or any one of a dozen phone apps, make it possible to collect information on aspects of worker performance that would not have been feasible a few years ago. Technology is not a panacea, however. Setting clear expectations about check-ins and workflow benchmarks is now a standard part of the interview and hiring process in many industries. Often some dimensions of the output will be difficult for you to measure and evaluate yourself. As a practical necessity, then, you will build a hierarchical team in which workers submit materials to a project manager who evaluates the quality of the work and reports back to you. Investing heavily in finding a trustworthy manager and then paying a competitive salary ("input-based pay," distinct from particular outcomes) is likely to yield better overall performance. A manager's ability to monitor others' work can be hard to assess directly, but a project manager with better information than you about the quality of worker labor can form a critical link in the research chain. You can try to create arrangements to verify the project manager's work, but this can come to have the feel of second-guessing their authority. Many project-specific subjective judgment calls are necessary in evaluating the quality of academic project inputs. If you have a manager who doesn't understand what you are trying to do, train her patiently. If it still isn't working, politely dismiss her and get a new project manager. ("*This isn't personal. It is a business decision . . .*")

Structure hierarchies such that discipline and bad news come from you and good news from middle management. When it comes time to discipline or dismiss someone, be specific about the cause. Fine-grained performance data, such as referencing a sloppy effort on a particular day, communicates to the worker (and to other workers still on the project) that you carefully monitor the quality of their work. You may also communicate this through occasional performance reviews. People tend to work a bit harder when they know they will be held accountable for their performance, but this insight must balance the preservation of worker autonomy and the sense that you see them not as socially distant subordinates but rather partners in the research.

At some point, you will return home. If you have nurtured a close relationship with the project manager, try to surprise him or her with an unexpected exit bonus. Consider remaining in touch professionally. If you have additional grant money to spend, it may be possible for the manager to continue to work for you, becoming both a friend and a valuable long-term asset. Subcontracting short-term work is a weak substitute for spending time in the field yourself, but having someone you trust to answer time-sensitive questions in a pinch is better than nothing.

HOW TO THINK ABOUT FIELDING SURVEYS

The semistructured interview techniques described in the previous chapter facilitate data collection of a particular kind. As you delve into personal histories in a fluid setting, in which subjects' judgments of authenticity of your effort to "get the story right" determine the quality of the data you receive, you can sometimes learn things that change your perspective. Immersion allows cooperative theory-building with your subjects and celebrates the co-production of meaning.

Surveys function differently. They are best-suited for testing hypotheses developed in advance. Survey methods reward deliberate design choices and facilitate a transparent kind of quantitative analysis. Survey technologists, even amateurs, can rely on generally accepted properties of sampling and statistical theory to make careful generalizations about an entire population. While no substitute for coursework, Peter V. Mardsen and James D. Wright's *Handbook of Survey Research* (2nd edition)[4] presents a starter review of sampling, attrition, nonresponse, paying respondents for their time, and other topics you should care about.[5]

In exchange for a sufficiently large sample size to employ statistical methods, the survey format can provide only a thin layer of information on each unit of observation. An overloaded survey instrument will guarantee attrition by subjects and noisier data. You won't publish most of it anyway. Good short surveys, well-planned, can test five or six hypotheses to anyone's satisfaction. Even the kinds of low-budget small-sample surveys that are most likely to be conducted by a self-funded graduate student can impress editors. It is often clearly true that if it were not for the original survey questions, we simply would not know a particular social fact. Many research papers are published each year with samples of just a few hundred observations.

While exceptions exist, surveys are generally ill-suited for the study of questions related to identity, subjective understandings of historical events, side-switching in a civil war, or other matters that involve nuance that is not easy to code. Surveys are well-suited to studies of public opinion, family spending decisions, health outcomes (sickness, mortality), migration, living arrangements, "have you heard gunfire on your street in the last week?," and other matters of fact. Through gradual and thorough exploration of these data, you can convince yourself that there is either support for your theory or insufficient evidence for your theory, forcing a revision.

In most parts of the world there is a commercial demand for consumer surveys and political polling. A competitive marketplace of firms willing to conduct surveys exists in most major cities. These companies' reputations are their primary asset, so it is no secret which entities are trustworthy. It is possible to train enumerators and conduct a survey oneself and this may be necessary in rural areas, but for the most part one can identify a trusted survey firm by contacting embassies or local academic researchers. You can even price out a survey from your home institution using a combination of internet searches and polite telephone inquiries. The best time to do this is during the pre-prospectus research design phase. Most research universities employ multiple survey specialists (spread across political science, economics, sociology, and even psychology) whose expertise one can tap. Interdisciplinary collaboration is facilitated by some aspects of the behavioral revolution, and dipping one's toe into this literature may inspire a much deeper dive. Even for dabblers, try to anticipate exactly the data you will need for a publication. Neil Malhotra calls a paper-ready vision "the MPU" (minimum publishing unit). Then approach a few vendors. Get quotes. Including specific price quotes from these companies in grant solicitations and IRB paperwork adds an air of seriousness to your enterprise.

If you are planning a survey, you may benefit professionally from preparing code in advance, running models on simulated data, and preregistering your designs. However, this is controversial. In a now-famous 2013 blog post ("Monkey Business"), Macartan Humphreys laid out the case for a voluntary preregistration regime.[6] A few years later, in an article published in the *American Political Science Review*, he and his coauthors encourage scholars to declare four research design features voluntarily—their background (M)odel, (I)nquiry, (D)ata strategy, and (A)nswer strategy, or MIDA framework—and write up their results in a manner consistent with declarations.[7] If you believe in your design, why not tie your hands and declare your favored test and robustness checks before looking at the data? Why not promise to share datasets, non-results, and replication code in advance? Who would deny that our community would benefit from a centralized searchable database, organized by location, of all fieldwork being proposed or attempted?[8] The debate is fueled by the ongoing replicability crisis in the social sciences (and natural sciences) and a few high-profile cases of outright fraud.[9]

Clearly stated initial data collection and analysis goals could be consistent with improvisational pluralism. Serious thinking about which statistical tests ought to be run and what specific role those tests should play in the dissertation's argument is not something to do at the last minute. Public planning allows critical feedback to be solicited and is good scholarly practice. Sharing data and replication code, keeping one's data organized, and encouraging researchers to educate themselves about various data repositories (QUALIDATA, the Open Science Framework, or the Harvard Dataverse) are all basically unobjectionable goals. Preregistration could even make the submission and reporting of findings that are not statistically significant more common. If you are in the planning stages of a survey, the preregistration process can probably help you streamline the collection and analysis. Certainly studies planned years in advance, with trending measurement techniques brought to bear (and grants secured, and IRB paperwork stamped, and a preregistration plan on file, and . . .) will have the best chance of publication in top journals. Do not make the perfect the enemy of the perfectly good, however. A little bit of systematic data often goes quite a long way.

Vice versa, even a little bit of high-integrity qualitative work, if it is conducted with integrity, can vastly increase the appeal of quantitative work. The ethos of improvisational pluralism would insist that even if you locate your work primarily in one of the rows of table 1.1, you should strive to triangulate inferential methods and look for opportunities to widen your aperture.

Consider recent contributions by three leading lights in Central Asian scholarship, all of whom I consider exemplars of the qualitative research tradition. In Regine Spector's *Order at the Bazaar* ethnographic study of Kyrgyz bazaar culture, she also organized systematic newspaper coding of bazaar representations in print media. Though the theory-building and empirical reconstruction of protest dynamics in *Weapons of the Wealthy* clearly emerged from Scott Radnitz's interviews, he also fielded an original survey. Madeline Reeves is an anthropologist whose methodology in *Border Work* is militantly antipositivist, but she still found it valuable to provide systematic evidence to buttress claims relating to demography and migration by presenting descriptive statistics from two original surveys ($N=361$ and $N=225$, 120–32).[10]

HOW TO NEGOTIATE WITH SURVEY FIRMS

What if you have a research design that is fundamentally qualitative and observational in nature, but, by serendipity, an opportunity emerges to collaborate with a survey group? Sometimes a pitch to embed a question or two (*"that is going to occur anyway . . ."*) occurs over drinks in a hotel lobby, with people just asking (*"hypothetically!"*) what questions you would add to their survey. This can be framed as a favor to help out a young researcher who might someday be inclined to bring her business back or say nice things to powerful community friends, or as part of a labor exchange where you act as a free consultant with methods and sampling, question design, analysis, or preparation of materials for donors, in exchange for data and access. Often opportunities of this sort occur unpredictably and on a short timetable. If your social network opens a window, prepare to hustle for a few days to jump through it. The upside is tremendous.

Your first step is to immediately make contact with your home institution's IRB. This may require calling in a favor, but many research universities have separate, streamlined, and much faster IRB processes for anonymous surveys. You should not acquire a reputation for being the kind of person who goes rogue, but people in your home institution probably will not want to stop you if you make an earnest effort to keep them informed.

Next, to get the most out a few questions, select two trusted associates who are fluently bilingual in the language of your host country. Send one to another room while you hammer out the specifics of question wording (paying attention to the choice set for responses). Ask the other for a finished translation of the questions from English into the other language that you believe preserves the exact meaning you hope for. Then bring the other associate in. Have them translate the questions back into English. Confirm that the meaning was preserved. This is called "back-translation." If the survey is being conducted on a sample who speak more than one relevant language, obviously this step will need to be repeated more than once.

If you have time, also arrange for a focus group in the local language. Involve one of your trusted associates if you do not consider yourself fluent in the language of the field site. Letting an assortment of strangers talk through issues related to your research can itself be useful (see chapter 4), but the narrower purpose of this exercise is question design: to listen to how people discuss the topic. Take note of which words occur in the regular flow of speech. The result may be that you change how you ask certain questions—or it may suggest to you that there will not be much variation in the answers, that the question is actually a "screen" for some secondary characteristic. (Note also that this supposition could be rephrased as a hypothesis you could test by examining correlation patterns across survey answers at a later time, if you desire.)

Finally, sit down with the person in the highest position of authority in the survey group. Treat this as you would a formal informational interview. Dress professionally and begin by handing over your business card. Also hand the person a personal copy of the translated question you would want to add to the survey (English and local language variants). This sends a costly signal of how serious you are about the collaborative opportunity, and that you understand some basic survey practices. Discuss the structure of the survey in which the question would be admitted.

Begin with some softball questions, which may reflect genuine ignorance on your part. Make sure that you understand enough about the sampling procedures that are going to be used in the survey. Repeat everything back and make sure you understand it well enough that you could explain it extemporaneously. Inquire about the terminal client and what they really want out of the survey. Exactly what claims to population representativeness are being made? Are there subgroups that you would want to know more about, but whose opinions are not solicited in the sample (which is often nationally representative)? How costly would it be to oversample these potentially interesting populations? ("*Hypothetically?*") Make sure that you understand the recruitment procedures. Enumerators often record the characteristics of buildings approached, the genders of respondents selected, or the language that the speaker used prior to acceptance or refusal. It is always good to know nonresponse rates for sensitive questions, so make sure those will be recorded. Then, if the moment seems right, consider volunteering to analyze them for free. Say that overall attrition rates are good indicators of how engaged subjects are with the exercise, or if the instrument is just too long. (The best predictor of an upcoming nonresponse or refusal to answer is a prior one.) If enumerators geotag interview locations using smartphones or tablets and code characteristics of houses or respondents, it becomes possible to assess sample bias in a sophisticated manner. You should show off a little, and also try to act as though you are already a member of the team.

Ask about the length of the survey, the number of modules, and if the questions are always asked in the same order or randomized (possibly in blocks). Inquire about the questions that will be asked immediately prior to your own. This is what the subjects will be "primed" to be thinking about when your question hits. Some survey technologists draw inference from randomizing primes, but survey firms vary on their receptiveness to these costly techniques.

It is important that an understanding emerge organically on data sharing. You will desire variables from elsewhere in the survey to conduct multivariate analysis, so it is best to not delay this conversation indefinitely. This can be a sensitive point and may be an unusual ask. Approach it delicately. If someone does not understand why you would want other variables, steer the conversation to enumerator effects— whether some people systematically answered questions differently for male than for female enumerators, whether the language they speak at home has an effect on their responses, etc. This will convey your intent to get the full data. Emphasize that you will explore patterns for the firm. Publication can take years, which allows plenty of time for relationships to form. If you find that collaboration is made easier by a handshake arrangement to not publish without accreditation and consultation, then shake on it.

Later, once the relationship has solidified a bit, consider suggesting a few advanced survey techniques. Some of these—such as asking open-ended questions at the beginning of a survey and using discourse analysis on responses—are potentially costly to implement and analyze, but they might be a novelty from the perspective of your local partner. Working with an academic researcher like you is, after all, free public relations for them.

HOW TO THINK ABOUT FIELD EXPERIMENTS

University–NGO partnerships are surely here to stay. Returning to chapter 1, table 1.1 suggests that designing and managing a large-scale field experiment is the most expensive way to do research. If the salaries of all of the local-party implementers are included, the scale of up-front sunk costs for these kinds of activities dwarfs those for other kinds of research projects. From the perspective of an entrepreneurial academic with the right training, however, it might not be all that much *more* expensive than doing anything else: your time is your most valuable asset. One reason, in fact, that field experiments have gained popularity stems from a logic of pragmatism. They facilitate a positive-sum exchange relationship between academics (who desire original data) and nonacademic field practitioners (who want to be able to report to donor constituencies that they are doing their best to figure out whether, and how, their programs are working).

As field experiments implemented by local partners emerge as a standard part of the comparative politics toolkit, I strongly suspect that the filter the guild uses to determine whose careers should flourish and who must be made to fail publicly will have as much to do with ethics as technique. The fact that much of this section grapples with woolly questions of professional ethics is a hint that not everyone is in favor of the new incentive structure driving new kinds of fieldwork. There may be no way to put brakes on the train, but that does not mean that everyone is a happy passenger. The guild has traditionally socialized scholars into the view that data collected via "vertical" power relationships are vulgar compared to data collected via "horizontal" relationships, due to some combination of personal politics, jealousy over salary differentials between academics and the professional class, presuppositions about what our comparative advantage is (or ought to be) in an era where computer language skills and papers few want to read seem to be overvalued, and a craftsman's guild ethos. There is anxiety that an industrial organization approach to research is displacing some virtues of the traditional craft.

Moral discomfort with the experimental paradigm tends to be most acute if study designs involve deception or absence of consent.[11] There is also broader anxiety within the discipline about incentivizing research for the next generation. Was randomizing roundworm treatment in the Kalahari the nose of the camel under the tent, creating incentives for young scholars (myself among them) to push the limits? Why not randomize election monitor placement? Why not spread information to try to increase voter turnout? Does it feel different if we try to *decrease* it? Why does this feel normatively different when the sample is rural Pakistani women and when it is sixty-one million Facebook users? Why not use different information treatments? Why not deliberately (randomly) induce fear? Why not randomize district electoral characteristics?[12]

Concerns about ethics are often framed as conversations about high-status publications, which can easily bleed into interest group politics pitting perceived "haves" against "have nots." Data collection in the social sciences is always a social enterprise. It relies on a hybridization of people skills (the purported comparative advantage of social psychology) and getting the incentives right (the purported comparative advantage of economics). When one is considering large-scale field experiments, however, there is a blurring of pragmatics (*"is the juice worth the squeeze in terms of publishing and impact?"*) and ethics (*"does a treatment group do better or worse than a control group . . . and what does that mean?"*). It can be difficult to tease these issues apart.

Most experimental research interventions historically sold themselves as positive-sum enterprises: everyone wins, but a control group may win less. This makes the most sense for an experimental intervention too small to possibly do much harm. Large interventions are becoming more common, however, and are trickier. The typical mode of argumentation is to assert that what is being proposed is "just" a randomization of practices that happen all the time, or is the kind of thing that was going to happen anyway (*"but now we'll have a better idea of how it works . . ."*). What governs the frontier of innovation, therefore, is the entrepreneurialism of the scholar who makes the pitch for randomizing programming. Academics with powerful personalities use personal connections in organizations who strike bargains, and the subjects affected (*"who, recall, were going to be affected anyway . . ."*) are not consulted in advance, often not even *told* afterward, and have no obvious mechanism of redress (especially if they are not US citizens).

Professionally, it can be genuinely difficult to signal to non-experimentalists that you took the first step of the scientific method—observation—seriously before beginning to tinker with the lives of your subjects. If a graduate student arrives on site prepared to take charge, spend money, and issue orders to subordinates, the project description afterward can feel as if there was no authentic scientific inquiry, just a well-funded entrepreneur who scored seed money and went through the motions at a steady pace. I have heard it said after a job talk: *"I see empire-building, not empathy-building, so I don't see why I should trust the results."* This criticism, if it is on the nose, can really be damning for early-career scholars trying to get their hands on the ladder.

The questions below are calibrated toward defusing the criticism, but if you are like me you will find you need a personal code (chapter 1). You have a long memory. I have also found that for those of us on the frontier and trying to think systematically about the risk areas, the IRB framework is simply not well-enough designed to provide very much guidance in key areas. Potential harms may come to people who are not subjects, such as the experiment's implementers or people who are just at the wrong place at the wrong time. All advice that follows assumes an ability to justify your plan to your university's IRB, given that if you spend a lot of time in the field you will, with time, become *the* area expert on risks there. Before you commit to randomizing NGO programming or beginning to shoulder the (substantial) costs of organizing a field experiment, ask yourself four questions and give yourself a bit of time to reflect honestly on the answers:

1. Might your study legitimize authoritarian behaviors or perpetuate bad government?
2. Is your experiment mostly an excuse to engage in confrontational activism?
3. How will you publish if (a) there are no results or (b) the results are the opposite of what you and the donors/readers want the results to be?
4. Are you a Missionary considering "going native"? Are you a Tourist collecting exotic passport stamps? Why do you imagine you have the right to administer a treatment in the first place? Are you actually confident that your answers to all of these questions will not change in time?

PRISON STATES

It is certainly vulgar for a foreign tourist to assume a right to treat just because she got IRB permission from bureaucrats. In a badly governed country, however, it is not always clear who the local domestic moral authority is who can legitimize the enterprise.

In some cases, it is possible to argue that any findings that could serve to legitimize certain very bad states, or make these very bad states more efficient and effective at controlling their populations, is morally compromising. Are some places *so badly governed* that we should not study them at all? Every researcher is responsible for finding an individual threshold of comfort for answering this question, which is why this book continues to emphasize a personal code. The hard-won ethical intuitions that IRB professionals have developed about the experimental paradigm, however, are generally calibrated to the harms that can arise for subjects who reside on college campuses. There are many states with ruthless security services, with leaderships desperate for foreign aid and hungry to validate certain outcomes for donors. What "informed consent" means when the study is backed by a state of this kind is by no means clear.

There are even stickier ethical problems on the near horizon. It is becoming widely understood that many states function like prisons filled with cameras. We have ethical intuitions that study populations who cannot easily opt out of a study—especially prisoners—are somehow deserving of different protections than are regular subject pools. It is difficult for a researcher to extract herself from the background level of coercion in a prison by blithely invoking the language of informed consent, however, once the ghosts of the Zimbardo experimental subjects at Stanford have been summoned forth. The entire conversation about randomizing scarce public goods can be implicated by the prison analogy. Perhaps no individual social scientist has a uniquely negative impact on a study population, but—thinking as an ethicist—where is it appropriate to construct the rhetorical "analogous to a prison population" boundary? In certain authoritarian police states? On reservations that are home to native populations? In refugee camps? In nations under military occupation where citizens' cell phone and email communications are monitored? As social scientists, there are reasons to be wary of the top-down, "eyes of the sovereign" perspective. I study Soviet history, and I know that social scientists who think they are good people sometimes do bad things.

GAMES OF CHICKEN

The Roving Activist from the upper-right cell of table 3.1, if she were to hear the previous section related in a conference setting, might well use this moment to put on an indignant and earnest counterperformance: "If you can't morally work *with* a government, then doesn't it follow that the only moral thing to do with our privilege is to try to *confront* that government?"

It isn't that simple, though. Thomas Schelling compared bargaining in the shadow of violence to a game of chicken, where two cars speed toward each other to see which driver swerves first. Most of the time at least one player swerves. Sometimes both of them miscalculate the resolve of their opponent and a collision occurs. I think this is a useful analogy. I have a very strong suspicion that when the experiments *do* stop, they will stop all at once. I can easily envision scenarios in which the whole conversation changes rapidly. I can imagine a high-profile disaster where an election result is altered, where implementation agents are rounded up en masse and accused of espionage, or in which it becomes widely known that well-funded Russian or Chinese social scientists have been conducting experiments on US subject pools.

In the best-case scenario, the proliferation of randomized controlled trials (RCTs) in the NGO community and the growing confidence of the experimental ethos in our guild can allow young researchers to get a lot of early advice, interface early and often with advisors and home IRB institutions, learn the relevant local laws, acquire local allies, consult with relevant civil society actors about best practices, and precommit to data analysis plans. In the context of games of chicken, all of this early work must also be understood as a mechanism for locking in one's commitment. With a large organization mobilized, tenure clock pressures, and a donor waiting for results, the researcher could come to see herself as fully committed to a symbolic confrontation.

Let me put my cards on the table: The scenario I believe is likeliest to "go nuclear" and draw unwanted attention to our discipline is a cascade of unexpected events that ends in violence. If this happens, I fear it will be due to the entrepreneurial labor of an activist playing a game of chicken in an unpredictable semiauthoritarian environment: someone who can be described as idealistic, sympathetic, professionally vulnerable, desperate for personal and professional validation, trying to get out ahead of the curve, fighting the tenure clock, who has only selectively internalized the advice heaped upon her, but who *also* earnestly believes that she is working on behalf of a brutalized population that needs helping, thinks that her position is functionally unique, and has faith her labor can change the world. So far, when social scientists have worked in solidarity with political campaigns or local activists (on election monitoring and "get out the vote" campaigns to help opposition candidates) the state security entities have swerved. Our community should not expect this to continue indefinitely. I'll leave it at that.

PUBLISHING UNEXPECTED RESULTS

The only field experiment I have personally overseen was conducted in Georgia in 2008, in collaboration with another then–graduate student (Daniel Hidalgo, now tenured at MIT). It was an information-dissemination randomized controlled trial intended to lower the cost of election-day malfeasance reporting. The subjects behaved in ways completely consistent with our theoretical priors. Treated groups engaged in more election-day reporting of malfeasance and were more likely to make changes to the voter list. We had a good plan. We got permission. We implemented it. We had an optimistic narrative of citizen empowerment. Case closed, right?

Wrong. The experimental design allowed us to see an unexpected downstream effect of the intervention. For every person we contacted, two people stayed home on election day. Then we examined heterogeneous treatment effects. The most plausible causal narrative is that voters knew someone was observing their behavior. Maybe they felt intimidated, or maybe they felt disgusted. We still do not really know what happened. We *do* know that where our teams showed up, people who would otherwise have cast votes for the opposition tended to stay home. This led to guilt-induced paralysis (which no one wants while on the tenure clock). I tried to remain focused on the fact that if we had not conducted the work experimentally *we would never have even known about the troubling downstream finding.* The guilt finally passed completely when it sank in that doing a preelection voter attitude survey—just showing up to ask questions in randomly sampled Georgian villages—had a voter suppression effect analogous to distributing information. Some subjects, it seems, didn't vote if they were being studied. This was a more interesting finding, at least to me, than the self-congratulatory story we initially set out to tell.

Ethical navel-gazing for its own sake is not the point of this anecdote. The professional problem that my coauthor and I had as a result of our investigation is that we quite suddenly lost our ability to put on a gambler's smile and pitch an "activist" framing for the project. Our literature review was suddenly useless. The working paper floating around the internet needed to be pulled from our websites. And then we had a very difficult time getting our study into print. Noticing that our experimental interventions were interacting with authoritarian legacies opened a can of worms with referees. After a particularly stinging rejection, I recall wishing that we had just buried the suppression finding in an appendix no one would ever read and just written the self-congratulatory paper that we had initially planned, for which we knew there would be a readership. We could have published multiple short, easy papers instead of hunting big game.

Even with the benefit of hindsight, I am not sure what we ought to have done. Perhaps a mature preregistration regime would have helped streamline the submission and writing process. It would have provided tools to think about how to separate core results from secondary results, giving the community of referees better tools to decide whether "fishing" for heterogenous treatment effects that supported our story was a valid move, and much else.[13] We may have just gotten unlucky with referees, and certainly our paper could have been written better (we were young). On the other hand, I still think the interaction effect of our scientific measurement efforts on Georgian voting behavior is interesting, and was a politically relevant fact about Georgia to document at the time. An ethos of improvisational pluralism requires flexibility. I worry about the capture of such reasonable-sounding preregistration proposals by other "ideological purists."[14] I also worry about how easily I can easily recognize a younger version of myself in those purists.

"PARACHUTING IN?"

Imagine a spectrum.

At one end, non-American graduate students gravitate to comparative politics in order to write credibly about their home societies. They do not need to "go native"—they *are* native, and cannot jettison this status. These scholars enjoy substantial comparative advantages over their non-native counterparts in terms of fieldwork start-up costs. They speak the language fluently. They know the history. They have a feel for the possible. They can get things done quickly with their network of family, friends, and contacts. They don't feel they need much of the advice in this book.

At the other end of the spectrum are what might be called Roving Technologists: academics who would never be confused with having any real interest in going native. They may have no real knowledge of the language spoken by their experimental subjects or even be able to produce a credible map of the country. They do know what the paper needs to look like in order to please reviewers, however.

I am not trying to sound sanctimonious, but notice, friend, that the kinds of experiments one will consider worthwhile—worth writing grants and recruiting labor for—differ depending on where you are on this spectrum. As one gets closer to opposite ends of the spectrum *the same RCT* can be deemed urgently necessary or a stupid stunt; *the same experimental study* can be described as normal science or a gratuitous waste of valuable energy. Experimentally demonstrating uncomfortable social facts is an important facet of how political science works its magic and changes the world. The real high-level spells require authentic engagement. Otherwise it is like a cheap magic trick—a kind of performance art to get attention on stage from captive audiences. Are you *really* committed to sticking around to help explain results and pushing social change? Or are you pretending you care in order to get noticed?

If you really plan to go native and come back to this site for the next five, ten, or twenty years, it may make more sense to do small things to demonstrate small local ironies and self-censor certain opinions on larger matters so that you can go along to get along. On the other hand, it may *only* make sense to engage in large-scale confrontational activist politics in a society that you have embraced as your own, since that is where you are most likely to have a well-calibrated model of the risks of escalation. Performances of "going native" are an unattractive affect that may be inevitable in your mid-twenties. Be really honest with yourself. Locals, at least in my experience, become cautious and nationalistic on behalf of their co-nationals when they feel that they are being experimented on. The problem of "parachuting in" becomes especially difficult and vexing because the most dangerous frontier of scholar–NGO collaborations occurs in the shadow of states where the principal investigator does not really want to reside long-term, and is gradually testing her own threshold for dealing with agents of state security bureaucracies.

RECAP: COSTS, BENEFITS, AND PERSONAL ETHICS REDUX

Many young scholars get into this business hoping to write things that other people will want to read. This can lead to an obsession with high-impact venues. Having veered into woolly matters of ethics, I will end this chapter with a few personal anecdotes about my own research redlines.

About a decade ago I invested many hundreds of hours lobbying to randomize the placement of police cameras in the city of Newark, New Jersey. Before that, in December of 2007, I made a decision to travel in person overland to the unrecognized Caucasian state of Abkhazia, and to spend two weeks living with no security, attempting to secure political permissions from elites in the de facto government to conduct a representative household survey. Both projects would have involved substantial cooperation with "the state." Both would have involved populations that could not easily opt out of the study. Neither effort panned out, but I am positive that a younger version of myself would have been able to talk himself into doing the research and fairly sure I could have sold IRBs into agreeing that the research was aboveboard. I am also pretty sure I wouldn't be living in either Newark or Abkhazia as I write this today.

I noticed something important in pursuing these research projects. In the preliminary scouting stages of the research, no one—no one at Yale, at Stanford, at Harvard, at UCSD, no one, not once—suggested that randomizing the placement of police cameras in Newark was anything other than a *Nature* paper, or that the Abkhazia work would be anything but historic and a "slam dunk tenure file." These experiences influenced my decision to write this book with an emphasis on personal responsibility. Everyone improvises, project by project. It may be that no one, not even your dissertation chair or your advisors, will be better positioned than you to evaluate the risks of whatever experimental interventions you propose. It will fall on you.

It is tempting to speculate about how rules governing research ought to change. Because there is no overarching mechanism to hold cowboy scholars to conservative standards, however, for the foreseeable future scholars are going to be operating with a lot of autonomy. There may eventually be a reckoning. Until that day, methodical tinkering continues apace. I think there is little to be gained by exaggerating the possible harms, allowing oneself to become selectively indignant on behalf of distant subject pools, or invoking language such as "playing God." This is not *Star Trek*. Our human subjects are not alien species. There is no Prime Directive. As long as foreign aid flows from the core to the periphery—in the name of security or charity—donors will demand justifications in results-oriented language. At the policy school where I work, our students think they should randomize what interventions they can, when they can, as best they can. Our best students then take their quantitative skill sets to investment banks, multinational corporations, the World Bank, Facebook, advertising conglomerates, democracy promotion NGOs, the US military, and other well-resourced actors that do not have IRBs. More than one cell of table 3.1 values this methodology. Even if you stop, or subtly coerce a colleague to stop, or write mean-spirited referee reports, the experimentation will not. Not for a long while.

The most ethically troubling problems for researchers often involve risk assessment. Are you exposing your subjects or your research team to more risk than they would be in if not for your study? There are ways to collect data that are legible to our discipline *and* dangerous *and* potentially ethically troubling. This needs not have anything to do with experiments. Browse some of the exemplar studies listed in table 1.1 to see what I mean. In my case, I found my redlines in the city of Mogadishu. In the weeks after Al Shabaab stopped holding territory there, I oversaw a survey. No one was hurt when our UCSD team did its work, and we took great care to minimize risks and ensure that enumerators were not putting themselves at more risk than normal in Mogadishu.[15] There were some close calls, though, and the following year I made the decision to cancel a follow-up survey and not oversee a cell phone–enabled cash transfer program. That decision had less to do with any weighing of professional costs and benefits and more to do with my own personal code. The decision to stop the research continues to weigh on my conscience at times, if I am honest. There may well have been people who might have benefited from more research. I will never know. Somalia represents something of an edge case, of course, and is not representative of the kinds of sites most readers of this book are considering. Because some might be, however, the next chapter presents a general framework for risk assessment that can be applied to a wider range of uncomfortable and dangerous field sites.

FREQUENTLY ASKED QUESTION #5

I did not expect this, but I have developed a . . .

complicated . . . personal relationship with someone

I work with in the field. What do I do?

There are important issues related to power and personal responsibility to consider. There are salient issues related to the integrity of your research and your professional reputation. The most important thing to say at the outset, as a framing issue, is that you are not alone. My sense is that this situation is more common than we acknowledge, especially in the subcommunity of fieldworkers who spend many months in a single site. One of the reasons that the field is so isolating and lonely is that you come to feel that your work is your life, as if the things you write are your only value. It is empowering to be reminded that you are more than your work. (*"Advisors, academic peers . . . they don't love me. They just love what I do . . . and that isn't real love, is it?"*) This person makes you feel attractive and needed. Everyone deserves to feel loved. It is normal to seek it.

That said:

- It is better to formally disentangle work and extracurricular relationships, if you can, as soon as you can. Date non-colleagues, friends of colleagues only if you must. The blurring of lines is inevitable for anyone navigating emotionally intense experiences, but it may not be desirable in the short or long term. If you cannot disentangle these parts of your life, figure out why not. Maybe you are sabotaging your research because you haven't been enjoying it. Maybe the relationship is more important than the research. Consider the possibility that you might be creating drama needlessly, playing out a melodramatic script. Spend some time with your diary. Reflect honestly on why you have arrived here.

• You need to decide if this is the beginning of something or a disposable hook-up. If the latter (no judgment), use protection. Realize you are being both watched and judged. At some point you must ask: "Who back home do you want to share this news with?"

If you answer "no one," that's a revealing answer.

If the answer is "I'm not sure," then think of a sibling or parent or close friend. Think about why you would want to share it, what they would say. But before you jump on Skype, think about someone back home with whom you would *not* want to share this news. It is difficult to keep information compartmentalized.

If the answer is "I am sure I want to tell everybody!," sit on that for a while. Your instincts might change. Or they might not. If, after some time, you truly believe strongly that this is "the one"—not a "green card marriage" but the real deal, life-partner stuff—congratulations! Logistical questions follow. How *will* it work? Will you stay there? Will the person go home with you?

If you come to realize that you can actually see to the end of the battery of logistical questions and answers, and the final answer is "this isn't possible," recognize that you, with your relatively easy ability to come and go, may have all the power over the timing of the end of the relationship. You owe it to the other person to make sure that no one is operating under any illusions. That conversation can be very difficult but should not be unduly delayed.

This situation can be even more difficult if it is a homosexual relationship taking place in a country where homosexuality is forbidden by law or strongly prohibited by social mores. If your partner must remain closeted for reasons of safety, or to avoid irreversible social shunning, you will feel special responsibility.

• The question presupposes something ongoing. I would likely disapprove of it, if we are being honest. Consider the possibility that part of what is attractive about you is that you represent a vector of exit. You could radically alter someone else's life opportunities. Sexual desire under these circumstances is never straightforward. Watch out for the savior complex. Something transactional may be occurring. There may be egregious ethical issues, at least in the eyes of some purists in the discipline, if you are perceived to be involved romantically with informants.

• Keep in mind that this relationship may continue to have complications for your ongoing relationship with the field site. The possibility of reopening old wounds may make you less inclined to return there for a variety of reasons.

6

HOW TO WEIGH RISKS IN DIFFICULT SETTINGS

I f you can conduct research that you think is meaningful *without* putting yourself at risk, many people will tell you that you should. And yet this advice is insufficient for so many young people. It was for me. I recall distinctly a phase of my life when I was not looking for the path of ease. I felt a deep personal need to demonstrate, to various audiences, that I was capable of doing something hard. I am certain I am not the only one for whom that is true. There *are* advantages, epistemological and professional, to getting the story yourself. You *are* only young once and some stories *are* intrinsically more worthy of telling than others, both from the perspective of science and the positioning of a young scholar in a crowded marketplace of ideas.[1]

A "hero's journey to the field" is a common rite of passage, in part because ambitious young students continue to intuit that a whiff of danger can be an important market signal, yielding a more impactful first book or a better chance at a good job. Linguistic acumen, good advising, a clever research design, careful data collection, mastery of the current technical measurement fads, good ethnographic instincts, all of it—these virtues may be necessary, but not sufficient, for a candidate's excellence to stand out. For a variety of personal and professional reasons, many young scholars decide that, in order to write something important enough for people to want to read it, they should use their time in graduate school to expose themselves to extreme social conditions, to find out how the world really works, and to dramatize their commitment to the guild by exposing themselves to danger before settling down into the life of the mind. Badly governed corners of authoritarian states, militarized borders, ungovernable slums, peripheral parts of weak states, and contested sovereignty continue to exert a strong pull.

Site-specific risk assessment is among the researcher's most important tasks. Institutional review board paperwork tends to focus on risks to individuals involved in the project as subjects. However, sometimes it is the researcher who may be put at risk. Risk to yourself, to your co-travelers, to your host family, to research collaborators, or to staff is generally not what the IRB is there for. You should incorporate up-to-date knowledge from the field site at the research proposal stage, when you will be best positioned to solicit candid advice from mentors. Maintaining knowledge of the current political situation on site is the most important single aspect of your job, especially if you are acting as a team manager and taking responsibility for others' safety.

It is usually not difficult to tell if you are heading into a setting where the security situation is volatile. If you remember only one thing from this chapter, it should be this: Set your redlines for ending research in writing, in advance. Share them with at least one friend who cares about you and is not invested in your academic work or career. Be specific about the people you plan to talk to (and those you do not plan to talk to), where you will go (and where you will not go), and why. If you find yourself violating the commitments you made in this conversation as you improvise and adapt to the field, at least you will notice that you are doing so.

This chapter addresses two kinds of potential harm. The first relates to physical safety and security. Most of what it takes to stay safe is a good head for observation, a conservative attitude toward exposure to risk, and basic common sense. An important component of planning is to be systematic about developing a theory of how your research will be perceived. In zones of contested sovereignty, the material in chapter 3 is not just a matter of data bias: self-presentation can literally be a matter of life and death. The higher the risk that social scientists are perceived as partisans, the higher the inherent risk of engaging in the study.

The second set of challenges relates to mental health. Previous research emphasized the taxing effects of stress and exposure to trauma. This chapter adds *paranoia*, meant in the clinical rather than the pejorative sense of the term. The point, quite simply, is that academic researchers working on politically sensitive topics may come to wonder who is watching them work.

A FRAMEWORK FOR ANTICIPATING RISKS PRIOR TO FIELDWORK

The spaces most commonly associated with the greatest degree of fieldwork danger are the places where borders are contested or state sovereignty is compromised. This anchors the matrix shown below. A separate concern for field workers from the United States is targeted violence against them qua Americans, especially in ongoing war zones. Hatred and contempt for this nationality is probably the best predictor overall for risk of kidnapping or exposure to violence. You can easily gauge in advance from journalistic reports whether a war zone features groups that are opting to use indiscriminate tactics (such as IEDs or suicide bombings). It is generally safer to conduct research, even in a war zone, if the United States is not seen as a participant or the face of evil and imperial hypocrisy and the technology of warfighting does not favor indiscriminate terror.

In order to assess the risks associated with different field sites comparatively, consider a stylized 2 × 2 matrix for zones of contested sovereignty. Table 6.1 draws on a study of the concept of sovereignty by Stephen Krasner.[2] He emphasized that the word is useful because it bundles together different meanings. Sometimes people use it to mean an absence of foreign interference. Sometimes they use it to mean mutual recognition under international law. Sometimes the word is employed as a state's ability to monopolize law enforcement, impose order over its entire territory, and patrol its borders.

The vertical dimension operationalizes the state's monopoly on the provision of domestic order. Our strange world no longer contains truly "stateless" spaces, but fieldwork often occurs in areas where the state is absent and a nonstate actor engages in performances of governance (such as social-service provision or overt rebel efforts to contest control

TABLE 6.1 A Framework for Field Site Risk Assessment

	Negligible rebel antiair capability	Demonstrated rebel antiair capability
Uncontested terrestrial control	"Weak states" Examples: Haiti, rural Guatemala, rural Kyrgyzstan, inner-city Alexandria, Nairobi, Durban, Chicago, etc. *Can be dangerous at unpredictable intervals*	Conventional battlefronts: disputed maps Examples: Donbas in Ukraine in 2020, Kosovo, Israel–Palestine, Turkish Kurdistan, etc. *Least dangerous*
Militarily contested terrestrial control	Irregular conflict with strong consensus on the identity of "good guys" and "bad guys" Examples: Rural Nepal in 2000, Afghanistan in 2003, Mali or Mogadishu in 2020 *Pretty dangerous*	Irregular conflict with great power proxy-war undertones Examples: Syria in 2020, Afghanistan in the 1980s *Extremely dangerous*

of territory). If this is so, the site resides in the lower half of the 2 × 2. Many institutions manage violence and contest state authority, of course: gangs in inner cities, illicit corporate actors (e.g., cartels with diversified assets), and more. For the purpose of this exercise, reserve the lower dimension of this 2 × 2 for countries engaged in long-running civil wars in which a standard map might show shaded areas outside state control.

The horizontal dimension operationalizes the degree of third-party (great power) foreign military interference in the field site. But some countries have embassies everywhere, so how are we to compare the extent of great power foreign interference across cases? An easy coding rule is whether the air force of that state cannot operate military aircraft without a risk of planes being shot down. The Georgian state cannot fly helicopters over the territory of Abkhazia, for instance, nor can the Ukrainian state fly planes over the Donbas. The vertical dimension is terrestrial contestation; the horizontal dimension sorts conflicts where the state has unrestricted control of the airspace (left) from those where the state has ceded the skies above contested territory (right). Because anti-air assets are difficult to hide, they are typically the first thing destroyed when professional armies engage. The presence of rebel anti-air capabilities in a war zone is evidence that a rebel group has a great power patron. Rebels who can shoot down planes have demonstrated an ability to hold territory *and* acquired an external patron to supply the hardware. If a state cannot safely fly planes over part of its territory, but persists in armed struggle for hearts and minds, it resides in the lower-right cell. If it has de facto ceded territory where it cannot safely fly planes to insurgents—if rebels run an unrecognized state-within-a-state—it resides in the upper right.

A vast mosaic of variation exists in the upper-left sector. There are very unsafe parts of the world where state sovereignty is nonetheless unquestioned and there is no ongoing civil war. The level of danger in this upper-left cell varies widely, given that it contains most of the world's population. The baseline level of insecurity on rural Native American reservations or in parts of inner-city Chicago is harrowing. The deaths in places like Rwanda, Syria, Afghanistan, the South Sudan, and Chechnya capture our imaginations, but credible estimates suggest that for every battlefield death in a civil war there are nine homicides globally.[3] One can expose oneself to terrible risks, and observe a lot of extreme variation on social variables, by close investigation of life in the slums of Mumbai, Lagos, Port au Prince, Naples, Bombay, or Newark, or in rural Idaho, or the suburbs of Tbilisi, or the exurbs of Bishkek, or the favelas of Brazil, or parts of Boston, Los Angeles, or San Diego. How to attenuate the risks you will face is context- and project-specific.

In the upper-right cell one finds de facto states: places where nonstate actors have acquired the capacity to essentially secede from the internationally recognized state. In most cases they fail to achieve widespread international recognition. This results in diplomatically contested maps. The conflict is frozen. A de facto border allows militias to avoid clashing directly. When things go well, over decades the orderly equilibrium that maintains these states can sometimes evolve in the direction of Somaliland, Hezbollah-controlled Lebanon, Taiwan, South Ossetia, or Kosovo. The upper-right cell is the functional aftermath of a conventionalized civil war, not an ongoing irregular war. Fixed front-lines and stable zones of control are evidence that rebels have moved through Mao's three stages of rebellion and defeated the state's army (quite often, though not exclusively, with substantial foreign military assistance). In these areas, civilian hearts and minds are not being directly fought over. Civilians may be pawns or victims of aggrandized extortion. Critically, however, the researcher's day-to-day work, even if closely observed, is unlikely to appear threatening so long as it is well-planned. Observational research designs are feasible. In some cases, the risk of random violence and street crime in the upper-right cell is negligible.

The top row of table 6.1 does not contain active war zones. In general, therefore, it is less dangerous than the bottom row. Ongoing irregular wars are dangerous places for researchers. One of the main reasons civilians die in war zones is that they are suspected of feeding information to either the government or the insurgents.[4] This is true in contemporary Mogadishu (where Weberian state capacity is so weak that the de jure reach of the state is just a few dozen city blocks) and parts of contemporary Chechnya (where would-be insurgents are boxed in by an extremely high-capacity state). When a well-meaning social scientist arrives in a situation like this, it brings up the question: Why are you here, really? If you are gathering information, who are you gathering it for? To the extent that you are a neutral observer, you can be accused of naïve tragedy tourism. To the extent that you are something *other than* a neutral observer, you are either an aspirational partisan or, worse, thoughtlessly doing science that could be repurposed for seek-and-destroy missions without your knowledge or permission.

The lower left cell describes most of the world's complex humanitarian emergencies. Since the September 11 attacks, the permanent five members of the United Nations Security Council tend to agree on how to talk about many of the world's irregular war zones, at least at the level of describing the legitimate actor ("the state") and the illegitimate actor ("the terrorists" or "the bad guys") who cannot be allowed to hold on to anti-air weapons (because they could target commercial airplanes). Debates over appropriate policy recommendations vary, but agreement by agents of the great powers on the identity of the "bad guys" is a useful, and codable, analytic starting point. One will travel far to find a professional diplomat willing to voice sympathy for the position of the Al Shabaab rebels in Somalia or the Moro Islamic Liberation Front in the Philippines. The United Nations, the World Bank, and other social actors have been very active in attempting to settle wars in the lower-left-cell areas. Some researchers arrive and observe ongoing processes at close proximity, assuring themselves that it is a war in the process of being settled and that risks to their safety are manageable. Think about why you chose this setting for your research, and why others will likely assume you chose this setting for your research.

The lower-right cell encompasses proxy wars: higher-intensity civil wars, often with both irregular and conventional fighting technologies on display. Military helicopters are expensive. If rebels are capable of threatening to shoot them down, but the government contests the territory by continuing to fly them, foreign powers are likely subsidizing a war of attrition. An even more straightforward indicator that a great power proxy conflict is taking place is when different members of the P-5 of the United Nations Security Council employ different language to describe the legitimacy of the same conflict actors. The Vietnam War is an obvious example, but many of the civil wars that took place in the 1980s against the backdrop of Cold War competition could be cited, as could the contemporary war in Syria. These are essentially the most dangerous places on the globe. Field research there is not advised.

ANTICIPATION OF RISKS DURING THE RESEARCH DESIGN PHASE

The first thing to discuss with your advisors is whether the potential benefits of the research are worth the possible repercussions. This kind of work has costs that twenty-somethings are poorly prepared to weigh even if they consider them soberly. If you think the work is worth these risks, you are an adult, but you must proceed with deliberate care or you will be accused of recklessness that will invalidate you as a scholar and future mentor, and you will be gradually encouraged to seek work outside the guild. Consider that the costs of something going terribly wrong accrue not just to you, but also to your affiliates who cannot flee the jurisdiction with a one-way ticket out of the country. In zones of compromised sovereignty, research can also cause indirect harm. Our writing can enflame political polarization. Our research methods can retraumatize populations who have been exposed to violence. Our very presence can draw unwanted attention, even retaliation, from state security services against our subjects. In certain war zones and some authoritarian regimes, it is not hyperbole to suggest that locals with whom you come into contact are pre-positioned hostages. These are serious ethical concerns.[5]

Also realize that your word may not count for very much with your subjects. Locals will have assumptions about who you are and what you are actually doing. These assumptions vary systematically and predictably across the four quadrants of table 6.1. If you are going to a place where researchers need to wear flak jackets, be accompanied by armed guards, and travel in armored vehicles, it *is* difficult to distinguish your research from partisan participation. If one is considering research in either of the lower cells, how will you credibly commit to not being an agent of the United States government? What if people do not believe you? If you are working in a country where the population or government sees itself as at war with the United States, what implications might this have for the integrity of your data?

Another topic to discuss is that one of the hallmarks of zones of contested sovereignty is the weak enforcement of property rights. Often there are overlapping local property rights claims. There may be assumptions of different distributional consequences in different future versions of conflict settlement. Material self-interest is a powerful motivator, and people are more likely to speak to you if they have a theory that your science will reify a version of reality in which their assets are worth more. This has implications for sample bias and attrition. Even high-integrity surveys, or qualitative designs based on long-form interviews, likely overrepresent certain voices.[6]

Relatedly, you should also consider "the state behind the state" in zones of contested sovereignty. Over the last two decades, the ability of strong states to monitor what goes on in weak states has expanded with the march of technology and the fear of terrorism. Whether or not formally validated by the United Nations, an external presence often has the effect of anchoring political order in the fragmented aftermath of civil war. A foreign military presence is often palpable. This fact, in turn, interacts with local perceptions of research in complex ways. I talked to many Tajiks in 2006 and 2007 who feared speaking on a cellular phone.

One memorably quipped, "We know there are ghosts in the phones." To ask whether they were Russian ghosts, Uzbek ghosts, or American ghosts would miss the point. It was a rationalizable paranoia (see below).

Finally, reflect honestly on your terminal intended audience. A complex blend of motivations brings the researcher into contact with extremely vulnerable communities. The wrong way to go about this, incidentally, is to stare at table 3.1 from chapter 3 to try to figure out which cell is "the real you." Our real identities are much more complicated than our public performances. Biases leak into our writing unconsciously if we do not confront them explicitly and build them into our research designs. Your diary is an important tool to track your own personal reflections. Try to keep private reflections separate from your professional voice. If you opt into this sort of work, highly emotional representational debates will be a predictable part of the write-up. Your private politics and personal motives will be exposed to hostile scrutiny and adversarial speculation. Historians call these "memory wars." They are not entered into lightly. Young graduate students may not fully appreciate the difficulty of starting an academic career writing about contested or polemicized parts of history. A sense that you are desperate for attention magnifies mistrust of your data. Selection bias is impossible to ignore if a case is selected to attract a wide nonacademic audience. Some readers will never trust you. Others will pity you. They will say you are desperate for attention and trying too hard.

ANTICIPATION OF RISKS AND PHYSICAL SECURITY

Careful planning can minimize certain risks. Identify a researcher who has recently returned from your chosen area, or identify which individuals in an embassy or trusted local organization are responsible for security briefings. In the planning stage, well before departure to the site, reach out cordially by phone or email. Schedule a time for a lengthy telephone call to vet concerns. Discuss the prevalence of violent crime and robbery. Discuss step-by-step procedures for an emergency exit.

Before departure, identify at least one trusted emergency support person. Ideally this person will be in-country but outside the conflict zone, but under some circumstances a collaborator at your home institution provides a reasonable substitute. He or she must share your risk assessment, your redlines for stopping the research, and must be the kind of person you respect enough to give you advice that you may not want to hear. Establish routines for checking in with this person. Make sure that your family and embassy contact know that this person has your proxy. If you fall out of contact unexpectedly, this person will become a critical contact node for your institution and for your family and friends.

To repeat a piece of advice from chapter 2, purchase *Where There Is No Doctor*, *The Pocket Guide to Emergency First Aid*, or some similar guidebook meant as a complement to first-responder training for backpackers. Familiarizing yourself with emergency medicine can help you keep your head in a crisis.

Once in-country, it is important to take the basic precaution of registering yourself with the embassy. Schedule a personal face-to-face security briefing, as well. Use active listening techniques. Depending on the circumstances, it may make sense to ask about armed checkpoints, land mines, random gun violence, epidemic outbreaks, or natural disaster responses. These people will (attempt to) extract you from a situation if you get in over your head. They likely have the most pull with the security services of the host state. Consider also making contact with practitioners in the humanitarian relief community—especially the International Committee of the Red Cross. These professionals often have subtly different perspectives than your embassy's on the conflict. Meet with them in person if you can to discuss your research plans and troubleshoot logistics, feasibility, points of vulnerability, entrance strategies, and exit strategies. They may be able to make helpful introductions on your behalf.

A practical inconvenience in zones of contested sovereignty is lack of access to banks with ATMs. Western Union is not a bad option, and mobile money seems to be changing the landscape, but transmitting money in and out of conflict zones can run afoul of US Treasury regulations. This leaves researchers with the practical problem of how to safely carry large sums of money into the site in order to pay cash for services as they go. Manage the threat of coercion (robbery or extortion at checkpoints) by stashing a few hundred dollars away in clothing or different parts of different bags, while keeping a good-looking sum to hand over on demand without losing all of it. Get a trusted local driver/bodyguard to act as an intermediary.

If you suspect that you might not be able to gain access to a particular area regardless of your story, your research design may need to adapt. Getting a research visa may be harder than you anticipate. Getting permission to access the parts of the country most interesting to you may require additional steps. Even if you cross this hurdle, you will constantly risk being accused of espionage or of being a sympathizer. These risks also extend to your fixers, translators, drivers, host family, research associates, and interview subjects. The matter of negotiating basic access to a zone of contested sovereignty is often fraught, even with a trusted fixer. If you try to gain access to restricted areas, people will want to know who you are and why you are there. At the time of this writing, the Chinese government effectively keeps researchers from getting too close to Xinjiang, just as the Indian government keeps researchers from getting too close to Northeast India. Extended negotiations are often necessary, but are often still not sufficient. Some areas of the planet are simply not studied. It is too difficult for researchers to get in.

Making tactical alliances with organizations that have already secured government favor in order to do work may be a viable strategy for accessing certain parts of conflict zones. My overland trip from Tbilisi to Abkhazia in December 2007 would have been impossible without brokerage from the NGO Conciliation Resources and my longstanding reputation as an affiliate of the Caucasus Research Resource Centers. Once there, everyone knew within a few days who I was and broadly what I was there to do (*"planning a representative survey"*). It took approximately a week to schedule a meeting with the de facto state's foreign minister. If this kind of brokerage is necessary to ensure your physical security, affiliate with a prestigious organization that has a reputation for political neutrality if you can. Working with a parastatal NGO or subcontractor for the government, a political party, or a foreign state may skew access.

Travel to certain places carries a risk of kidnapping. Although men are not used to thinking of themselves as a vulnerable population, they are, statistically, at slightly greater risk than women in many parts of the world. If you are traveling alone and planning to stay in unfamiliar hotels, you are a soft target indeed. Many people you will never meet will observe your schedule and track your daily comings and goings. They might be tempted to sell that information to a broker. Kidnapping is distinct from concerns about physical safety (related to highway robbery or street crime). In my experience, kidnapping is neglected by researchers for the simple reason that it is too scary to contemplate.

The best way to protect yourself is to have many friends invested in keeping you safe. The worst way to protect yourself is to carry a weapon or imagine that you can fight your way out. Martial arts training may give you confidence in the opening seconds of a fight, but what next, friend? If you ever hear gunfire, drop flat on the ground. Don't try to hide behind or in a car: bullets fired from a high-caliber weapon can rip through most of the metal. Maybe try to get behind the wheel wells or the engine block.

ANTICIPATION OF RISKS AND MENTAL HEALTH

Graduate school is hard. It is not easy to sustain years of momentum through the psychological peaks and valleys that accompany academic labor. For those who magnified the anxiety by living far away and especially alone, the peaks are higher and the valleys are lower. The habits of mind that you must cultivate to thrive in these environments are taxing.

EXHAUSTION AND DEPRESSION

Elizabeth Wood famously identified "fieldwork blues" produced by social isolation, loneliness, disorientation, and the accumulated grind of enduring discomforts (bedbugs, stomach bugs, harassment, surveillance, etc.).[7] Ambient discomfort takes its toll. Fieldwork can be lonely even when it is comfortable. Fieldwork in zones of contested sovereignty is much more difficult. Countless war journalist memoirs confirm that boredom and monotony define much of life in war zones. Writing ethnographic field notes is hard when your subjects are clearly going through the motions in dull pain. All of this is further complicated by the knowledge that, once one gets home, there is a perceived need to engage in insincere performances and humblebrag.[8] Many people feel strong in-guild pressure to pretend they enjoy the field when they actually do not.[9] If you want to conduct high-integrity research on counterinsurgency and civil war violence, it is often the case that the people you most want to observe and interview do not reside in the capital.[10] The process of going to find that sample face to face is neither exciting nor self-justifying, however. It is actually banal to notice that life in contested sovereignty zones is difficult—every city is full of taxi drivers who can tell you that. People are sad and scared. They wish they could leave, but the exit options are as undocumented migrants or prostitutes. Your presence as an interloper raises jealous suspicions. (*What else do you want to know, friend?*)

The work is isolating. As we do it, and reflect on why we are doing it, we often do not feel as heroic as we imagined we would. Personal reflection on why one is shouldering extreme challenges demands introspection, which can yield uncomfortable answers. The subject matter is itself quite depressing. While we may have anticipated some of this in the abstract, the reality in the dull hours of the night can be crippling. Self-reinforcing cycles of loneliness, isolation, and withdrawal are difficult to break out of. The support network you would normally use to remind yourself of the good times is so very far away.

TRAUMA

In most research settings, the most serious threats to human security come from normal accidents compounded by lack of access to basic care. People die from late-night collisions between trucks and taxis on mountain roadways, or from avalanches, exposure, domestic violence that escalates, accidental gunfire, fires, blood poisoning, or water-borne illnesses.[11] In the event of tragedy, you will confront the fact that you have no ability to change the behaviors that reproduce violence and inequality, only to observe and document them. Faced with this, you may come to feel you are not doing enough. Sometimes we experience things in the field that we want to forget, but since we can't, we want to write . . . but then the words aren't the right ones. Negative emotional experiences in the field can change the fieldworker irrevocably. The deepest scars are invisible. At some level, you must have understood that you needed to see some ugly things in order to tell the nonfiction story that you wanted to tell. Now you've seen them. You may be paralyzed by how difficult it is going to be to write something worthy of what you've seen. Read the World Health Organization's *Psychological First Aid: Guide for Field Workers*. Seek professional care upon your return (and skim the section on secondary trauma in chapter 7 of this book).

PARANOIA

Many authoritarian states rule through some combination of violence and fear—and it is the latter that is pervasive. The sense that you might be being watched can change your behavior. In zones of contested sovereignty, things are quite a bit less ambiguous. You usually *are* being watched. Life goes on under multiple states' collection nets, and since some of us are technologically savvier than most, the kinds of tools our security state doppelgängers would use to sift through email communications systematically (down to the Python line coding specifics) are not arcane to us. Part of the process of acculturation is developing strategies to circumvent monitoring of online activity (e.g., expectations that someone is reading emails or tracking IP addresses), app banning, and more. State efforts to control online spaces can be clumsy or sophisticated. The purpose of this section is not to provide best practices for evasion, which would go out of date anyway. The larger point is that our data—beginning with pixelated photographs of us taken from airport cameras—are being archived on foreign servers. These data may never be analyzed, but they will remain after we depart. Paranoia in the field comes from the interaction of the dual realizations that we are being tagged and tracked and that we may be doing work that is even more important than we thought it was.

Paranoia of this sort has three additional pernicious characteristics. The first is that surveillance occurs in secret and is thus difficult to falsify. State actors lie systematically about whether they engage in it, so it is hard to prove to yourself that you aren't crazy or imagining things. Second, academics often infuse their research with totemic meaning. It is tempting, when what you are writing is very important to you, to imagine that it might also be important to someone nefarious. Third, and perhaps most importantly for your mental health, this paranoia can easily follow you home. Unlike exhaustion and trauma, paranoia has some practical remedies.

- Begin taking internet security seriously. You may not be able to convince yourself that you are not being followed. You can easily convince yourself that the camera on your computer isn't recording you by putting a piece of tape over it when you aren't on Skype. Consult the Electronic Frontier Foundation website for current best practices.
- Depending on the circumstances of your research, consider securing a safe or a safety deposit box in a major city. Original copies of sensitive materials can be stored in this manner—plus you can always inquire if anyone has come around asking about the box.
- Remember that border agents may confiscate any information in your possession as you cross border checkpoints. If data exist in only one place, it can be a source of stress.
- Consider whether you are serious about making good on promises to destroy identifiers in order to make anonymity promises credible. Using pencil and paper, ideally with a private code (that you will not lose track of yourself), is the best way to accomplish this.
- You may, by contrast, make digital copies of materials and back everything up on a timed cloud-link (such as Dropbox). This functionally ensures that data will always exist in more than two places. Trade-offs are complicated and specific circumstances matter. Researchers who imagine themselves to be curating public digital archives behave differently from those who imagine themselves curating single rooms of museum exhibits.
- In the worst-case scenario, in which a researcher is declared a person of interest, the downstream risks might include retaliation against human subjects after he or she departs. The IRB line varies by institution, but in general, priority is placed on methods of collection that can occur without "naming names." Credible promises

of confidentiality are important. Interview identifiers should be recorded and stored in a location separate from the interview notes. A dedicated agent might still be able to confiscate everything and piece identities together, but you can raise the costs of doing so. Take precautions consistent with evolving best practices.[12] Whole-disk encryption and PGP (NortonLifeLock's Pretty Good Privacy program) when emailing data through a virtual private network is fairly easy to set up if you have concerns about a malevolent actor snooping, but this kind of security is always an imperfect defense.

Finally, attempts to raise the costs of stealing your data higher than what a potential intruder might pay can backfire. Consider the scenario where you have aggressively encrypted some data that a state-level actor considers to be very desirable, and the password to decrypt it exists only inside your head.[13] What might they be willing to do in order to acquire that password? What are you willing to lose to keep them from getting it? Sit on these questions before you settle on a costly data security plan. Many professional researchers hand-write field notes. If data only exist

FIGURE 6.1 What you win when you win a data security arms race (Randall Munroe, *xkcd* #538, from http://xkcd.com)

in one place, on paper, a $1 cigarette lighter can be a very reasonable data security plan.

Then again: This all starts to sound a bit paranoid, doesn't it?

RECAP: HOW CLOSE IS TOO CLOSE?

Specifics of research design and self-presentation matter before and after fieldwork. If you pretend to have experienced things you did not, that is fraudulent. If you describe a well-executed research design that occurred in a country at war, the results can be impressive. Consider carefully whether it is necessary for you to position yourself physically in the war zone to collect the data you need to make inferences. If you seem to be trying too hard, as I hinted above, people will question what motivates you. How is one supposed to act in order to "get full credit" for going to a dangerous place? The frustrating answer is that it depends on who one is trying to impress. The job market puts complex market pressures and severe psychological pressures on graduate students who are trying to establish their professional reputations.

You are never going to make everybody happy. There are different pathways to satisfying professional success sketched in tables 1.1 and 3.1. Qualitative case studies for dissertations in the security subfield of international relations put a value on original data collection, but also demand a comparative dimension across multiple cases. This can reward a peripatetic approach easily caricatured as war tourism. Those seeking to make common cause with rigorous anthropology, by contrast, would prefer to heap professional recognition on demonstrations of deep, committed, long-term investigation of a field site with participant observation. These designs often leverage unusual strategies that allow access to rebels or illicit actors, who then share an unusual perspective. Development economists, in contrast to both of these communities, are willing to tolerate their graduate students' parachuting into a conflict zone to oversee a staff collecting data for them and leaving with only a superficial understanding of what the war is about or its effects, so long as the design is 100 percent bulletproof. There are more communities than these, but it is worth reflecting on the fact that these three do not always respect each other's work. They barely tolerate each other's presence, truth be told.

If a field site is dangerous, but you intuit that it is also the most interesting place in the world and you do not want to switch sites or topics, you are going to have to improvise. This book can help you with that. Dangerous work inevitably becomes personal. This is why, as I hinted at the end of the previous chapter, the biggest risks involve research designs that blur the lines between guerrilla journalism, social activism, and espionage. I think most people can agree, in the abstract, that nothing in academic life—nothing—ought to be worth the risk of being shot at a checkpoint, of having shrapnel from an IED lodged in one's leg, of being kidnapped, of seeing a gun put to the head of a friend or partner, or of the specter of being handcuffed to a desk in an interrogation room. On the other hand, weighed against this is the fact that these same risks are political realities faced by some of our human subjects. If we are going to reappropriate them in our writing, perhaps it is not inappropriate to suggest that we walk the walk as we learn to talk the talk.

FREQUENTLY ASKED QUESTION #6

What do I do if I am detained at a border or checkpoint?

Do not offer a bribe. If you have a driver who is paying one for you, that's a normal checkpoint interaction. If you fear the situation is more serious, remember: Bribery is a criminal offense.

Three things are true:

1.   The people in the uniforms have all the power. They bully you and allow you to feel your vulnerability—which has been there all along, but you've been allowed to ignore it. You are a guest. The theory that you are a spy is hard to falsify. Type the words "Matthew Hedges UAE" or "Xiyue Wang Iran" or "Kylie Moore-Gilbert Iran" into Google. You tell yourself it will not happen to you—but why not? Because you didn't break any laws? Don't be naïve, friend. Sure you did. You tried to bribe an officer. Two witnesses saw everything and have already signed affidavits. Or maybe they "found something" in your bag. Drugs, for example. Near the end of my time in Tajikistan, someone put an empty syringe in my luggage at the airport as I was leaving. I found it upon reentry into the United States. It was empty—but the message was clear: if I kept doing what I was doing, someone was going to plant evidence that I was a drug smuggler. I might have ended up with an INTERPOL record. I might well have simply disappeared.

2.   You represent paperwork. What you are waiting for, probably, is for someone to call a boss, who will then call his boss—a whole chain of bureaucratic CYA. Likely all of these people would rather be doing other

things, but aren't sure what to do with you. It costs nothing to make you wait.

3.   While the worst-case scenario for you is bad, it isn't great for the bureaucrats, either. The paperwork for espionage goes on and on. The security services of neighboring countries, and eventually the great powers, can become involved. Security assistance may be threatened. If it is, someone will look for a scapegoat. No one wants to have his name on paperwork for a high-profile incident that involves interacting with the part of the government that interacts with INTERPOL.

So you are playing a risky game. It could be modeled with payoffs analogous to a game of chicken between teenage drivers. If this is correct, it is a game defined by its high stakes and the fact that neither of you wants the worst outcome. Signals of resolve matter. You can wait and stay calm, reminding yourself that you cannot make your situation better by doing anything other than being submissive and polite, so smile, try to make small talk, and wait. Or you can up the ante. Calmly convey to the bureaucrats that you are above their pay grade. Ask for their full names. Ask calmly for a pencil and a piece of paper. Write the names down.

The scariest part is that you are being made aware that your choices may no longer matter. In a worst-case scenario, the correct analogy is not teenage chicken, but geopolitical chess. You may already be a sacrificed pawn.

You now see the risks inherent to conducting fieldwork in zones of contested sovereignty up close. This juncture rattles all of us. Most researchers opt to go home.

7

HOW TO COME HOME

Many fieldworkers are more confident in their ability to collect high-quality data than their ability to write an academic paper or book. Time in the field can delay the day of reckoning, so it is tempting to never quite leave. For some, the field provides comfort, a role that you can play, and a welcoming stage. It can be an addiction. The ease of transportation combined with global internet connectivity blurs the distinction between your time in the field and your time after the field. However, a book of advice about taking a journey would be incomplete without reiterating the real importance of having somewhere that feels like home.

Different mechanisms keep the field "present" for you even after you return to the ivory tower: ongoing research, social ties, and your personal psychology. Research is straightforward. Often dangling threads of project-based research have been left unfinished. You have plans for follow-up papers or entire chapters and sketches of research designs half filled out, an interview that got away but with a promise to catch up next time, etc. You have a stock of data from your trip, but desire a flow, perhaps acquired at low cost remotely via trusted research assistants, a reliable fixer, or various Facebook friends. Social ties are similarly straightforward. Real people made it possible for you to do your work. You became friends with them. You may have left the field promising that you would be back to see them as soon as you could.

Less straightforward is ongoing engagement with a field site through one's writing, which is fundamentally a matter of personal psychology. The responsibility inherent in one's chosen role can be acute for some scholars. Academic writing is a form of political engagement, though few appreciate the craft, and it is a subtle game (but an engrossing and enjoyable one) to compete to change other people's syllabi. Many researchers get grants, get IRB sign-off, vet their designs, go to the field, and collect original data, but still do not fully come to grips with the responsibility implied by their privilege until they return and begin writing.

Once you can resist the voice in your head offering the temptation to go back to the field for "just one more piece of data," you should take stock. Your home department probably feels less like the exclusive club it did in the excitement of your first year of grad school and more like a way station before a high-stakes game of musical chairs. Something that surprises many fieldworkers upon their return is how much more solidarity they have come to feel with people they met in the field than with the crop of graduate students squatting in department cubicles or the professorate at their home institution. The sociology of the ivory tower may feel more artificial, more exploitative, or just more "thin" than it did before. Reentry is bruising.

This chapter will help you take stock of your professional portfolio. The next stage of academic life involves a winner-take-all tournament. To compete, you need to turn your fieldwork into data, turn the data into inferences, turn those inferences into dissertation chapters that begin to have the feel of an important book manuscript, send individual chapters (as papers) to journals, get them provisionally accepted, use the momentum, convince your advisors to write you letters, use those letters to get your hands on the rungs of the ladder, then begin to climb. This short prescriptive chapter, therefore, provides closure in the form of guidance for professional reentry after fieldwork. It considers three distinct processes: physical return, emotional return, and professional return. It is dominated by concerns relating to emotional reentry. Writing a dissertation involves virtual reliving, reprocessing, commodifying, and ascribing meaning to an intense period of your life. Common sources of post-fieldwork emotional stress are secondary trauma, survivor guilt, and impostor syndrome. I conclude with an optimistic conjecture: that writing in the structures of the guild can be therapeutic.

PHYSICAL REENTRY

The world is a smaller place than it once was. One can Skype with advisors or colleagues for advice, get assistance with R or LaTeX code from a satellite internet connection even in rural areas of developing countries, fly home on short notice if there is a family emergency—all good things. The flip side of "home" being closer while you are in the field is that "the field" is closer once you get home. Stutter-stepping back and forth from the field site for months (or even years) is not uncommon.

If you find yourself doing extended fieldwork, keep careful track of the moment at which you decide to stop. It is often a hard-won moment. What happened to you on that day may be dramatic (the kind of thing that could make for a compelling story to tell later) or it may be a completely internal change, noticing something about yourself and your relationship with your work or the site. It is probably worth an entry in your diary.

You have proven to yourself that you can make it adrift, but mental health and bodily health both suffer on the road. When you are ready to return home, consider the following:

• Decide if you need to go back to your field site. If the answer is "yes," then decide if that return trip will be in the next six months. If the answer is "yes," then you are not actually engaging in reentry: you are keeping one foot here and one foot there.

• Coming and going is always more time-consuming than you think it will be. Certain aspects of start-up are always a chore. The logistical boxes that you checked in chapter 2 must be unchecked. Make a list. Many things you delayed because you were out of the country—the trip to the DMV, a checkup with your dentist—can easily add up to a week of "must dos" on top of obligations that have nothing to do with research (moving boxes from your car's trunk into your apartment once the subleaser has gone). If you dedicated a full day to organizing and cleaning your workspace before you left, it pays off now.

• There is almost always a serious personal matter left unfinished before going to the field, or else something that came up when you were too far away to do anything about it—a real-life event involving a parent or a sick loved one or a divorce or a birth. To recenter, exit your academic fieldwork bubble and partition work stress from life stress. Prioritize certain follow-up visits. There is only so much time.

• During this awkward "crash landing" period, you will naturally depend on the kindness of friends. They are happy to see you, but do not overstay your welcome. Get back on your feet and back in your own space as quickly as you can, then revisit.

• Do not delay the ritual of closure with donors. They usually expect a write-up and may invite you to come in person and share your research. A quick telephone call can confirm expectations, but put something in writing as soon as is convenient and put a face-to-face meeting on the calendar if appropriate. A handwritten follow-up note is always appreciated.

• Get your computer checked out by someone who knows what to look for (university IT support). This is particularly important if you have been in a part of the world where you have reason to suspect the government use of surveillance and malware.

• Prioritize getting back into a regular exercise routine to get your constitution back. The cumulative stress of travel, jet lag, long plane rides—it all takes a toll. The dislocations can provide a good impetus. Revisit the campus gym. Eat better. Drink more water.

EMOTIONAL REENTRY

The field probably *has* changed you in complex and subtle ways. There is work to be done, however. As you adapt to the consequences, let some knowledge of commonly identified side effects of emotionally intense fieldwork aid you.

SECONDARY TRAUMA

Some of your subjects live in your head like ghosts. Their voices can be hard to ignore. If your most critical interview subjects are tied to some of your most intense memories, the process of looking at your notes and trying to remember why you wrote what you did, or why you switched pen colors, can be like a séance. It evokes strong emotions—including horror—that you once suppressed. The sense of personal responsibility to record everything, to honor the experience of someone who was herself traumatized, is itself traumatic. The additional burden of trying to get the story right from the perspective of your subjects (or else dishonor the trust they put in you) can overload your emotional coping mechanisms, especially if the trip to the field was inspired by a strong desire to "get the story right." First-time fieldworkers who did not have any idea what to expect will feel it most.[1] Secondary trauma is often difficult to self-diagnose or process, and is often conflated with writer's block or the simple absence of motivation.

I find the séance analogy potent and apt, but with an important difference: There is no spiritual medium. Ghosts visit when you are alone. The decision of which voices to include in your writing is artisanal. You cannot delegate the choices. What parts of the data to include in a manuscript as paragraph-long quotes, which parts to code for tests and visualizations, and which to leave in their notebooks are permanent decisions. You can tell yourself that you can always go back and publish with what is in those notebooks, or that you'll make the information available to future researchers and that someday they will be found, but probably omitted voices are lost.

Begin by learning to keep your diary separate from your professional voice. The reality of academic writing is that you will throw away most of what you start to write. You will throw away most of what you found in the field. You will reduce from complexity and, as you do, you will silence some voices. Everyone who does research returns from serious fieldwork with many competing voices—enough material for multiple books. But only one book will exist in the real world.

SURVIVOR GUILT

Our discipline rewards clinical analytic approaches to the normatively disturbing aspects of our subject matter. Even the most distant ascetic observer or practiced cynic, after the discomforts of the field are safely in the rearview mirror, feels occasional pangs of guilt, helplessness, sadness, hopelessness, anxiety, and anger on behalf of research subjects.[2]

This emotional transference is well-studied. We *do* enjoy a privileged role as transient observers, with the freedom to come and go, confident and precredentialed by our graduate courses and empowered by our guild protections to serve as translators of ground truth to a distant academic community. Every cell of table 3.1 presupposes an archetype who will write something important at the end of the journey.

Sometimes we feel that privilege while in the field. We feel it equally acutely when we are safely at home, surrounded by our notes, with just a few photographs for company. Feelings of guilt can be especially paralyzing if the researcher is motivated by Missionary ideals, especially if he identifies strongly with one faction in an ongoing struggle, *especially* in the tragic event of an informant, collaborator, or colleague being imprisoned (or worse), *especially* if active listening was a part of the data collection. Transforming qualitative data into prose is essentially inseparable from reliving the memory of the interview itself.

But now, here you are, where life is easy, while your subjects are still there, where it is hard. That's the privilege that you have—and that your subjects knew you had in the field when they talked to you. You get to come and go. Most people don't.

Being deliberate and self-aware can help avoid unattractive affects in your writing (e.g., a "savior complex" voice, "selective vision" problems that systematically bias your findings, etc.). Respectful conversations with trusted advisors and the IRB can help establish the appropriate context for destroying notes or selectively omitting information from replication data. You should also talk to friends who know you well and have a sense of what you want the final product to look like. They are distant from your data and may be well-positioned to help you remember the dissertation that you set out to write.

At the level of personal psychology, however, many questions do not have generalizable answers. Is it your job to speak truth to power, or to "leave no footprints"? Is it to ensure the safety of your research associates—the fixers and drivers and friends who were observed with you and made your work possible, but who do not enjoy your social protections—or to write the kinds of things they would want to write if only they could? Is it your job to try to get as many people out as you can, to change broken societies from within, or to maximize the probability of access for future researchers? Sometimes values conflict.

Overidentification with one's human subjects and immersion in their suffering can lead to months of paralysis on the part of the writer. It is common to respond by withdrawing emotionally. Other common defense mechanisms include cynicism toward the whole academic super-structure, apathy, nihilistic humor, and chemical dependence. In my case, it took a long time before this was diagnosed for me by a profes-sional therapist for what it was: self-loathing, displaced to academic structures that had been embraced by a younger version of myself. The root cause of the self-loathing was survivor guilt, which led me to con-clude (incorrectly, I now believe) that I had more in common with my subjects than with my future colleagues. The larger point is that some of your behavioral responses to the trauma of the return from fieldwork are serious. Some of the damage you do to relationships during this period cannot be undone.

IMPOSTOR SYNDROME

Most of this chapter (and others before it) spoke directly to the experi-ences of someone going to a war zone or a dangerous space. A third kind of psychic harm awaits people who did work in the Czech Republic or Japan, who were not in any real danger doing fieldwork and enjoyed it.

You are about to go on the job market and trade on the experiences of your subjects, even though you are not those people. You repress it, but the possibility that you are not actually qualified to speak with their voices haunts the periphery of your consciousness and attacks you in quiet moments. Acute impostor syndrome while in the field simply comes with the territory. Much of the advice scattered throughout this book takes aim at this problem without naming it directly. The advice intends to instill confidence, and improvisational pluralism requires a fake-it-till-you-make-it attitude—but because it *does* involve faking, the risk of impostor syndrome looms. Some researchers *are* better prepared than others in terms of language training and genuine area expertise. (Some academics are even studying their home societies.) Some people *are* prepared to see more clearly, hear more accurately, and interpret more correctly. Overcoming impostor syndrome vis-à-vis key informants, senior scholars, academic area specialists, and old embassy hands is a part of professionalization that occurs over the course of extended fieldwork.

A different kind of impostor syndrome may confront you, the intrepid fieldworker, as you approach the return threshold, however: the question of whether you were cut out for the academic tournament to begin with. The prize—a tenure-track job—looms large in the background of reentry conversation. The "field blues" follow so many researchers home, in part, because the end of fieldwork coincides with the difficult transition of the end of graduate school, which brings its own kinds of blues, whether or not you go to the field at all. Your "home department" is not going to be "home" for much longer. Because fieldworkers had the self-confidence to leave the academy, they may have delayed certain psychological trials by *presupposing* that if they did their work with integrity they would receive a professional reward. The question "What if I was wrong for this all along?" is a difficult one to confront directly, but the physical return from the field coincides with the phase of the graduate student "life cycle" when the question can no longer be delayed. There are dozens of new first-, second-, and third-year faces filling the ranks of the army coming up from behind. With the market in front of you and the field behind you, no place feels like home. To return to the mundane incentives of the guild while the floor disappears beneath your feet can feel humiliating and humbling. At a minimum, it is disorienting.

The academic job market winnows down an extremely competitive field, overcrowded with dedicated and talented specimens, to just a few. University professors are like professional concert musicians or NBA players in that respect. In our guild, we acquire highly specific skills that we try to sell to local monopsonies with virtually no turnover. You must have known this before you left for the field. Your strategy for signaling seriousness and getting noticed involved the field. Some of your classmates chose a different strategy: buckling down at a desk, reading, writing, getting senior mentors to read multiple drafts, and rewriting. You have delayed that part of the job while collecting your data. But you are all competing now, head to head, for scarce ladder jobs. They've been disciplined and writing (they will say) while you have been having self-indulgent adventures (they will say). Let us posit that you have done what this book advocates and done it well: You identified a set of debates in a literature, chose a good case, formed a committee, took your lumps, adapted, found measures, ran tests, and, along the way, justified the journey with a faith that contributing to a canon by adding new data sourced from foreign streets was a good way to spend your valuable time. You could have done a lot of things, but what you did do was to send a costly market signal that you actually want into this guild, one that involved a high-stakes journey. Notice that the implied claim (*"Since there aren't jobs for everyone!"*) is that those who do *not* take a similar journey are missing something and, yes, may well be less worthy of a ladder (journeyman) job than you. But this is, predictably, not something those cohort-mates and social peers want to hear. From their perspective, you all started at the same time, but just as you were beginning to reap the benefits of the habits of mind associated with a chosen discipline, you packed your bags and departed for a journey with a DIY attitude and no real rules or supervision. They may point this out with "gotcha" questions or by asking why one of your unpublished papers is supposed to be worth more than two (*"or is it three?"*) of theirs that are already peer-reviewed.

This is all so cruel. It is intended to reinforce impostor syndrome, to make you wonder if you ever had what it takes to do the job, and to make you wonder if you *want* to do it.

In summary, upon return many young scholars are destined to struggle. The isolation of the writer is confounded by the pressure of self-knowledge as a privileged observer. Trauma in the field can lurk in your notes, PTSD can go undiagnosed, and old demons can reincarnate in unexpected forms. Making it all worse is that return from the field coincides with the period in graduate school in which market forces naturally dissolve old cohorts and place first-year friendships under strain. Six general pieces of advice:

• Secondary trauma and survivor guilt should not go undiagnosed or unaddressed. Cycles of shame and fear of being open lead many people to avoid therapy and delay self-correction. Make an appointment to see a professional therapist once per week. Prioritize the time in your schedule. Talk therapy works. Your university health insurance almost certainly covers it. Survivor guilt, secondary trauma, and PTSD are all real. Some of the symptoms are treatable. Professionals can teach you techniques that can help you hurt less, understand your own situation better, and write more confidently. Being self-aware helps at the margins, so keep a few mantras on hand, even after the therapy runs its natural course.

• Managing the logistics of physical reentry frees up space for both psychological realignment and the work you need to do. You are not your ideas. You are not your work. You are a person living in three-dimensional space. Don't mistreat yourself.

• Let your advisors help you with the things that they can help you with. Advisors have a professional role to play—an important one—in preparing you psychologically for the job market. If you want help over-coming impostor syndrome vis-à-vis your colleagues who did not go to the field, ask for that help. Graduate students often unconsciously turn advisors into something not unlike parents. Let them, then, provide the comfort that only they can provide. If you can summon the courage to ask, advisors are well-positioned to say things tailored to your circum-stance that you need to hear.

• While every cohort has a few bad apples, consider that negative and unproductive feedback often comes from a place of insecurity. Those who didn't go into the field often feel the mirror-image of your impostor syndrome. Even if they have a publication or two, they may have a sneak-ing suspicion that *you're* the one doing the job right and that *they* are the ones engaging in a cosplay of academic discovery. Perhaps they have a theory that *you* are the one belittling *them* behind *their* backs, calling them second-rate economists or third-rate computer programmers to devalue their contributions to the field. If you are lucky, and willing to grow, you may find a way to surprise yourself and even make new friends. Listen to them talk about their work. Engage in earnest, courteous, and professional transaction. See what happens.

• In my experience, real reentry can be delayed for months (even years) after stepping off the airplane. It is not easy to sort personal from professional matters in a job that involves so much writing, aggressive marketing of ideas, itinerant travel (predocs to postdocs to first jobs) and performance. A diary is useful as a reminder that there is a version of your written voice that should not be shared. I can recall the exact moment it became real to me that I would actually be happier if I could reclaim certain very bad experiences that I'd had *as data*, separate from the trauma of the experiences. It still took a long time to make real changes based on that insight.

• The only way to overcome impostor syndrome is to rejoin academic society.

PROFESSIONAL REENTRY

The purpose of your journey was to collect the material to write something great. You owe it to yourself to produce the academic paper or book that provided the impetus for the planning and the experience. The academic job market is a good opportunity to begin to see yourself more in solidarity with some parts of the academy than others, to consider yourself a professional with unique skills that can be priced by the market, and to begin to consider the natural readerships for your dissertation work.

It is natural to view professional reentry from the perspective of the academic job market. A tenure-track job in the US or European academy is obviously not the only thing you can do with a PhD in political science, but it is a common goal, and one that your department will expect you to be pushing toward with urgency.[3] You are better prepared to contribute than you would have been if you had not gone to the field. You have demonstrated a passion for a topic, for a field site, for the human connections you get from social science research. This moment, right now, may be the best time in your life. Write as if it were your calling and let the chips fall.

A good way to begin to treat the discipline as a profession is conferencing. If you can time your return from the field to coincide with your discipline's yearly annual meeting, do so. For political scientists it is the American Political Science Association's annual meeting, colloquially APSA. It is a hard conference to get into, but volunteer to act as a discussant if you feel comfortable, or plan ahead and organize a panel. Consider attending even if you are not presenting. Find a place to sit. Observe what you see through new eyes, honed by ethnography. You are looking at a scholarly society. You are seeing a lot of people who hang around each other for a few days a year, for years or decades at a time. They gradually get to know each other. Friends embrace or share quick handshakes. Even frenemies make eye contact, smile a bit, nod heads. There is excitement. There is energy. People are ready to share their ideas. Some of their work may be unpolished.

Be ready to look the part. If your fieldwork took place over many years, your body may have changed a bit. You may need to make a relatively costly investment in new professional workplace attire before going on the job market. A poorly fitting suit sends the wrong message.

Go to panels that sound interesting to you. Listen critically as people explain their work product. Certain market stars are going to have impressive figures, designed to reinforce everyone else's impostor syndrome—but don't fall for the glamor tricks. Yes, there are a lot of impressive people, but also a fair number of poseurs and dog-ate-my-homework presenters. What parts of these performances can you emulate with the data you already have? Where are the holes? How can you "sell" what you have more effectively? There is fierce competition along the full spectrum of jobs, but terms of competition are subtly different. Begin to see the academic market as a kind of a game, if you can. Begin to think about how you can market yourself.

Given that attendance may be a financial stretch if your departments will only offer travel grants to students who are presenting, remember that there are many other good first-time/post-fieldwork conferences, such as the International Studies Association or an area studies conference. My first conference post-fieldwork was ASN (the Association for the Study of Nationalities), and I continue to try to attend every year. Area studies conferences are where you are most likely to be able to remind yourself of the universe of other academics, some outside your discipline, who have a genuine interest in the politics of your field site for its own sake.

Begin to define a niche for yourself and a narrative about why the work that you chose to do makes you the most qualified person in the world for a particular set of jobs. Your fieldwork will give you a huge leg up over your professional competition if you frame it right, so do not be psyched out. Very few people go on the market with a polished paper based on original data like yours. The choices you made years ago to take yourself out of the ivory tower and into the field gave you a story that differentiates you from the herd. Consider the following program.

First, revisit your old methods syllabi with new eyes. Notice that, armed with your own data, you are now an empiricist—a real empiricist, with none of whatever impostor syndrome you might have felt in your second year of grad school. You had an intuition that in order to be the best version of yourself you wanted to have an original dataset. You have it. Now is a good time to seek advice from other empiricists who are not fieldworkers on how to reconcile challenges in design, methods of data analysis, and write-up. No one is really going to be able to challenge your interpretation of your data. They may not hire you, or put your interpretation into print in the journal you think it deserves to be in, but that isn't necessarily the point. The point is that you are, right now, not a junior academic or a fake academic. This is it. This is the job, right here. You can get a lot of help transforming *your* (!) data into something inspiring.

Second, recognize that you have some catching up to do. The field did go on without you. The only way to catch up is to get serious about reading to make up for lost time. Acquire a mature appreciation of the important advances that took place while you were self-absorbed in the field. Do so as fast as you can, but you cannot skip this step. You will have to work harder than some of your peers for the next few years. Do not pretend that you and your story are so special that you did not fall behind while writing it. Leaving, as you did, does come with disadvantages compared to the majority of research scientists who remain focused and reap the social and intellectual benefits of sticking around graduate school for five to seven uninterrupted years.

Third, after resettling, sit down with each member of your committee individually. Debrief them on your fieldwork experience and let them debrief you on what you have missed in the ivory tower. The goal is not self-critical reflection (which should be done periodically and separately) but rather clinical criticism of what you have and where it fits into the current trends. You took a reading break while in the field. They did not. Listen hard when they tell you what you need to catch up on. Propose emendations to the chapter structure now, and make sure to get buy-in from the whole committee. Discuss the first draft of your marketing plan for yourself.

Fourth, decide which part of your dissertation will be your job market paper—the centerpiece of your brand. Craft a dissertation writing plan with this chapter polished by next fall. You'll submit it and go on the market. If you strike out, you'll roll the dice again.

Or you will decide that you have had it with the academic rat race and you will go do something else. It is beyond the scope of this book to explain what that thing is going to be. The landscape of the natural sciences is filled with labs populated by graduate students and directed by postdocs, all weighing reservation options of going into pharmaceutical drug development or software engineering, keeping track of which PIs are spinning off companies based on patentable intellectual property. We are a humble guild by comparison, but you can repurpose your skills for other kinds of work. It is very important to remember that if you do not succeed on the academic job market your life does not end. You will soon have a doctorate and your area expertise (and life experiences) will set you apart from most other people. There are nine cells in table 3.1, some of which include quite attractive alternatives to the pure life of the mind. Or maybe you will put both the discipline *and* your field site in the rearview mirror. Maybe you have just gone through five or six formative years. Your real calling may be something else entirely. Life is long, friend.

Whatever you do, you owe it to yourself to finish the dissertation to your satisfaction. High-quality academic papers are very difficult to write. The process of dealing with rejection after rejection from journal editors and referees will be frustrating for the rest of your life—but the "start-up costs" for your first paper are huge, and writing a high-quality academic book, or a dissertation that is destined to become one, is even harder. It quickly becomes very personal (more personal than a modular paper). It has all the psychological difficulties of a first novel, but with additional self-imposed pressure to write something worthy of years of experiences or the baggage of your subjects' experiences. One of my best friends called it "being in the presence of something much bigger than yourself," which ably captures the unease I felt knowing that I might be writing nonfiction that would outlive me. I pass along twelve professional tips for writing, all paraphrased from various of my social science heroes:

• Nobody cares about anger. Let that part of your story go. Let it all go, if you can.

• Getting your career started requires learning to write in a way pleasing to journal referees and journal editors. This may require unlearning habits, since science writing is clear but rarely beautiful. This observation goes double for social scientists writing about topics that can inflame emotions, such as racism or violence. Do not write to be understood. Write rather so that you cannot possibly be misunderstood as you argue something very narrow. In Daniel Dennett's words, "We are to some degree just as responsible for *likely* misunderstandings of what we say as we are for the 'proper' effects of our words."[4]

• You are not your subjects. Do not try to reappropriate their experiences. It takes a lot of conscious effort and discipline—as a writer, as a reader of the notes you made as a listener—to include others' voices at the expense of your own. Go where the data lead to the extent you can. Don't "talk over" your subjects. Readers can tell.

• At some point in the process, someone in authority may tell you to "put yourself back into the book." At other points you will get the opposite advice, to "take whatever in this book is closest to your heart and just cut it out—because whatever remains on the page will be truer as a result of it." Both kinds of advice can be useful.

• First drafts are never good enough. You are writing for people with a lot on their desks but potentially quite long attention spans. Rewrite it. Make it shorter. Make it clearer.

• The dry voice is wisest and best.

• You are not funny. Your topic matter is deadly serious. The discipline is humorless.

• It is OK to admit ambiguity or uncertainty. Demonstrate that the empirical correlations are real, make the case for why the test is compelling, show as many robustness checks as you can, and then be honest. Every researcher discovers some things that do not fit the theory. If the data fit too perfectly, something may smell fishy. It is even OK to be completely wrong. It happens all the time in science. If you find this discouraging, remember: our ability to voice sentences like "I don't know" and "I used to be confident I knew, but now I'm not certain anymore" is one of the main things that separates academic authority from clerical authority.

• Some positivists pride themselves on their ability to define the exact moment at which certainty ends and speculation begins. Whether this is a good way to go about the process of social inquiry is disputed, but it becomes easier to write in this way if you cultivate an appreciation of small and precise questions. You can state what you know with certainty and point out where others may be exaggerating *their* certainty.

• Fads change. In order to keep up, you must continue to read. There is no alternative.

• A lot of people helped you do your research. You probably owe them something. It falls on you to make sense of what that is, but it likely has something to do with how you write their story. Pay those people back if you can. If you can't, pay it forward.

• It is much easier to motivate yourself to write about politics in difficult places when an underlying theory of social change motivated the fieldwork in the first place. Otherwise you tend to get discouraged.

CONCLUSION: WHY DO WE DO THIS?

Comparative politics has historically encouraged young scholars to learn difficult languages, travel to uncomfortable places, and live for long periods of time far away from loved ones, all to bring back data from understudied parts of the world. If I did not believe this was valuable in itself, regardless of professional success, I would not write a book like this. The guild justifies the journey with the claim that it is necessary in order to ensure that the material filling our dusty libraries is not completely out of touch with the lived experience of our human subjects. Those of us who go walk the walk, serving as living reminders that if one wants to know more about the world outside the ivory tower, at some point one must shoulder the burden of going there.

The journey changes you. It changes how you read and what you think is worth reading. Social scientists acquire habits of thinking, of observation, and of evidence-based reasoning constrained by probabilistic intuitions. What counts as cutting-edge research varies across disciplines, but multiple fields claim the same classic works. Thomas Schelling and Elinor Ostrom are claimed by both political science and economics. Charles Tilly is claimed by sociologists, European historians, and political scientists. James C. Scott is claimed by anthropology, area studies, and political science. Eric Hobsbawm is claimed by both history and literature. This suggests a convergence of aesthetic tastes across diverse academic disciplines. Some scholars find this convergence of perceptions reassuring. I certainly do.

Over the arc of a career, success depends on our reputations as writers as well as readers. We construct a complex hierarchy of prestige gradually, out of the accumulation of thousands of judgments by senior guild members on the value of artisanal books and papers. Our guild product is valuable to those who desire an ongoing and structured conversation, curated collectively, about outcomes relevant to the human experience. Taking part in this conversation is an end in itself. That is what we tell ourselves, anyway.

Professional gratification for empirical data collected is often delayed years or decades, if it comes at all. Even if this is elusive, however, more than the other subfields of political science, comparative politics dangles the possibility of getting inside other cultures. We respect and try mightily to heap professional rewards on students who take risks, leave the comfort of the academy, get their hands dirty, see for themselves how theories interact with the messy details of the real world, and come back to share important stories. There *is* virtue in the kind of labor that this book promotes, and personal rewards, which can make it worthwhile. Pluralism rewards gradual development of ethical awareness. The constraints of the real world inevitably require adaptation. If your experience is like mine, you will look back with kind eyes on your youthful mistakes like the trail at the end of a long backpacking trip: you will remember the sunsets and the card games, not the mosquitos and sunburns and the painful uphill climb.

It isn't all sunsets. You will deal with a lot of rejection in this business, and a lot of different kinds of frustrations. They all take a toll. It is easy, from a pious and distant abstract, to resign oneself to the fact that rewards for intellectual labor are indirect and that this job requires an ability to delay gratification. In day-by-day reality, uncertainty and poverty is hard to take. Our guild has been overproducing apprentice entrants for a long time. In 1952, Erving Goffman observed:

> In organizations patterned after a bureaucratic model, it is customary for personnel to expect rewards of a specified kind upon fulfilling requirements of a specified nature. Personnel come to define their career line in terms of a sequence of legitimate expectations and to base their self-conceptions on the assumption that in due course they will be what the institution allows persons to become. Sometimes, however, a member of an organization may fulfill some of the requirements for a particular status, especially the requirements concerning technical proficiency and seniority, but not other requirements, especially the less codified ones having to do with the proper handling of social relationships . . . The necessity of disappointing the expectations that a person has taken for granted may be infrequent in some organizations, but in others, such as training institutions, it occurs all the time. The process of personnel selection requires that many trainees be called but that few be chosen.[5]

Making an original and recognized contribution to an established field of knowledge while also properly handling all of the necessary relationships is difficult—a great deal harder than I imagined it would be. Even if you do everything as well as you can, professional satisfaction is not automatic. If you look to the guild for more than labor protections, moreover, you are bound for disappointment. It is easier to convince yourself to work hard if you labor under the illusion that the words you write might change politics, but what we write does not change the world directly. It might not change it at all. We do make changes as teachers, and it is fine to dwell on that, but there are not enough "good jobs." While many unhappy people imagine they would be happier if only they had a "good job" with tenure (and they might) there are also thousands of unhappy unsympathetic people with tenure at "good places."

Taking that into account, for those of you who have not left for the field but have flipped to the back of the book, my last piece of advice is to try to take a step back. Because your dissertation committee members are likely going to be with you for a very long time, try to see your mentors as people. Read some of their early work that no one cites. Ask them why they started writing when they sat where you do. Listen hard. Now they are older, and familiar with the rhythms of the job. Ask how their motivations have changed. Who seems happy? Why? Notice there is variation. Our guild is not designed to produce joy, but rather to cartel access to something very valuable.

Welcome to the guild.

ACKNOWLEDGMENTS

A few years ago Caelyn Cobb, an unusually forceful and patient editor, approached me to solicit a "how to" book for fieldwork. I hid this conversation from my wife, Emma Salustro, for as long as I could. A practitioner guide for fieldworkers had been her advice for a decade, and she loves being right about my career. Her codename for this book became "Operation Common Sense."

The first political scientist whose advice I solicited was my sister, Amanda Driscoll. When I asked for her favorite nugget of fieldwork saddle-wisdom, she distilled: "There's the thing that you tell people you're going to do to get the grant, then there's the thing you actually do while in the field, then there's the thing you write up." The phrase *improvisational pluralism* appeared in my notes shortly afterward. The course at Stanford University that did the most to prepare me for fieldwork was designed by Jeremy Weinstein. I started this book by going back to those class notes.

Other than Amanda and Jeremy, within my discipline my most memorable conversations on fieldwork were with Lee Ann Fujii, Roger Petersen, Scott Desposato, David Laitin, James Fearon, Yuhki Tajima, Nicholai Lidow, Bethany Lacina, Dara Cohen, Desha Girod, Claire Adida, Nahomi Ichino, Barbara Walter, Sam Popkin, Elaine Denny, Charles King, Peter Gourevitch, David Lake, Eric Gartzke, Macartan Humphreys, Phil Roeder, Mark Beissinger, Rose McDermott, Yoshiko

Hererra, Jorge Dominguez, Timothy Blauvelt, Kara Downey, Fotini Christia, Jon Lindsay, Zoe Marks, Erica Chenoweth, Yuri Zhukov, Ana Bracic, Gabrielle Kruks-Wisner, Mike Seese, John Porten, Rich Nielsen, Sasha Klayachkina, Anastasia Shesterinina, Will Reno, Christian Davenport, Jennifer Muratashvili, Lisa Wedeen, and Libby Wood. I am also grateful to cross-disciplinary fellow-travelers who shared expertise and helped me clarify my own thoughts, especially Caroline Schuster and Erin McFee on matters related to ethnographic methods, Mike Ambrogi and Nick Cox on data security, Sarah Cameron and my old roommate Seth Perry on using archives, Craig McIntosh on field experiments, and Liz Lyons on personnel management.

The first draft of this book was written in the summer of 2019. Peter Cowhey, my dean at the School of Global Policy and Strategy at the University of California, San Diego, was an early supporter of the project. John Porten, then a PhD student at UCSD, served as a sounding board from the initial drafting stage to the end. John's engagement and camaraderie helped give this book its shape. Table 3.1, in particular, owes a great debt to his editorial emendations. James Robinson and the Pearson Institute at the University of Chicago opened their doors to me as a visiting scholar.

My aunt by marriage, Anita Salustro, copyedited every chapter of the first draft manuscript at least twice, provided needed enthusiasm for the project in early stages, and helped unformed ideas congeal. Katherine Harper and Kathryn Jorge worked in tandem to provide magnificent copyediting for the final manuscript. Elliot Linzer constructed the index.

Between the first and final draft, I shopped the manuscript around a bit and was humbled by extensive written feedback from Sasha Klyachkina, Sarah Parkinson, Austin Wright, Steph Haggard, Edward Schatz, and especially Andrew Roberts and Richard Nielsen. I also received useful comments from graduate students and faculty at the University of California at San Diego (Adam Fefer, Brian Engelsma, Charles McClean, Duy Duc Trinh, Gareth Nellis, Lauren Gilbert, Marco Alcocer, Mariana Carvalho Barbosa, Megumi Naoi, Mike Seese, Syeda ShahBano Ijaz), Harvard (Zoe Marks, Erica Chenoweth, Jay Lyall, Chris Shay, Averell Schmidt, Yegor Lazarev, Anina Schwarzenbach, Sarah Dumant, Leonore Reese, Anna Pikcha), Northwestern (Elizabeth Good, Ely Orrego, Issrar Chamekh, Lauren Baker, Miruna Barnoschi, Qin

Huang, Rana Khoury, Salih Noor, Sarah Moore), the University of Chicago (Maria Gonzales, Alex Chinchilla, Jong Yoon Baik, Genevieve Bates, Evgenia Olimpieva, Noah Schouela), The University of Michigan (Christian Davenport, Chris Fariss, Tom O'Mealia, Tim Jones, Rebecca Savelsberg, Zhi Bin Ye, Hannah Leszczynski, Sasha Devogez), Michigan State University (Ana Bracic, Ethan Santangelo, Gerson Guevara, Hyerin Seo, Markus Reason, Max Welch, Nicholas Frantzeskakis, Torie Fritz), the University of Virginia (Gabrielle Kruks-Wisner, Ahmed Teleb, Dana K. Moyer, Sunggun Park, Tolulope Odukoya, Layla Picard, Hayley Elszasz, Alexis Bibeau-Gagnon, Mylène Freeman, Ferdinand Flagstad, Sally Bonsall, Carolyn Anh Dang), George Washington University (Janet Lewis, Omar Garcia Ponce, Caleb Schmotter, Anum Syed, Dan Trombly, Dan Ziebarth, Dennis Li, Gabriel Kelly, Mark Berlin, Sean Givnish, Stephen Rangazas, and Barbara Stallings), and the University of Wisconsin at Madison (Yoshiko Herrera, Nils Ringe, Kathy Cramer, David Bates, Sasha Klyachkina, Michael Masterson, Siying Fu).

I am grateful to my daughter Eleanor for encouraging me with her daily art creations and to my son Max for all he does to keep Eleanor's ego in check. As parents, it is impossible to overstate the debt that both Emma and I feel toward Emily Cox. If it were not for Emily, our lives in Chicago would probably not be possible. This book would certainly not exist.

I dedicate this book to my mother, Mary Driscoll, who watched me grow up playing imagination games. When teaching formal theory, I argue that the result of a model's application can be an abstracted storytelling, treating places and people's lived experiences as evidence consistent with a theory. That is not the entire story, though. My mother has watched me model probabilities my whole life, long before the discipline of political science gave structure to my world-building efforts. She will locate this book in a lineage that runs from *The Hobbit* to Gary Gygax and Madeleine L'Engle, through *The Bard's Tale* and Lloyd Alexander to David Eddings, Ursula K. Le Guin, and Neal Stephenson to Ben Robbins to this. Look, mom: A gold ring.

APPENDIX I

HOW TO RETELL THE STORY OF YOUR JOURNEY TO THE FIELD

The terminal goal of fieldwork is usually a written product that takes the form of an academic paper or a book. The burden will eventually fall on you, the author, to make all the pieces fit coherently. One way is to argue that you were inspired to go on a special journey in order to code a hard-to-measure variable and conduct a test. The results of that test are important. They allow you to correct a misunderstanding in the literature. To get the story, though, you had to go.

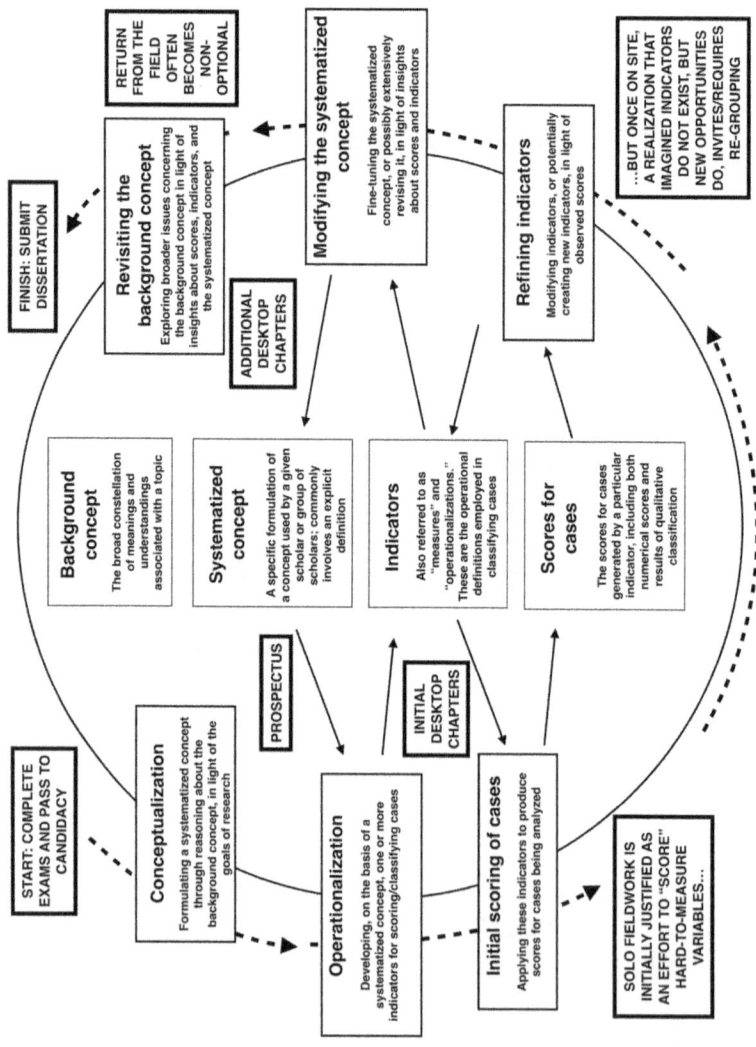

FIGURE A.1 An adaptable template for a compelling narrative of scientific discovery. Adapted from Robert Adcock and David Collier, "Measurement Validity: A Shared Standard for Qualitative and Quantitative Research," *American Political Science Review* 95, no. 3 (2001): 531.

The figure contains the following labeled elements:

START: COMPLETE EXAMS AND PASS TO CANDIDACY

FINISH: SUBMIT DISSERTATION

RETURN FROM THE FIELD OFTEN BECOMES NON-OPTIONAL

Revisiting the background concept — Exploring broader issues concerning the background concept in light of insights about scores, indicators, and the systematized concept

Modifying the systematized concept — Fine-tuning the systematized concept, or possibly extensively revising it, in light of insights about scores and indicators

Refining indicators — Modifying indicators, or potentially creating new indicators, in light of observed scores

...BUT ONCE ON SITE, A REALIZATION THAT IMAGINED INDICATORS DO NOT EXIST, BUT NEW OPPORTUNITIES DO, INVITES/REQUIRES RE-GROUPING

Background concept — The broad constellation of meanings and understandings associated with a topic

Systematized concept — A specific formulation of a concept used by a given scholar or group of scholars; commonly involves an explicit definition

Indicators — Also referred to as "measures" and "operationalizations." These are the operational definitions employed in classifying cases

Scores for cases — The scores for cases generated by a particular indicator, including both numerical scores and results of qualitative classification

ADDITIONAL DESKTOP CHAPTERS

PROSPECTUS

INITIAL DESKTOP CHAPTERS

Conceptualization — Formulating a systematized concept through reasoning about the background concept, in light of the goals of research

Operationalization — Developing, on the basis of a systematized concept, one or more indicators for scoring/classifying cases

Initial scoring of cases — Applying these indicators to produce scores for cases being analyzed

SOLO FIELDWORK IS INITIALLY JUSTIFIED AS AN EFFORT TO "SCORE" HARD-TO-MEASURE VARIABLES...

APPENDIX II

ADDITIONAL READING

While preparing this manuscript, I leaned heavily on the following works. All are worth the time.

ON RESEARCH DESIGN

Geddes, Barbara. *Paradigms and Sand Castles: Theory Building and Research Design in Comparative Politics*. Ann Arbor: University of Michigan Press, 2003.

Goertz, Gary. *Multimethod Research, Causal Mechanisms, and Case Studies: An Integrated Approach*. Princeton, NJ: Princeton University Press, 2017.

Mardsen, Peter V., and James D. Wright. *Handbook of Survey Research*. 2nd ed. Bingley, UK: Emerald, 2010.

Schatz, Edward. *Political Ethnography: What Immersion Contributes to the Study of Power*. Chicago: University of Chicago Press, 2009.

ON LISTENING AND WRITING WHAT YOU HEAR

Cyr, Jennifer. *Focus Groups for the Social Science Researcher*. New York: Cambridge University Press, 2019.

Emerson, Robert M., Rachel I. Fretz, and Linda L. Shaw. *Writing Ethnographic Fieldnotes.* 2nd ed. Chicago: University of Chicago Press, 2011.

Fujii, Lee Ann. *Interviewing in Social Science Research: A Relational Approach.* New York: Routledge, 2017.

Gallaher, Carolyn. "Researching Repellent Groups: Some Methodological Considerations on How to Represent Militants, Radicals, and Other Belligerents." In *Surviving Field Research: Working in Violent and Difficult Situations,* ed. Chandar Kelha Sriram, John C. King, Julie A. Mertus, Olga Martin-Ortega, and Johanna Herman, 127–46. New York: Routledge, 2009.

Jacobs, Alan, Tim Buthe, Ana M. Arjona, Leonardo R. Arriola, et al. "Transparency in Qualitative Research: An Overview of Key Findings and Recommendations." Working Paper Series: Qualitative Transparency Deliberations, Working Group Final Reports, 2019. https://papers.ssrn.com/sol3/papers.cfm?abstract_id=3430025.

Mosley, Layna. *Interview Research in Political Science.* Ithaca, NY: Cornell University Press, 2013.

ON DANGER

Electronic Frontier Foundation. "Pocket Border Crossing Guide." 2018. https://www.eff.org/files/2018/01/11/border-pocket-guide-2.pdf.

Werner, David. *Where There Is No Doctor: A Village Health Care Handbook.* Revised ed. Berkeley, CA: Hesperian Health Guides, 2017.

World Health Organization, War Trauma Foundation, and World Vision International. *Psychological First Aid: A Guide for Field Workers.* 2011. https://www.who.int/mental_health/publications/guide_field_workers/en/.

ON MATH (RE: "I REALIZE MATH IS NOT MY COMPARATIVE ADVANTAGE, BUT I NEED HELP")

Angrist, Joshua D., and Jörn-Steffen Pischke. *Mostly Harmless Econometrics: An Empiricist's Companion.* Princeton, NJ: Princeton University Press, 2009.

Humphreys, Macartan. *Political Games: Mathematical Insights on Fighting, Voting, Lying, and Other Affairs of State.* New York: Norton, 2016.

Lohr, Sharon L. *Sampling: Design and Analysis.* 2nd ed. Boston: Cengage Learning, 2009.

Singh, Simon. *The Code Book.* New York: Anchor Books, 1999.

ON STEPPING BACK FROM THE GAME

Elster, Jon. *Nuts and Bolts for the Social Sciences.* Cambridge: Cambridge University Press, 1989.

Rojas, Fabio. *Grad Skool Rulz: Everything You Need to Know about Academia from Admissions to Tenure.* Smashwords (ebook). Published Oct 2, 2011.

Shapiro, Ian. *The Flight from Reality in the Human Sciences.* Princeton, NJ: Princeton University Press, 2005.

NOTES

1. WELCOME TO THE GUILD

1. Joshua D. Angrist and Jörn-Steffen Pischke, *Mostly Harmless Econometrics: An Empiricist's Companion* (Princeton, NJ: Princeton University Press, 2009); Edward Schatz, *Political Ethnography: What Immersion Contributes to the Study of Power* (Chicago: University of Chicago Press, 2009).

2. This is not a direct quote, but I should attribute the spirit of the quote to David Lake. He would surely add that this is actually the purpose of all qualitative research, whether or not it involves travel.

3. Donald P. Green and Alan S. Gerber, "Reclaiming the Experimental Tradition in Political Science," in *Political Science: The State of the Discipline*, ed. Ira Katznelson and Helen V. Milner (New York: Norton, 2002), 829.

4. I am grateful to Elizabeth Wood for this analogy.

5. Diana Kapiszewski, Lauren M. Maclean, and Benjamin L. Read, *Field Research in Political Science: Practices and Principles* (Cambridge: Cambridge University Press, 2015), xi.

6. Paul Castañeda Dower, Evgeny Finkel, Scott Gehlbach, and Steven Nafziger, "Collective Action and Representation in Autocracies: Evidence from Russia's Great Reforms," *American Political Science Review* 112, no. 1 (2018): 125–47. Dower et al. exists only because Scott Gehlbach accidentally stumbled across a multivolume chronicle of peasant unrest in nineteenth-century Russia that, by some serendipity, made its way to the stacks of the University of Wisconsin at Madison. He describes this in "Serendipity," *Scott Ghelbach* (blog), February 10, 2018, https://scottgehlbach .net/serendipity/.

7. Matters of corporate reputation and liability are probably paramount to institutional university actors (see main text), but there are also well-understood reasons why the

process has been institutionalized. Carolyn Gallaher, "Researching Repellent Groups: Some Methodological Considerations on How to Represent Militants, Radicals, and Other Belligerents," in *Surviving Field Research: Working In Violent And Difficult Situations*, ed. Chandar Kelha Sriram, John C. King, Julie A. Mertus, Olga Martin-Ortega, and Johanna Herman (New York: Routledge, 2009), 129–32; Sarah Curran, "Ethical Considerations for Research in Cross-Cultural Settings," in *A Handbook for Social Science Field Research*, ed. Ellen Perecman and Sara R. Curran (London: Sage, 2006), 197–216.

8.   IRBs may also simply decide that certain research designs carry too much liability. Participant observation of soccer hooligans as they brutalize innocent bystanders for fun is the kind of thing intrepid investigative journalists can do but intrepid graduate students cannot. See, e.g., Bill Buford, *Among the Thugs* (London: Vintage, 1993).

9.   Sarah Brooks, "The Ethical Treatment of Human Subjects and the Institutional Review Board Process," in *Interview Research in Political Science*, ed. Layna Mosley (Ithaca, NY: Cornell University Press, 2013), 45–66.

10.   Reno provides an overview of legal issues related to interpretation of the 2001 USA PATRIOT Act as they may relate to overseas research on armed groups. The subpoena of researcher data is not a purely hypothetical concern. See William Reno, "The Problem of Extraterritorial Legality," in *Interview Research in Political Science*, ed. Layna Mosley (Ithaca, NY: Cornell University Press, 2013), 173–78; Beth McMurtie, "Secrets from Belfast," *Chronicle of Higher Education*, January 26, 2014, https://www.chronicle.com/interactives/belfast; Shamus Khan, "The Subpoena of Ethnographic Data," *Sociological Forum* 34, no. 1 (2019): 253–63.

11.   Fabio Rojas, *Grad Skool Rulz: Everything You Need to Know about Academia from Admissions to Tenure* (Smashwords ebook, October 2, 2011), 74.

12.   Gartzke writes with delicious self-awareness on this illusion. Piven describes interactions with policy processes as "political theater, played to wide audiences, and increasingly important to politicians trying to sway voting publics," noting that the pantomime is especially common practice for scholars working in the law and economics tradition. See Eric Gartzke, "Zombie Relevance," published by Dan Drezner, "Gartzke on Policy, Political Science, and Zombies," *Foreign Policy*, February 27, 2011, https://foreignpolicy.com/2011/02/27/gartzke-on-policy-political-science-and-zombies/; Frances F. Piven, "The Politics of Policy Science," in *Problems and Methods in the Study of Politics*, ed. Ian Shapiro, Rogers M. Smith, and Tarek E. Masoud (Cambridge: Cambridge University Press, 2004), 84–85.

13.   I am grateful to Austin Wright for articulating this point in this way.

14.   David Laitin, "Comparative Politics: The State of the Subdiscipline," in *Political Science: The State of the Discipline*, ed. Helen Milner and Ira Katznelson (Washington, DC: American Political Science Association, 2000).

15.   Charles King, *Gods of the Upper Air: How a Circle of Renegade Anthropologists Reinvented Race, Sex, and Gender in the Twentieth Century* (New York: Doubleday, 2019).

2. HOW TO PREPARE TO LEAVE YOUR HOME INSTITUTION

1. Barbara Geddes, *Paradigms and Sand Castles: Theory Building and Research Design in Comparative Politics* (Ann Arbor: University of Michigan Press, 2003).

2. Sudhir Venkatesh, "'Doin' the Hustle': Constructing the Ethnographer in the American Ghetto," *Ethnography* 3, no. 1 (2002): 91–111.

3. Aisha Ahmad, *Jihad & Co: Black Market and Islamist Power* (New York: Oxford University Press, 2017); Georgi Derluguian, *Bourdieu's Secret Admirer in the Caucasus: A World Systems Biography* (Chicago: University of Chicago Press, 2005).

4. ILGA World: The International Lesbian, Gay, Bisexual, Trans and Intersex Association, https://ilga.org/. I am grateful to Erica Chenoweth for recommending this resource.

5. Roger Petersen, *Western Intervention in the Balkans: The Strategic Use of Emotion in Conflict* (Cambridge: Cambridge University Press, 2011), 55.

6. Geddes, *Paradigms and Sand Castles*, 144–48.

7. For those seeking examples of this move from typology to measurement that have been dramatized in a teachable way, see Colin Elman, "Explanatory Typologies in Qualitative Studies of International Politics," *International Organization* 59, no. 2 (2005): 293–326; David Collier, Jody LaPorte, and Jason Seawright, "Putting Typologies to Work: Concept Formation, Measurement, and Analytic Rigor," *Political Research Quarterly* 65 no. 1 (2012): 217–32; Derek Layder, *Doing Excellent Small-Scale Research* (Los Angeles: Sage, 2013).

8. Evan S. Lieberman, "Preparing for Field Research," *Qualitative Methods* 2, no. 1 (2004): 5, emphasis mine.

9. William Reno, *Warlord Politics and African States* (Boulder, CO: Lynne Rienner, 1998).

10. Jonathan Rodden, *Hamilton's Paradox: The Promise and Peril of Fiscal Reform* (Cambridge: Cambridge University Press, 2006).

11. Jesse Driscoll, *Warlords and Coalition Politics in Post-Soviet States* (Cambridge: Cambridge University Press, 2015), 162–66, 213–19.

12. Geddes, *Paradigms and Sandcastles*, 143. Gary Goertz and James Mahoney, *A Tale of Two Cultures: Qualitative and Quantitative Research in the Social Sciences* (Princeton, NJ: Princeton University Press, 2012) and Gary Goertz, *Multimethod Research, Causal Mechanisms, and Case Studies: An Integrated Approach* (Princeton, NJ: Princeton University Press, 2017) complement Geddes well.

13. I am grateful to Yuri Zhukov for articulating this point in this way.

14. Sarah Cameron, *The Hungry Steppe: Famine, Violence, and the Making of Soviet Kazakhstan* (Ithaca, NY: Cornell University Press, 2018).

15. Scott A. Frisch, Douglas B. Harris, Sean Q. Kelly, and David C. W. Parker, eds., *Doing Archival Research in Political Science* (Amherst, NY: Cambria Press, 2012), 1; Linda A. Whitaker and Michael Lotstein, "Pulling Back the Curtain: Archives and Archivists Revealed," in *Doing Archival Research in Political Science*, ed. Scott A. Frisch et al. (Amherst, NY: Cambria Press, 2012), 99.

16. A full-throated defense of my discipline on this point would be tedious and lead us astray. I'll bet the early-career work of Yuri Zhukov stands the test of time for "real historians." Other exemplary uses of archival data that have appeared on my own teaching syllabi include: Mark Beissinger, *Nationalist Mobilization and the Collapse of the Soviet State* (Cambridge: Cambridge University Press, 2002); Michele Leiby, "Digging in the Archives: The Promise and Perils of Primary Documents," *Politics and Society* 37, no. 1 (2009): 75–99; Evgeny Finkel, *Ordinary Jews: Choice and Survival During the Holocaust* (Princeton, NJ: Princeton University Press, 2017); Laia Balcells, *Rivalry and Revenge: The Politics of Violence During Civil War* (Cambridge: Cambridge University Press, 2017); Francisco Garfias, "Elite Competition and State Capacity Development: Theory and Evidence from Post-Revolutionary Mexico," *American Political Science Review* 112, no. 2 (2018): 339–57; Yuri Zhukov and Roya Talibova, "Stalin's Terror and the Long-Term Political Effects of Mass Repression," *Journal of Peace Research* 55, no. 2 (2018): 267–83; Yuri Zhukov and Arturas Rozenas, "Mass Repression and Political Loyalty: Evidence from Stalin's 'Terror by Hunger,'" *American Political Science Review* 111, no. 2 (2019): 569–83; Yuri Zhukov, "Population Resettlement in War: Theory and Evidence from Soviet Archives," *Journal of Conflict Resolution* 59, no. 7 (2015): 1155–85.

17. Leonard Schatzman and Anslem L. Strauss, *Field Research* (Englewood Cliffs, NJ: Prentice Hall, 1973), 19.

18. Schatzman and Strauss, *Field Research*, 24.

19. I am grateful to Yoshiko Hererra for forcefully insisting I include this point. See also Jesse Driscoll, "Being Watched and Being Handled," in *Doing Fieldwork in Areas of International Intervention: A Guide to Research in Violent and Closed Contexts*, ed. Berit Bliesemann de Guevara and Morten Bøås (Bristol, UK: Bristol University Press, 2020).

20. I am grateful to Sasha Klyachkina for articulating this point in this way.

3. HOW TO THINK ABOUT SELF-PRESENTATION
ONCE YOU ARRIVE

1. I owe this phrasing to Kylea Liese. The observation that one's social structure (cultural predispositions, class inheritance, and language) shapes behaviors is much older than Bourdieu. Aristotle observed it, for example. Some constraints are unconscious. In some cases, constraints (even these precognitive ones) are deliberately chosen by social actors (or their parents) who make strategic (or nonstrategic) choices to condition themselves (or their children) and thereby alter constraints' salience. Rawi Abdelal, Yoshiko M. Herrera, Alastair Ian Johnston, and Rose McDermott, "Identity as a Variable," *Perspective on Politics* 4, no. 4 (2006): 695–711. See also Pierre Bourdieu, *Outline of a Theory of Practice* (Cambridge: Cambridge University Press, 1977); Sadiya Akram, "Fully Unconscious and Prone to Habit: The Characteristics of Agency in the

Structure and Agency Dialectic," *Journal for the Theory of Social Behavior* 43, no. 1 (2012): 45–65.

2. The 1973 Clifford Geertz essay "The Deep Play" is the text most responsible for convincing me of the value of ethnographic observation. The attack on this Geertz contribution by Vincent Crapanzano and the merciless interrogation of Ernst Gellner (another of my heroes) by Talal Asad in the same volume, as well as my lifetime of engagement with students of Edward Said have cumulatively convinced me that any attempt to model things from others' points of view will open one up to the charge of speaking out of turn. This charge will be leveled even if one is careful, even if one is speaking about (what seem to you to be) the simplest and self-evident small truths. See Clifford Geertz, "The Deep Play: Notes on the Balinese Cockfight," in *The Interpretation of Cultures*, ed. Clifford Geertz (New York: Basic Books, 1973), 412–53; Vincent Crapanzano, "Hermes' Dilemma: The Masking of Subversion in Ethnographic Description," in *Writing Culture*, ed. James Clifford and George E. Marcus (London: University of California Press, 1986), 74; Talal Asad, "The Concept of Cultural Translation in British Social Anthropology," in *Writing Culture*, 141–64; Edward Said, *Orientalism* (New York: Pantheon, 1978). My training has also attuned me to a Geertzian "deep play" in the discipline of political science: We publicly act as if we have faith in a search for general laws, even though many of us privately suspect the enterprise is Sisyphean. There is nothing to be done but to grow a thick skin. See David Laitin, "The Perestroika Challenge to Social Science," *Politics & Society* 31, no. 1 (2003): 163–84.

3. See George Herbert Mead, *Mind, Self, and Society* (Chicago: University of Chicago Press, 1934).

4. Christian Davenport, "Researching while Black: Why Conflict Research Needs More African Americans (Maybe)," *Political Violence at a Glance*, April 10, 2013, http://politicalviolenceataglance.org/2013/04/10/researching-while-black-why-conflict-research-needs-more-african-americans-maybe/.

5. Thomas S. Kuhn, *The Structure of Scientific Revolutions*, 3rd ed. (Chicago: University of Chicago Press, 1996).

6. Anne Norton, "Political Science as a Vocation," in *Problems and Methods in the Study of Politics*, ed. Ian Shapiro, Rogers M. Smith, and Tarek E. Masoud (Cambridge: Cambridge University Press, 2004), 67. Her chapter title references the famous essay by Max Weber. Elsewhere in the prose she includes his observation that "the professor has other fields for the diffusion of his ideals" and "should not demand the right as a professor to carry the marshal's baton or the statesman or reformer in his knapsack." See Max Weber, "The Meaning of Ethical Neutrality," in *Methodology of the Social Sciences*, trans. Edward Shils and Henry Finch (New York: Free Press, 1949), 5.

7. Writing these words in 2020, it is important to acknowledge, if only in a note, that those claims of political neutrality are often criticized by powerful social actors as being absurd on their face (with some evidence). For evidence, see Mitchell Langbert, Anthony J. Quain, and Daniel B. Klein, "Faculty Voter Registration in Economics,

History, Journalism, Law, and Psychology," *Econ Journal Watch* 13, no. 3 (2016): 422–51.

8.   Ian Shapiro, *The Flight from Reality in the Human Sciences* (Princeton, NJ: Princeton University Press, 2005), 15.

9.   Rose McDermott, "Experimental Methods in Political Science," *Annual Review of Political Science* 5 (2002): 31–61; Macartan Humphreys and Jeremy Weinstein, "Field Experiments and the Political Economy of Development," *Annual Review of Political Science* 12 (2009): 367–78; Dimiter Toshkov, *Research Design in Political Science* (London: Palgrave, 2016), 166–99.

10.   Helen Margetts and Gerry Stoker, "The Experimental Method," in *Theory and Methods in Political Science*, 4th ed., ed. Vivien Lowndes, David Marsh, and Gerry Stoker (London: Palgrave, 2018), 293.

11.   At some risk of repetition: If a guild novice needs an entry-level primer on the value of local knowledge, that novice ought to consider a long sit with Geertz, "The Deep Play."

12.   Norton, "Political Science as a Vocation," 66.

13.   I put these phrases in quotes because (1) they are exactly what certain political scientists say all the time to score points and (2) it is perhaps worth reflecting on how pompous and insulting they can sound when they do.

14.   While there are well-rehearsed arguments against the evangelical variants of modernization theory, high levels of economic growth and good governance measures are correlated. For studies that emphasize different caveats, see Carles Boix, "Democracy, Development, and the International System," *American Political Science Review* 105, no. 4 (2011): 809–28; Daron Acemoglu, Suresh Naidu, Pascual Restrepo, and James A. Robinson, "Democracy Does Cause Growth," *Journal of Political Economy* 127, no. 1 (2019): 47–100.

15.   William Easterly, *The White Man's Burden: Why the West's Efforts to Aid the Rest Have Done So Much Ill and So Little Good* (New York: Penguin, 2006).

16.   What it means to "jump ship" on academia, commodify one's experiences and degree, and (as one coauthor put it) *"get on the gravy train"* varies by individual. While filling out a budget to fund solo fieldwork in Ukraine in 2015, my university grants manager casually suggested that we use the US federal government's "per diem" amount as an estimate to justify day-to-day expenses. I only realized later that the number being proposed was $374 per day. According to World Bank estimates, Ukraine's per capita GDP was $4,000 per year in 2014, closer to $2,000 per year in 2015.

17.   Barbara Shapiro, *A Culture of Fact: England, 1550–1720* (Ithaca, NY: Cornell University Press, 2000), 65. Her account traces the rise of modern social sciences from replicable procedures for distinguishing fact from fable (73, 77–84). Foreshadowing modern transparency debates, she documents distrust and disdain four hundred years ago for "travel liars" (71) who rely on uncorroborated narrative.

18.   Stephen King, *On Writing: A Memoir of the Craft* (New York: Scribner, 2000), 249. Elsewhere he describes writing as telepathy (103–7). This book is hard to improve upon, incidentally, as a no-nonsense guide for those seeking advice on how to write.

19.   I am aware that advice on computer-related subjects rarely ages well, and making ref-
      erence to Instagram and Twitter, or even the notion of "blogging," may well date this
      book. So be it.

20.   Herbert J. Rubin and Irene S. Rubin, *Qualitative Interviewing: The Art of Hearing
      Data*, 2nd ed. (London: Sage, 2005), 102.

21.   Anastasia Shesterinina, "Collective Threat Framing and Mobilization in Civil War,"
      American Political Science Review 110, no. 3 (2016): 411–27; Egor Lazarev, "Laws in
      Conflict: Legacies of War, Gender, and Legal Pluralism in Chechnya," *World Politics*
      71, no. 4 (2018): 667–709.

4. HOW TO THINK ABOUT SOLO DATA COLLECTION

1.   Ellen Pader, "Seeing with an Ethnographic Sensibility," in *Interpretation and Method:
      Empirical Research Methods and the Interpretative Turn*, ed. Dvora Yanow and
      Penegrine Schwartz-Shea, (New York: M. E. Sharpe, 2006), 161–75; Edward Schatz,
      "Ethnographic Immersion and the Study of Politics," in *Political Ethnography: What
      Immersion Contributes to the Study of Politics* (Chicago: University of Chicago Press,
      2009), 1–22.

2.   David Laitin, *Hegemony and Culture: Politics and Change among the Yoruba* (Chicago:
      University of Chicago Press, 1986); Michael Barnett, "The UN Security Council, Indif-
      ference, and Genocide in Rwanda," *Cultural Anthropology* 12, no. 4 (1997): 551–78;
      Roger Petersen, *Western Intervention in the Balkans: The Strategic Use of Emotion in
      Conflict* (Cambridge: Cambridge University Press, 2011); Timothy Pachirat, *Every
      Twelve Seconds: Industrialized Slaughter and the Politics of Sight* (New Haven, CT: Yale
      University Press, 2013); Katherine J. Cramer, *The Politics of Resentment: Rural Con-
      sciousness in Wisconsin and the Rise of Scott Walker* (Chicago: University of Chicago
      Press, 2016); Richard Neilsen, *Deadly Clerics: Blocked Ambition and the Path to Jihad*
      (New York: Cambridge University Press, 2017); Gabrielle Kruks-Wisner, *Claiming the
      State: Active Citizenship and Social Welfare in Rural India* (New York: Cambridge
      University Press, 2018); Ana Bracic, *Breaking the Exclusion Cycle: How to Promote
      Cooperation between Majority and Minority Ethnic Groups* (Oxford: Oxford Univer-
      sity Press, 2020).

3.   The claim of nonreplicability strikes me as the most serious. Though Burawoy explains
      how revisitations can be valuable, it is not common for political scientists to spend
      their careers revisiting their dissertation field sites. While in theory, revisits can be
      undertaken by other scholars, this does not occur much in practice, and certainly not
      with the reflexivity Burawoy advocates. Michael Burawoy, "Revisits: An Outline of a
      Theory of Reflexive Ethnography," *American Sociological Review* 68, no. 5 (2003): 645–
      79. Because the field is preoccupied by data transparency debates and concerns about
      replicability, if you work with qualitative data it is a good idea to rehearse defenses of
      your methodology that you find persuasive.

4.   Lisa Wedeen, "Ethnography as Interpretive Enterprise," in *Political Ethnography: What Immersion Contributes to the Study of Power*, ed. Edward Schatz (Chicago: University of Chicago Press, 2000), 83.

5.   Tariq Thachil, *Elite Parties, Poor Voters: How Social Services Win Votes in India* (New York: Cambridge University Press, 2014).

6.   Lee Ann Fujii, "Five Stories of Accidental Ethnography: Turning Unplanned Moments in the Field into Data," *Qualitative Research* 15, no. 4 (2015): 525–39.

7.   Erica S. Simmons and Nicholas R. Smith, "Comparison with an Ethnographic Sensibility," *PS: Political Science & Politics* 50, no. 1 (2017): 126–30.

8.   Mitchell Duneier, "Race and Peeing on Sixth Avenue," in *Racing Research, Researching Race: Methodological Dilemmas in Critical Race Studies*, ed. France Winddance Twine and Jonathan W. Warren (New York: New York University Press, 2000); Begoña Aretxaga, "Dirty Protest," in *States of Terror: Begoña Aretxaga's Essays*, ed. Joseba Zulaika (Reno: Center for Basque Studies, University of Nevada, 2005), 57–74.

9.   Robert M. Emerson, Rachel I. Fretz, and Linda L. Shaw, *Writing Ethnographic Fieldnotes*, 2nd ed. (Chicago: University of Chicago Press, 2011); Schatz, *Political Ethnography*.

10.   Herbert J. Rubin and Irene Rubin, *Qualitative Interviewing: The Art of Hearing Data*, 2nd ed. (London: Sage, 2005), 64.

11.   A colleague stumbled across Scott Cunningham's very compelling description on Twitter of his discovery of an instrumental variable relevant to the study of sex workers. Scott Cunningham (@causalinf), "So im a big believer that the best natural experiments (instruments) favor the prepared, the patient observer who is doing her work and just waiting and looking 14/n," Twitter, January 18, 2020, 7:38 p.m., https://twitter.com/causalinf/status/1218694069708382209.

12.   Jesse Driscoll and Nicholai Lidow, "Representative Surveys in Insecure Environments: A Case Study of Mogadishu, Somalia," *Journal of Survey Statistics and Methodology* 2, no. 1 (2014): 78–95.

13.   E.g., Gerardo L. Munck and Richard Snyder, *Passion, Craft, and Method in Comparative Politics* (Baltimore: Johns Hopkins University Press, 2007).

14.   Rubin and Rubin, *Qualitative Interviewing*, 4.

15.   Jeffrey M. Berry, "Validity and Reliability Issues in Elite Interviewing," *Political Science & Politics* 35, no. 4 (2002): 679–82; Cathie J. Martin, "Crafting Interviews to Capture Cause and Effect," in *Interview Research in Political Science*, ed. Layna Mosley (Ithaca, NY: Cornell University Press, 2013), 109–24.

16.   Anastasia Shesterinina, "Ethics, Empathy, and Fear in Research on Violent Conflict," *Journal of Peace Research* 56, no. 2 (2018): 190–202.

17.   Rautalinko, Lisper, and Ekenhammar provide a good summary of Rogerian Reflective Listening (alternatively called Active Listening) and define the toolkit of reflective listening as follows: (a) reflecting fact (b) reflecting emotion (c) questioning on fact, and (d) questioning on emotion. See: Erik Rautalinko, Hans-Olof Lisper, and Bo Ekenhammar, "Reflective Listening in Counseling: Effects of Training Time and Evaluator Social Skills," *American Journal of Psychotherapy* 61, no. 2 (2007): 191–209.

18. One color is for the main interview notes, the second for what Fujii (2017) calls "meta-data" notes (notes-to-self about the interview, usually written immediately afterward but sometimes jotted innocuously during the interview itself). The third color is for emergencies: if the interview changes tone at a critical point, I change colors to remind myself what happened.

19. Lauren Prather and Sarah Bush, "Do Electronic Devices in Face-to-Face Interviews Change Survey Behavior? Evidence from a Developing Country," *Research & Politics* 6, no. 2 (2019): 1–7, provides systematic evidence for this assertion, and a great deal more.

20. Jonah Lehrer, *Proust Was a Neuroscientist* (New York: Harcourt, 2007).

21. Diana Kapiszewski and Dessislava Kirilova, "Transparency in Qualitative Security Studies Research: Standards, Benefits, and Challenges," *Security Studies* 23 (2014): 699–707.

22. Lee Ann Fujii, *Interviewing in Social Science Research: A Relational Approach* (New York: Routledge, 2017).

23. A thoughtful meditation on these issues is found in Carolyn Gallaher, "Some Methodological Considerations on How to Represent Militants, Radicals, and Other Belligerents," in *Surviving Field Research: Working in Violent and Difficult Situations*, ed. ed. Chandar Kelha Sriram, John C. King, Julie A. Mertus, Olga Martin-Ortega, and Johanna Herman (New York: Routledge, 2009), 127–46.

24. Virginia Dickson-Swift, Erica L. James, and Pranee Liamputtong, *Undertaking Sensitive Research in the Health and Social Sciences: Managing Boundaries, Emotions, and Risks* (Cambridge: Cambridge University Press, 2008), 8.

25. Gerald Corey, *Theory and Practice of Counseling and Psychotherapy*, 8th ed. (Belmont, CA: Thomson, 2009).

26. Kenneth S. Pope and Melba J. T. Vasquez, *Ethics in Psychotherapy and Counseling: A Practical Guide* (San Francisco: John Wiley, 2007).

27. Keith Darden, "One Last Thing Before You Go," in *Stories from the Field: A Guide to Navigating Fieldwork in Political Science*, ed. Peter Krause and Ora Szekely (New York: Columbia University Press, 2020), 347.

28. I am grateful to Caroline Schuster for collaborating with me to bring the work of Trouillot and Borneman and Masco to wider attention. See Michel-Rolph Trouillot, "Anthropology as Metaphor: The Savage's Legacy and the Postmodern World," *Review (Fernand Braudel Center)* 14, no. 1 (1991): 29–54; John Borneman and Joseph Masco, "Anthropology and the Security State," *American Anthropologist* 117, no. 4 (2015): 781–85; Jesse Driscoll and Caroline Schuster, "Spies Like Us," *Ethnography* 19, no. 3 (2017): 411–30.

29. This also means no meaningful inferences can thus be squeezed from non-random patterns of "don't know" and "refuse to answer" responses, since the social ritual complicates the kinds of inferences one can draw from silence. In some of my own work, I eventually became more interested in what questions Somalis refused to answer than anything else about Mogadishu.

30. Michael Bloor, Jane Frankland, Michelle Thomas, and Kate Robson, *Focus Groups in Social Research* (London: Sage, 2001); Jennifer Cyr, *Focus Groups for the Social Science Researcher* (New York: Cambridge University Press, 2019).

31. There are exceptions. I have never seen this methodology used more effectively than in the data presented in Cramer, *The Politics of Resentment*.

32. I admit I have few of these war stories myself. The general advice that follows draws heavily on written communication with Timothy Blauvelt and Seth Perry and memorable conversations with Sarah Cameron and Yuri Zhukov. A special issue of the *Journal of Peace Research* (March 2018) is devoted to the use of archival work in conflict studies, and the essay by Balcells and Sullivan in particular ought to be essential reading for anyone considering work of this sort. Secret police archives and regime archives present separate challenges. See Laia Balcells and Christopher M. Sullivan, "New Findings from Conflict Archives: An Introduction and Methodological Framework," *Journal of Peace Research* 55, no. 2 (2018): 137–46; Kirsten Weld, *Paper Cadavers: The Archives of Dictatorship in Guatemala* (Durham, NC: Duke University Press, 2014).

33. Julia Lynch, "Tracking Progress While in the Field," *Qualitative Methods* 2, no. 1 (2004): 10–15.

5. HOW TO THINK LIKE A MANAGER

1. Debra Javeline and Sarah Lindemann-Komarova, "Financing Russian Civil Society," *Europe–Asia Studies* 72, no. 4 (2020): 644–85, DOI: 10.1080/09668136.2019.1637399.

2. This section draws heavily on Lee Ann Fujii, "Working with Interpreters," in *Interview Research in Political Science*, ed. Layna Mosley (Ithaca, NY: Cornell University Press, 2013), 144–68.

3. Nathan Jensen, Elizabeth Lyons, Eddy Chebelyon, Ronan Le Bras, and Carla Gomes, "Conspicuous Monitoring and Remote Work," *Journal of Economic Behavior and Organization* 176 (2020): 489–511.

4. Peter V. Marsden and James D. Wright, *Handbook of Survey Research*, 2nd ed. (Bingley, UK: Emerald, 2010).

5. If you are a complete novice but want to read just one thing on survey design—what kinds of questions to ask, why you should avoid asking double-barreled questions, etc.—carefully review Jon A. Krosnik and Stanley Presser, "Question and Questionnaire Design," in Marsden and Wright, *Handbook of Survey Research*, 263–314. A free eighty-page variant with a twenty-page bibliography can be found online.

6. Macartan Humphreys, "Monkey Business," reprinted in the *APSA Comparative Politics Newsletter*, 2013, https://www.bitss.org/2013/03/20/monkey-business/.

7. Graeme Blair, Jasper Cooper, Alexander Coppock, and Macartan Humphreys, "Declaring and Diagnosing Research Designs," *American Political Science Review* 113, no. 3 (2019): 838–59. The authors provide nonproprietary DeclareDesign software (https://declaredesign.org/) to reduce the start-up costs of a voluntary compliance regime.

8. If such a database exists at the time you are reading this, it should be a wonderful resource. Consult it. See who else is working on the same site as you. Consider

contacting them and collaborating. Make sure you do not reinvent the wheel, get blindsided, or get scooped.

9. Scott Ashworth, Christopher R. Berry, and Ethan Bueno de Mesquita, *Theory and Credibility: Integrating Theoretical and Empirical Social Science* (Princeton, NJ: Princeton University Press, forthcoming); Colin Elman, Diana Kapiszewski, and Lorena Vinuela, "Qualitative Data Archiving: Rewards and Challenges," *PS: Political Science & Politics* 43, no. 1 (2010): 23–27; Colin Elman, Diana Kapiszewski, and Arthur Lupia, "Transparent Social Inquiry: Implications for Political Science," *Annual Review of Political Science* 21, no. 1 (2018): 29–47.

10. Regine Spector, *Order at the Bazaar: Power and Trade in Central Asia* (Ithaca, NY: Cornell University Press, 2017), 197–99; Scott Radnitz, *Weapons of the Wealthy: Predatory Regimes and Elite-Led Protests in Central Asia* (Ithaca, NY: Cornell University Press, 2010); Madeline Reeves, *Border Work: Spatial Lives of the State in Rural Central Asia* (London: Cornell University Press, 2014), 54–56.

11. Scott Desposato, "Subjects' and Scholars' Views on the Ethics of Political Science Field Experiments," *Perspectives on Politics* 16, no. 3 (2018): 739–50.

12. None of these are hypotheticals. On roundworm pills in the Kalahari, see Edward Miguel and Michael Kremer, "Worms: Identifying Impacts on Education and Health in the Presence of Treatment Externalities," *Econometrica* 72, no. 1 (2004): 159–217. Examples of other studies are drawn from Nahomi Ichino and Matthias Schündeln, "Deterring or Displacing Electoral Irregularities? Spillover Effects of Observers in a Randomized Field Experiment in Ghana," *Journal of Politics* 74, no. 1 (2012): 292–307; Xavier Giné and Ghazala Mansouri, "Together We Will: Experimental Evidence on Female Voting Behavior in Pakistan," World Bank Policy Research Working Paper 5892, 2011; Robert Bond, Christopher J. Fariss, Jason J. Jones, et al., "A 61-Million Person Experiment in Social Influence and Political Mobilization," *Nature* 489 (2012): 295–98; Lauren Young, "The Psychology of State Repression: Fear and Dissident Decisions in Zimbabwe," *American Political Science Review* 113, no. 1 (2019): 140–55; Katherine Casey, Abou Bakarr Kamara, and Niccolo Meriggi, "An Experiment in Candidate Selection," NBER Working Paper No. 26160, 2019, DOI: 10.3386 /w26160.

13. Coffman and Niederle argue that replication studies could solve most of these harms. See Lucas C. Coffman and Muriel Niederle, "Pre-Analysis Plans Have Limited Upside, Especially Where Replications Are Feasible," *Journal of Economic Perspectives* 29, no. 3 (2015): 81–98. I sometimes worry that this whole set of debates is creating a generation that is inclined to be skeptical toward all non-preregistered empirical work, as if all noncompliers are p-hackers and curve-fitters. As of this writing, the following practices are increasingly common: (1) writing exhaustively complete (sixty-plus-page!) plans that account for all possible directions of effects; (2) ignoring entire sections of these plans when convenient; and/or (3) filing a plan but then running (and reporting) post-hoc tests anyway.

14. David Laitin, "Fisheries Management," *Political Analysis* 21, no. 1 (2012): 45.

15. See Jesse Driscoll and Nicholai Lidow, "Representative Surveys in Insecure Environments: A Case Study of Mogadishu, Somalia," *Journal of Survey Statistics and Methodology* 2, no. 1 (2014): 78–95; and Elaine Denny and Jesse Driscoll, "Calling Mogadishu: How Reminders of Anarchy Bias Survey Participation," *Journal of Experimental Political Science* 6, no. 2 (2019): 81–92.

6. HOW TO WEIGH RISKS IN DIFFICULT SETTINGS

1. For students seeking a methodological refresher on why "the most difficult places" might be appealing to scientists "for a broad range of discovery-related goals," consider Seawright as a useful complement to the discussion in Geddes on case selection on and off the regression line. See Jason Seawright, "The Case for Selecting Cases That Are Deviant or Extreme on the Independent Variable," *Sociological Methods & Research* 45, no. 3 (2016): 493–525; Barbara Geddes, *Paradigms and Sand Castles: Theory Building and Research Design in Comparative Politics* (Ann Arbor: University of Michigan Press, 2003).

2. Stephen Krasner, *Sovereignty: Organized Hypocrisy* (Ithaca, NY: Cornell University Press, 2000).

3. James Fearon and Anke Hoeffler, "Conflict and Violence Assessment Paper: Benefits and Costs of the Conflict and Violence Targets for the Post-2015 Development Agenda," Working Paper, Copenhagen Consensus Center, 2015, 1, https://www.copenhagenconsensus.com/sites/default/files/conflict_assessment_-_hoeffler_and_fearon_0.pdf.

4. Stathis Kalyvas, *The Logic of Violence in Civil War* (Cambridge: Cambridge University Press, 2006); Eli Berman, Jacob Shapiro, and Joseph Felter, *Small Wars, Big Data* (Princeton, NJ: Princeton University Press, 2018).

5. Elisabeth J. Wood, "The Ethical Challenges of Field Research in Conflict Zones," *Qualitative Sociology* 29, no. 3 (2006): 373–86; Kate Cronin-Furman and Milli Lake, "Ethics Abroad: Fieldwork in Fragile and Violent Contexts," *PS: Political Science and Politics* 51, no. 3 (2018): 607–14.

6. Elaine Denny and Jesse Driscoll. "Calling Mogadishu: How Reminders of Anarchy Bias Survey Participation," *Journal of Experimental Political Science* 6, no. 2 (2019): 81–92.

7. Wood, "Ethical Challenges of Field Research in Conflict Zones." See also Julie Mertus, "Maintenance of Personal Security: Ethical and Operational Issues," in *Surviving Field Research: Working in Violent and Difficult Situations*, ed. Chandra Lekha Siram, John C. King. Julie A. Mertus, Olga Martin-Ortega, and Johanna Herman (New York: Routledge, 2009), 165–66.

8. I remain grateful to Jennifer Muratashvili for articulating this point in a memorable way.

9. Amelia Hoover Green, "Successful Fieldwork for the Fieldwork Hater," in *Stories from the Field: A Guide to Navigating Fieldwork in Political Science*, ed. Peter Krause and Ora Szekely (New York: Columbia University Press, 2020).

10. Stathis Kalyvas, "The Urban Bias in Research on Civil Wars," *Security Studies* 13, no. 3 (2004): 160–90.

11. Raymond M. Lee, *Dangerous Fieldwork* (Thousand Oaks, CA: SAGE, 1995), 10–15.

12. Current as of this writing: Eva Bellin, et al., "Research in Authoritarian and Repressive Contexts," Working Paper Series: Qualitative Transparency Deliberations, Working Group Final Reports, 2019, https://papers.ssrn.com/sol3/papers.cfm?abstract_id=3333496; Ana M. Arjona, Zachariah C. Mamphilly, and Wendy Pearlman, "Research in Violent or Post-Conflict Political Settings," Working Paper Series: Qualitative Transparency Deliberations, Working Group Final Reports, 2019, https://papers.ssrn.com/sol3/papers.cfm?abstract_id=3333503; and Milli Lake, Samantha Majic, and Rashaan Maxwell. "Research on Vulnerable and Marginalized Populations," Research in Authoritarian and Repressive Contexts, Working Paper Series: Qualitative Transparency Deliberations, Working Group Final Reports, 2019, https://papers.ssrn.com/sol3/papers.cfm?abstract_id=3333511.

13. Simon Singh. *The Code Book* (New York: Anchor Books, 1999), 120–24.

7. HOW TO COME HOME

1. Ioannis Armakolas, "A Field Trip to Bosnia: The Dilemmas of the First-Time Researcher," in *Researching Violently Divided Societies: Ethical and Methodological Issues*, ed. M. Smyth and G. Robinson (London: Pluto Press, 2001), 169–70.

2. Virginia Dickson-Swift, Erica L. James, and Pranee Liamputtong, *Undertaking Sensitive Research in the Health and Social Sciences: Managing Boundaries, Emotions, and Risks* (Cambridge: Cambridge University Press, 2008).

3. Fabio Rojas, *Grad Skool Rulz: Everything You Need to Know about Academia from Admissions to Tenure*, Smashwords (ebook), October 2, 2011, 44–63.

4. Daniel Dennett, *Freedom Evolves* (New York: Penguin, 2004), 17.

5. Erving Goffman, "On Cooling the Mark Out," *Psychiatry* 15, no. 4 (1952): 455–56.

BIBLIOGRAPHY

Abdelal, Rawi, Yoshiko M. Herrera, Alastair Ian Johnston, and Rose McDermott. "Identity as a Variable." *Perspective on Politics* 4, no. 4 (2006): 695–711.

Acemoglu, Daron, Suresh Naidu, Pascual Restrepo, and James A. Robinson. "Democracy Does Cause Growth." *Journal of Political Economy* 127, no. 1 (2019): 47–100.

Adcock, Robert, and David Collier. "Measurement Validity: A Shared Standard for Qualitative and Quantitative Research." *American Political Science Review* 95, no. 3 (2001): 529–46.

Ahmad, Aisha. *Jihad & Co: Black Market and Islamist Power*. New York: Oxford University Press, 2017.

Akram, Sadiya. "Fully Unconscious and Prone to Habit: The Characteristics of Agency in the Structure and Agency Dialectic." *Journal for the Theory of Social Behavior* 43, no. 1 (2012): 45–65.

Angrist, Joshua D., and Jörn-Steffen Pischke. *Mostly Harmless Econometrics: An Empiricist's Companion*. Princeton, NJ: Princeton University Press, 2009.

Aretxaga, Begoña. "Dirty Protest." In *States of Terror: Begoña Aretxaga's Essays*, ed. Joseba Zulaika, 57–74. Reno: Center for Basque Studies, University of Nevada, Reno, 2005.

Arjona, Ana M., Zachariah C. Mamphilly, and Wendy Pearlman. "Research in Violent or Post-Conflict Political Settings." Working Paper Series: Qualitative Transparency Deliberations, Working Group Final Reports, 2019. https://papers.ssrn.com/sol3/papers.cfm?abstract_id=3333503.

Armakolas, Ioannis. "A Field Trip to Bosnia: The Dilemmas of the First-Time Researcher." In *Researching Violently Divided Societies: Ethical and Methodological Issues*, ed. Marie Smyth and Gillian Robinson, 165–83. London: Pluto Press, 2001.

Asad, Talal. "The Concept of Cultural Translation in British Social Anthropology." In *Writing Culture*, ed. James Clifford and George E. Marcus, 141–64. London: University of California Press, 1986.

Ashworth, Scott, Christopher R. Berry, and Ethan Bueno de Mesquita. *Theory and Credibility: Integrating Theoretical and Empirical Social Science*. Princeton, NJ: Princeton University Press, forthcoming.

Balcells, Laia. *Rivalry and Revenge: The Politics of Violence during Civil War*. Cambridge: Cambridge University Press, 2017.

Balcells, Laia, and Christopher M. Sullivan. "New Findings from Conflict Archives: An Introduction and Methodological Framework." *Journal of Peace Research* 55, no. 2 (2018): 137–46.

Barkey, Karen. *Bandits and Bureaucrats: The Ottoman Route to State Centralization*. Ithaca, NY: Cornell University Press, 1994.

Barnett, Michael. "The UN Security Council, Indifference, and Genocide in Rwanda." *Cultural Anthropology* 12, no. 4 (1997): 551–78.

Beissinger, Mark. *Nationalist Mobilization and the Collapse of the Soviet State*. Cambridge: Cambridge University Press, 2002.

Bellin, Eva, Seena C. Greitens, Yoshiko Hererra, and Diane Singerman. "Research in Authoritarian and Repressive Contexts." Working Paper Series: Qualitative Transparency Deliberations, Working Group Final Reports, 2019. https://papers.ssrn.com/sol3/papers.cfm?abstract_id=3333496.

Berman, Eli, Jacob Shapiro, and Joseph Felter. *Small Wars, Big Data*. Princeton, NJ: Princeton University Press, 2018.

Berry, Jeffrey M. "Validity and Reliability Issues in Elite Interviewing." *Political Science & Politics* 35, no. 4 (2002): 679–82.

Blair, Graeme, Jasper Cooper, Alexander Coppock, and Macartan Humphreys. "Declaring and Diagnosing Research Designs." *American Political Science Review* 113, no. 3 (2019): 838–59.

Blattman, Chris. "Field Work in the Tropics." Blog post. April 21, 2009. https://chrisblattman.com/2009/04/21/field-work-in-the-tropics/.

Blattman, Christopher, Donald Green, Daniel Ortega, and Santiago Tobón. "Place Based Interventions at Scale: The Direct and Spillover Effects of Policing and City Services on Crime." NBER Working Paper, Development Economics, 2019. https://www.nber.org/papers/w23941.

Bloor, Michael, Jane Frankland, Michelle Thomas, and Kate Robson. *Focus Groups in Social Research*. London: Sage, 2001.

Boix, Carles. "Democracy, Development, and the International System." *American Political Science Review* 105, no. 4 (2011): 809–28.

Bond, Robert M., Christopher Fariss, Jason Jones, Adam Kramer, Cameron Marlow, Jamie Settle, and James Fowler. "A 61-Million Person Experiment in Social Influence and Political Mobilization." *Nature* 489 (2012): 295–98.

Borneman, John, and Joseph Masco. "Anthropology and the Security State." *American Anthropologist* 117, no. 4 (2015): 781–85.

Bourdieu, Pierre. *Outline of a Theory of Practice*. Cambridge: Cambridge University Press, 1977.

Bracic, Ana. *Breaking the Exclusion Cycle: How to Promote Cooperation between Majority and Minority Ethnic Groups.* Oxford: Oxford University Press, 2020.

Brooks, Sarah. "The Ethical Treatment of Human Subjects and the Institutional Review Board Process." In *Interview Research in Political Science*, ed. Layna Mosley, 45–66. Ithaca, NY: Cornell University Press, 2013.

Buford, Bill. *Among the Thugs.* London: Vintage, 1993.

Burawoy, Michael. "Revisits: An Outline of a Theory of Reflexive Ethnography." *American Sociological Review* 68, no. 5 (2003): 645–79.

Cameron, Sarah. *The Hungry Steppe: Famine, Violence, and the Making of Soviet Kazakhstan.* Ithaca, NY: Cornell University Press, 2018.

Casey, Katherine, Abou Bakarr Kamara, and Niccoló Meriggi. "An Experiment in Candidate Selection." NBER Working Paper No. 26160, Political Economy, 2019. DOI: 10.3386/w26160.

Coffman, Lucas C., and Muriel Niederle. "Pre-Analysis Plans Have Limited Upside, Especially Where Replications Are Feasible." *Journal of Economic Perspectives* 29, no. 3 (2015): 81–98.

Cohen, Dara. *Rape during Civil War.* Ithaca, NY: Cornell University Press, 2016.

Collier, David, Jody LaPorte, and Jason Seawright. "Putting Typologies to Work: Concept Formation, Measurement, and Analytic Rigor." *Political Research Quarterly* 65, no. 1 (2012): 217–32.

Corey, Gerald. *Theory and Practice of Counseling and Psychotherapy*, 8th Ed. Belmont, CA: Thomson, 2009.

Cramer, Katherine J. *The Politics of Resentment: Rural Consciousness in Wisconsin and the Rise of Scott Walker.* Chicago: University of Chicago Press, 2016.

Crapanzano, Vincent. "Hermes' Dilemma: The Masking of Subversion in Ethnographic Description." In *Writing Culture*, ed. James Clifford and George E. Marcus, 51–76. London: University of California Press, 1986.

Cronin-Furman, Kate, and Milli Lake. "Ethics Abroad: Fieldwork in Fragile and Violent Contexts." *PS: Political Science and Politics* 51, no. 3 (2018): 607–14.

Curran, Sarah. "Ethical Considerations for Research in Cross-Cultural Settings." In *A Handbook for Social Science Field Research*, ed. Ellen Perecman and Sara R. Curran, 197–216. London: Sage, 2006.

Cyr, Jennifer. *Focus Groups for the Social Science Researcher.* New York: Cambridge University Press, 2019.

Darden, Keith. "One Last Thing before You Go." In *Stories from the Field: A Guide to Navigating Fieldwork in Political Science*, ed. Peter Krause and Ora Szekely. New York: Columbia University Press, 2020.

Davenport, Christian. "Researching while Black: Why Conflict Research Needs More African Americans (Maybe)." Political Violence at a Glance, April 10, 2013. http://political violenceataglance.org/2013/04/10/researching-while-black-why-conflict-research-needs -more-african-americans-maybe/.

Dennett, Daniel. *Freedom Evolves.* London: Penguin, 2004.

Denny, Elaine, and Jesse Driscoll. "Calling Mogadishu: How Reminders of Anarchy Bias Survey Participation." *Journal of Experimental Political Science* 6, no. 2 (2019): 81–92.

Derluguian, Georgi. *Bourdieu's Secret Admirer in the Caucasus: A World Systems Biography.* Chicago: University of Chicago Press, 2005.

Desposato, Scott. "Subjects' and Scholars' Views on the Ethics of Political Science Field Experiments." *Perspectives on Politics* 16, no. 3 (2018): 739–50.

Dickson-Swift, Virginia, Erica L. James, and Pranee Liamputtong. *Undertaking Sensitive Research in the Health and Social Sciences: Managing Boundaries, Emotions, and Risks.* Cambridge: Cambridge University Press, 2008.

Dower, Paul Castañeda, Evgeny Finkel, Scott Gehlbach, and Steven Nafziger. "Collective Action and Representation in Autocracies: Evidence from Russia's Great Reforms." *American Political Science Review* 112, no. 1 (2018): 125–47.

Driscoll, Jesse. "Being Watched and Being Handled." In *Doing Fieldwork in Areas of International Intervention: A Guide to Research in Violent and Closed Contexts,* ed. Berit Bliesemann de Guevara and Morten Bøås, 143–58. Bristol, UK: Bristol University Press, 2020.

Driscoll, Jesse. *Warlords and Coalition Politics in Post-Soviet States.* Cambridge: Cambridge University Press, 2015.

Driscoll, Jesse, and F. Daniel Hidalgo. "Intended and Unintended Consequences of Democracy: Promotion Assistance to Georgia after the Rose Revolution." *Research and Politics* 1, no. 1 (2014): 1–13.

Driscoll, Jesse, and Nicholai Lidow. "Representative Surveys in Insecure Environments: A Case Study of Mogadishu, Somalia." *Journal of Survey Statistics and Methodology* 2, no. 1 (2014): 78–95.

Driscoll, Jesse, and Daniel Maliniak. "Did Georgian Voters Desire Escalation in 2008? Experiments and Observations." *Journal of Politics* 78, no. 1 (2016): 265–80.

Driscoll, Jesse, and Caroline Schuster. "Spies Like Us." *Ethnography* 19, no. 3 (2017): 411–30.

Dube, Oeindrila, and Juan Vargas. "Commodity Price Shocks and Civil Conflict: Evidence from Colombia." *Review of Economic Studies* 80 (2013): 1384–421.

Duneier, Mitchell. "Race and Peeing on Sixth Avenue." In *Racing Research, Researching Race: Methodological Dilemmas in Critical Race Studies,* ed. France Winddance Twine and Jonathan W. Warren, 215–26. New York: New York University Press, 2000.

Easterly, William. *The White Man's Burden: Why the West's Efforts to Aid the Rest Have Done So Much Ill and So Little Good.* New York: Penguin, 2006.

Elman, Colin. "Explanatory Typologies in Qualitative Studies of International Politics." *International Organization* 59, no. 2 (2005): 293–326.

Elman, Colin, Diana Kapiszewski, and Arthur Lupia. "Transparent Social Inquiry: Implications for Political Science." *Annual Review of Political Science* 21, no. 1 (2018): 29–47.

Elman, Colin, Diana Kapiszewski, and Lorena Vinuela. "Qualitative Data Archiving: Rewards and Challenges." *PS: Political Science & Politics* 43, no. 1 (2010): 23–27.

Elster, Jon. *Nuts and Bolts for the Social Sciences.* Cambridge: Cambridge University Press, 1989.

Emerson, Robert M., Rachel I. Fretz, and Linda L. Shaw. *Writing Ethnographic Fieldnotes,* 2nd Ed. Chicago: University of Chicago Press, 2011.

Fearon, James, and Anke Hoeffler. "Conflict and Violence Assessment Paper: Benefits and Costs of the Conflict and Violence Targets for the Post-2015 Development Agenda."

Working Paper, Copenhagen Consensus Center, 2015. https://www.copenhagenconsensus
.com/sites/default/files/conflict_assessment_-_hoeffler_and_fearon_0.pdf

Finkel, Evgeny. *Ordinary Jews: Choice and Survival during the Holocaust.* Princeton, NJ: Princeton University Press, 2017.

Frisch, Scott A., Douglas B. Harris, Sean Q. Kelly, and David C. W. Parker. *Doing Archival Research in Political Science.* Amherst, NY: Cambria Press, 2012.

Frye, Timothy, Scott Gehlbach, Kyle L. Marquardt, and Ora John Reuter. "Is Putin's Popularity Real?" *Post-Soviet Affairs* 33, no. 1 (2017): 1–15.

Fujii, Lee Ann. "Five Stories of Accidental Ethnography: Turning Unplanned Moments in the Field into Data." *Qualitative Research* 15, no. 4 (2015): 525–39.

——. *Interviewing in Social Science Research: A Relational Approach.* New York: Routledge, 2017.

——. "Working with Interpreters." In *Interview Research in Political Science*, ed. Layna Mosley, 144–68. Ithaca, NY: Cornell University Press, 2013.

Gallaher, Carolyn. "Researching Repellent Groups: Some Methodological Considerations on How to Represent Militants, Radicals, and Other Belligerents." In *Surviving Field Research: Working in Violent and Difficult Situations*, ed. Chandar Kelha Sriram, John C. King, Julie A. Mertus, Olga Martin-Ortega, and Johanna Herman, 127–46. New York: Routledge, 2009.

Garfias, Francisco. "Elite Competition and State Capacity Development: Theory and Evidence from Post-Revolutionary Mexico." *American Political Science Review* 112, no. 2 (2018): 339–57.

Gartzke, Eric. "Zombie Relevance." *Foreign Policy*, February 27, 2011. https://foreignpolicy
.com/2011/02/27/gartzke-on-policy-political-science-and-zombies/.

Geddes, Barbara. *Paradigms and Sand Castles: Theory Building and Research Design in Comparative Politics.* Ann Arbor: University of Michigan Press, 2003.

Geertz, Clifford. "The Deep Play: Notes on the Balinese Cockfight." In *The Interpretation of Cultures*, ed. Clifford Geertz. New York: Basic Books, 1973.

Gehlbach, Scott. "Serendipity." Blog post, February 10, 2018. https://scottgehlbach.net
/serendipity/.

Giné, Xavier, and Ghazala Mansouri. "Together We Will: Experimental Evidence on Female Voting Behavior in Pakistan." World Bank Policy Research Working Paper 5892, 2011. https://elibrary.worldbank.org/doi/pdf/10.1596/1813-9450-5692.

Goertz, Gary. *Multimethod Research, Causal Mechanisms, and Case Studies: An Integrated Approach.* Princeton, NJ: Princeton University Press, 2017.

Goertz, Gary, and James Mahoney. *A Tale of Two Cultures: Qualitative and Quantitative Research in the Social Sciences.* Princeton, NJ: Princeton University Press, 2012.

Goffman, Erving. "On Cooling the Mark Out." *Psychiatry* 15, no. 4 (1952): 451–63.

Green, Amelia Hoover. "Successful Fieldwork for the Fieldwork Hater." In *Stories from the Field: A Guide to Navigating Fieldwork in Political Science*, ed. Peter Krause and Ora Szekely. New York: Columbia University Press, 2020.

Green, Donald P., and Alan S. Gerber. "Reclaiming the Experimental Tradition in Political Science." In *Political Science: The State of the Discipline*, ed. Ira Katznelson and Helen V. Milner. New York: Norton, 2002.

Habyarimana, James, Macartan Humphreys, Daniel N. Posner, and Jeremy Weinstein. *Coethnicity: Diversity and the Dilemmas of Collective Action*. New York: Russell Sage, 2011.

Humphreys, Macartan. "Monkey Business." CEGA Blog, Berkeley Initiative for Transparency in the Social Sciences, March 20, 2013. Reprinted in the *APSA Comparative Politics Newsletter*, 2013. https://www.bitss.org/2013/03/20/monkey-business/.

Humphreys, Macartan, and Jeremy Weinstein. "Field Experiments and the Political Economy of Development." *Annual Review of Political Science* 12 (2009): 367–78.

Hyde, Susan. "The Observer Effect in International Politics: Evidence from a Natural Experiment." *World Politics* 60, no. 1 (2007): 37–63.

Ichino, Nahomi, and Matthias Schündeln. "Deterring or Displacing Electoral Irregularities? Spillover Effects of Observers in a Randomized Field Experiment in Ghana." *Journal of Politics* 74, no. 1 (2012): 292–307.

Jacobs, Alan, Tim Buthe, Ana M. Arjona, Leonardo R. Arriola, et al. "Transparency in Qualitative Research: An Overview of Key Findings and Recommendations." Working Paper Series: Qualitative Transparency Deliberations, Working Group Final Reports, 2019. https://papers.ssrn.com/sol3/papers.cfm?abstract_id=3430025.

Javeline, Debra, and Sarah Lindemann-Komarova. "Financing Russian Civil Society." *Europe–Asia Studies* 72, no. 4 (2020): 644–85. DOI: 10.1080/09668136.2019.1637399.

Jensen, Nathan, Elizabeth Lyons, Eddy Chebelyon, Ronan le Bras, and Carla Gomes. "Conspicuous Monitoring and Remote Work." *Journal of Economic Behavior and Organization* 176 (2020): 489–511.

Kalyvas, Stathis. *The Logic of Violence in Civil War*. Cambridge: Cambridge University Press, 2006.

——. "The Urban Bias in Research on Civil Wars." *Security Studies* 13, no. 3 (2004): 160–190.

Kapiszewski, Diana, and Dessislava Kirilova. "Transparency in Qualitative Security Studies Research: Standards, Benefits, and Challenges." *Security Studies* 23 (2014): 699–707.

Kapiszewski, Diana, Lauren M. Maclean, and Benjamin L. Read. *Field Research in Political Science: Practices and Principles*. Cambridge: Cambridge University Press, 2015.

Khan, Shamus. "The Subpoena of Ethnographic Data." *Sociological Forum* 34, no. 1 (2019): 253–63.

King, Charles. *Gods of the Upper Air: How a Circle of Renegade Anthropologists Reinvented Race, Sex, and Gender in the Twentieth Century*. New York: Doubleday, 2019.

King, Stephen. *On Writing: A Memoir of the Craft*. New York: Scribner, 2000.

Krasner, Stephen. *Sovereignty: Organized Hypocrisy*. Ithaca, NY: Cornell University Press, 2000.

Krosnik, Jon A., and Stanley Presser. "Question and Questionnaire Design." In *Handbook of Survey Research*, 2nd ed., ed. James D. Wright and Peter V. Mardsen, 263–314. San Diego: Elsevier, 2010.

Kruks-Wisner, Gabrielle. *Claiming the State: Active Citizenship and Social Welfare in Rural India*. New York: Cambridge University Press, 2018.

Kuhn, Thomas S. *The Structure of Scientific Revolutions*. 3rd ed. Chicago: University of Chicago Press, 1994.

Laitin, David. "Comparative Politics: The State of the Subdiscipline." In *Political Science: The State of the Discipline*, ed. Helen Milner and Ira Katznelson, 630–59. Washington, DC: American Political Science Association, 2002.

——. "Fisheries Management." *Political Analysis* 21, no. 1 (2012): 42–47.

——. *Hegemony and Culture: Politics and Change among the Yoruba*. Chicago: University of Chicago Press, 1986.

——. "The Perestroika Challenge to Social Science." *Politics & Society* 31, no. 1 (2003): 163–84.

Lake, Milli, Samantha Majic, and Rashaan Maxwell. "Research on Vulnerable and Marginalized Populations." Research in Authoritarian and Repressive Contexts. Working Paper Series: Qualitative Transparency Deliberations, Working Group Final Reports, 2019. https://papers.ssrn.com/sol3/papers.cfm?abstract_id=3333511.

Langbert, Mitchell, Anthony J. Quain, and Daniel B. Klein. "Faculty Voter Registration in Economics, History, Journalism, Law, and Psychology." *Econ Journal Watch* 13, no. 3 (2016): 422–51.

Layder, Derek. *Doing Excellent Small-Scale Research*. Los Angeles: Sage, 2013.

Lazarev, Egor. "Laws in Conflict: Legacies of War, Gender, and Legal Pluralism in Chechnya." *World Politics* 71, no. 4 (2018): 667–709.

Lee, Raymond M. *Dangerous Fieldwork*. Thousand Oaks, CA: Sage, 1995.

Lehrer, Jonah. *Proust Was a Neuroscientist*. New York: Houghton Mifflin Harcourt, 2007.

Leiby, Michele. "Digging in the Archives: The Promise and Perils of Primary Documents." *Politics & Society* 37, no. 1 (2009): 75–99.

Lieberman, Evan S. "Preparing for Field Research." *Qualitative Methods* 2, no. 1 (2004): 3–7.

Lynch, Julia. "Tracking Progress While in the Field." *Qualitative Methods* 2, no. 1 (2004): 10–15.

Margetts, Helen, and Gerry Stoker. "The Experimental Method." In *Theory and Methods in Political Science*, 4th ed., ed. Vivien Lowndes, David Marsh, and Gerry Stoker, 290–305. London: Palgrave Macmillan, 2018.

Marsden, Peter V., and James D. Wright. *Handbook of Survey Research*, 2nd ed. Bingley, UK: Emerald, 2010.

Martin, Cathie J. "Crafting Interviews to Capture Cause and Effect." In *Interview Research in Political Science*, ed. Layna Mosley, 109–24. Ithaca, NY: Cornell University Press, 2013.

Mazumder, Soumyajit. "Becoming White: How Military Service Turned Immigrants into Americans." Working Paper. SocArXiv Papers, 2019. https://osf.io/preprints/socarxiv/agjsm/.

McDermott, Rose. "Experimental Methods in Political Science." *Annual Review of Political Science* 5 (2002): 31–61.

McMurtie, Beth. "Secrets from Belfast." *Chronicle of Higher Education*, January 26, 2014. https://www.chronicle.com/interactives/belfast.

Mead, George Herbert. *Mind, Self, and Society*. Chicago: University of Chicago Press, 1934.

Mertus, Julie. "Maintenance of Personal Security: Ethical and Operational Issues." In *Surviving Field Research: Working in Violent and Difficult Situations*, ed. Chandra Lekha Siram, John C. King. Julie A. Mertus, Olga Martin-Ortega, and Johanna Herman, 165–76. New York: Routledge, 2009.

Miguel, Edward, and Michael Kremer. "Worms: Identifying Impacts on Education and Health in the Presence of Treatment Externalities." *Econometrica* 72, no. 1 (2004): 159–217.

Munck, Gerardo L., and Richard Snyder. *Passion, Craft, and Method in Comparative Politics.* Baltimore: Johns Hopkins University Press, 2007.

Neilsen, Richard. *Deadly Clerics: Blocked Ambition and the Path to Jihad.* New York: Cambridge University Press, 2017.

Norton, Anne. "Political Science as a Vocation." In *Problems and Methods in the Study of Politics,* ed. an Shapiro, Rogers M. Smith, and Tarek E. Masoud, 67–82. Cambridge: Cambridge University Press, 2004.

Pachirat, Timothy. *Every Twelve Seconds: Industrialized Slaughter and the Politics of Sight.* New Haven, CT: Yale University Press, 2013.

Pader, Ellen. "Seeing with an Ethnographic Sensibility." In *Interpretation and Method: Empirical Research Methods and the Interpretative Turn,* ed. Dvora Yanow and Peregrine Schwartz-Shea, 161–75. New York: M. E. Sharpe, 2006.

Petersen, Roger. *Western Intervention in the Balkans: The Strategic Use of Emotion in Conflict.* Cambridge: Cambridge University Press, 2011.

Piven, Frances F. "The Politics of Policy Science." In *Problems and Methods in the Study of Politics,* ed. Ian Shapiro, Rogers M. Smith, and Tarek E. Masoud, 83–105. Cambridge: Cambridge University Press, 2004.

Pope, Kenneth S., and Melba J. T. Vasquez. *Ethics in Psychotherapy and Counseling: A Practical Guide.* San Francisco: John Wiley, 2007.

Prather, Lauren, and Sarah Bush. "Do Electronic Devices in Face-to-Face Interviews Change Survey Behavior? Evidence from a Developing Country." *Research & Politics* 6, no. 2 (2019): 1–7.

Radnitz, Scott. *Weapons of the Wealthy: Predatory Regimes and Elite-Led Protests in Central Asia.* Ithaca, NY: Cornell University Press, 2010.

Rautalinko, Erik, Hans-Olof Lisper, and Bo Ekenhammar. "Reflective Listening in Counseling: Effects of Training Time and Evaluator Social Skills." *American Journal of Psychotherapy* 61, no. 2 (2007): 191–209.

Reeves, Madeline. *Border Work: Spatial Lives of the State in Rural Central Asia.* London: Cornell University Press, 2014.

Reno, William. "The Problem of Extraterritorial Legality." In *Interview Research in Political Science,* ed. Layna Mosley, 159–78. Ithaca, NY: Cornell University Press, 2013.

——. *Warlord Politics and African States.* Boulder: Lynne Rienner, 1998.

Roberts, Margaret. *Censored: Distraction and Diversion inside China's Great Firewall.* Princeton, NJ: Princeton University Press, 2019.

Rodden, Jonathan. *Hamilton's Paradox: The Promise and Peril of Fiscal Reform.* Cambridge: Cambridge University Press, 2006.

Rojas, Fabio. *Grad Skool Rulz: Everything You Need to Know about Academia from Admissions to Tenure.* Smashwords (ebook), October 2, 2011.

Rubin, Herbert J., and Irene S. Rubin. *Qualitative Interviewing: The Art of Hearing Data,* 2nd ed. London: Sage, 2005.

Said, Edward. *Orientalism.* New York: Pantheon, 1978.

Schatz, Edward. "Ethnographic Immersion and the Study of Politics." In *Political Ethnography: What Immersion Contributes to the Study of Power,* ed. Edward Schatz, 1–22. Chicago: University of Chicago Press, 2009.

Schatzman, Leonard, and Anslem L. Strauss. *Field Research.* Englewood Cliffs, NJ: Prentice Hall, 1973.

Seawright, Jason. "The Case for Selecting Cases That Are Deviant or Extreme on the Independent Variable." *Sociological Methods & Research* 45, no. 3 (2016): 493–525.

Shapiro, Barbara. *A Culture of Fact: England, 1550–1720.* Ithaca, NY: Cornell University Press, 2000.

Shapiro, Ian. *The Flight from Reality in the Human Sciences.* Princeton, NJ: Princeton University Press, 2005.

Shesterinina, Anastasia. "Collective Threat Framing and Mobilization in Civil War." *American Political Science Review* 110, no. 3 (2016): 411–27.

——. "Ethics, Empathy, and Fear in Research on Violent Conflict." *Journal of Peace Research* 56, no. 2 (2018): 190–202.

Simmons, Erica S., and Nicholas R. Smith. "Comparison with an Ethnographic Sensibility." *PS: Political Science & Politics* 50, no. 1 (2017): 126–30.

Singh, Simon. *The Code Book.* New York: Anchor Books, 1999.

Soulemianov, Emil A., and David S. Siroky. 2016. "Random or Retributive? Indiscriminate Violence in the Chechen Wars." *World Politics* 68, no. 4 (2016): 677–712.

Spector, Regine. *Order at the Bazaar: Power and Trade in Central Asia.* Ithaca, NY: Cornell University Press, 2017.

Thachil, Tariq. *Elite Parties, Poor Voters: How Social Services Win Votes in India.* New York: Cambridge University Press, 2014.

Tomz, Michael, and Jessica Weeks. "Public Opinion and Foreign Electoral Intervention." *American Political Science Review.* Forthcoming, 2020. https://web.stanford.edu/~tomz/pubs/TomzWeeks-APSR-2020.pdf.

Toshkov, Dimiter. *Research Design in Political Science.* London: Palgrave, 2016.

Trouillot, Michel-Rolph. "Anthropology as Metaphor: The Savage's Legacy and the Postmodern World." *Review* (Fernand Braudel Center) 14, no. 1 (1991): 29–54.

Venkatesh, Sudhir. "'Doin' the Hustle': Constructing the Ethnographer in the American Ghetto." *Ethnography* 3, no. 1 (2002): 91–111.

Vonnegut, Kurt. *Mother Night.* New York: Fawcett, 1962.

Weber, Max. "The Meaning of Ethical Neutrality." In *Methodology of the Social Sciences,* translated by Edward Shils and Henry Finch, 1–47. New York: Free Press, 1949.

Wedeen, Lisa. "Ethnography as Interpretive Enterprise." In *Political Ethnography: What Immersion Contributes to the Study of Power,* ed. Edward Schatz, 75–95. Chicago: University of Chicago Press, 2000.

Weinstein, Jeremy. *Inside Rebellion: The Politics of Insurgent Violence.* New York: Cambridge University Press, 2006.

Weld, Kirsten. *Paper Cadavers: The Archives of Dictatorship in Guatemala.* Durham, NC: Duke University Press, 2014.

Whitaker, Linda A., and Michael Lotstein. "Pulling Back the Curtain: Archives and Archivists Revealed." In *Doing Archival Research in Political Science*, ed. Scott A. Frisch, Douglas B. Harris, Sean Q. Kelly, and David C. W. Parker. Amherst, NY: Cambria Press, 2012.

Wood, Elisabeth J. "The Ethical Challenges of Field Research in Conflict Zones." *Qualitative Sociology* 29, no. 3 (2006): 373–86.

Young, Lauren. "The Psychology of State Repression: Fear and Dissident Decisions in Zimbabwe." *American Political Science Review* 113, no. 1 (2019): 140–55.

Zhukov, Yuri. "Population Resettlement in War: Theory and Evidence from Soviet Archives." *Journal of Conflict Resolution* 59, no. 7 (2015): 1155–85.

Zhukov, Yuri, and Arturas Rozenas. "Mass Repression and Political Loyalty: Evidence from Stalin's 'Terror by Hunger.'" *American Political Science Review* 111, no. 2 (2019): 569–83.

Zhukov, Yuri, and Roya Talibova. "Stalin's Terror and the Long-Term Political Effects of Mass Repression." *Journal of Peace Research* 55, no. 2 (2018): 267–83.

INDEX

GPSR Authorized Representative: Easy Access System Europe, Mustamäe tee 50, 10621 Tallinn, Estonia, gpsr.requests@easproject.com